Handbook of Business and Financial Ratios

Michael R. Tyran

Prentice-Hall, Inc.
Englewood Cliffs, New Jersey 07632

Prentice-Hall International, Inc., *London*
Prentice-Hall of Australia, Pty. Ltd., *Sydney*
Prentice-Hall Canada, Inc., *Toronto*
Prentice-Hall of India Private Ltd., *New Delhi*
Prentice-Hall of Japan, Inc., *Tokyo*
Prentice-Hall of Southeast Asia Pte. Ltd., *Singapore*
Whitehall Books, Ltd., *Wellington, New Zealand*
Editora Prentice-Hall do Brasil Ltda., *Rio de Janeiro*
Prentice-Hall Hispanoamericana, S.A., *Mexico*

© 1986 by

PRENTICE-HALL, INC.
Englewood Cliffs, N.J.

Library of Congress Cataloging-in-Publication Data

Tyran, Michael R.
  Handbook of business and financial ratios.

  Includes index.
  1. Ratio analysis.   I. Title.
HF5681.R25T97 1986   658.1'51   85-25585

ISBN 0-13-375858-3

PRINTED IN THE UNITED STATES OF AMERICA

What This Book Will Do for You

Handbook of Business and Financial Ratios presents numerous ratios that represent useful and important guidelines in assessing, interpreting, and planning financial data to meet the objectives of managing a business entity more effectively.

There's no "theory" in this book; it shows you step-by-step how-to-use ratios as a prime tool in isolating, identifying, and highlighting operating performance and financial position events. The ratios will enable you to rapidly troubleshoot specific areas that need special attention. With the help of this *handbook,* internal and external data are more quickly and accurately interpreted, enabling your management to make more discerning and profitable decisions.

This *handbook* is complete with 50 models that illustrate how ratios are used for analysis and comparison by period, data element, account description, item variance, and so on by management. It's full of formulas and examples showing you how to make calculations, and further outlines various types of ratios, showing their use, both in common and special situations.

Here are some of the many ways ratio analysis and this *handbook* will help you:

- It isolates abnormal or changing situations in operational and financial activities that require management's attention and action.

- It gives you a basis for investigating and interpreting specific changes in data relationships. These data could indicate possible problem situations or undesirable trends.

- It logically arranges data so that you can rapidly assimilate and interpret the information in terms of the organization's objectives and planning goals.

- It allows you to see how the company is perceived by outsiders influencing the cost of capital, price-earnings ratio, and bond ratings.

- It visually plots the analysis so that significant variations and data results are not obscured.

v

- It offers suggestions for improving management's decision making in the areas of profitability, financial stability, liquidity, return on investment, and solvency.

- It can help you quickly review quantitative and varied information in a manner that is easy to understand.

- It helps you interpret and define significant relationships that exist among relevant financial data sets at a given point in time over varying time periods.

- It describes the significance of individual ratios as they apply to the control of direct and indirect costs, turnover rates of inventory, receivables, cash and capital employed, and allows a realistic assessment and maintenance of an adequate capital structure for operational stability and growth.

- It is of specific interest to management who may be concerned with ratios relevant to efficient performance at competitive costs, profitability, growth patterns, managing assets and liabilities, and planning and achieving financial objectives.

- It can be of interest to creditors who have a major concern in an organization's ratios pertinent to their solvency or financial leverage, liquidity, and ability to pay debt obligations on schedule.

- It can serve as an important reference guide to investors who are concerned with management's operating performance, the organization's financial stability, and return on investment.

Each chapter in the book provides specific information needed to interpret the ratio, applications highlighting how and when to use these ratios, their advantages and disadvantages, and pitfalls to avoid in their utilization. Throughout the book, you'll find:

- *Step-by-step illustrations and detailed procedures* that show how to calculate and more effectively use important ratios in analyzing past performance results, making industry comparisons, and formulating valid future objectives.

- *Ratio guidelines* for isolating problem situations for immediate corrective action and precautionary indicators in establishing future goals.

- *Chapter highlights* as a preface to each chapter to acquaint you with its specific contents and objectives.

- *Illustrative ratio formulas* as examples of ratio calculations and use that can help save time when it comes to applying the ratios to a specific situation.

- *Graphic and numerical charts* to illustrate relevant statistical techniques and processes involved in ratio analysis.

- *Comparative worksheet data* for the statement of financial position indicating the relationship and importance of each line item to the relevant total assets and total liabilities and equity.
- *Ratio development worksheets* for calculating processes, their use and objectivity in ratio analysis.
- *System design-processing flow charts* that describe computerized procedures for ratio analysis. These flow charts present the logic for establishing relevant mechanical systems.
- *Variable budget scattergraph diagrams* for assessing operating performance and establishing control procedures.
- *Trend-line computations and graphics* for developing future operating/financial anticipations that are likely to occur in the business environment.

In review, this *handbook* segments financial ratio analysis into these critical areas:

TOOLS FOR FINANCIAL ANALYSIS to assess and plan an organization's financial and operational activities

OPERATIONAL RATIOS to measure, plan, and control performance efficiency

DIRECT COST AND G & A EXPENDITURE RATIOS to assess, control and plan costs

EXPENSE RATIOS to monitor, control, and budget overhead expenses

PROFITABILITY RATIOS to gauge a firm's operational success

INDUSTRY COMPARISON RATIOS to assess and interpret data for planning, controlling, and maintaining a competitive operational effectiveness

FINANCIAL POSITION REPORTING to evaluate an organization's financial status and progress

CASH FLOW PLANNING to support operational activities, minimize problem areas, and achieve a favorable cash flow position

STATISTICAL TECHNIQUES to analyze results from operating events and achieve realistic financial objectives

INVESTMENT ANALYSIS RATIOS to improve equity capital position for sustaining operational growth

As a time saver, analytical tool, and troubleshooter the *Handbook of Business and Financial Ratios* will serve you well by helping you recognize changes and problem situations and highlight implications for management decisions and action.

Michael R. Tyran

The models throughout this book are provided to:

- *Illustrate* the calculation processes for using statistical tools and financial operations analysis and planning
- *Express* data relationships among relevant reporting items for operating trend analysis, interpretation, and measurement
- *Demonstrate* the use of significant ratios in making similar industry comparisons, sources of the information, and ratio objectives and assessment
- *Compare* time period and their vertical/horizontal ratio analysis in terms of profitability, liquidity, operating efficiency, working capital, and debt-paying capability
- *Present* data correlation comparisons and displays among pertinent financial items such as purchases, payables and disbursements and sales, receivables and receipts, and cash flow
- *Highlight* the importance of inventory and receivable turnover ratios as well as the aging process in the planning cycle
- *Illustrate visually* an assessment of changes to stockholders' equity between periods and describes the usefulness of this procedure in financial analysis and management actions
- *Graphically display* computerized accounting system flow charts and the development of information for ratio and statistical analyses such as gross profit, overhead expenses, direct costs, manpower, indirect to direct labor, and performance results
- *Provide* cost-volume-profit relationship charts and various aspects of break-even principles and analysis for operating and financial decisions
- *Illustrate* the development and application of the profitgraph and capitalgraph techniques as an aid to data assessment and financial projections
- *Highlight* the evaluation of an organization's capital structure and provides analytical measurement ratios for bonds, preferred and common stocks

Models

Contents

CHAPTER 6
HOW TO USE RATIO ANALYSIS FOR INDUSTRY COMPARISONS   143

CHAPTER 7
EVALUATING AN ORGANIZATION'S FINANCIAL POSITION   163

Chapter 8
UNDERSTANDING DATA RELATIONSHIPS FOR EFFECTIVE
CASH FLOW PLANNING   191

1

Tools for Financial Analysis and Planning Operations

CHAPTER HIGHLIGHTS

Financial reports are of interest to users both within and outside a business organization. Without adequate analysis, however, these reports may not be fully useful to their recipients. Statistical analysis therefore plays a vital role in the financial and business environments.

After explaining the vital role of statistical analysis, this chapter presents a step-by-step method for the collection, preparation, analysis, interpretation, and presentation of statistical data.

Most of the chapter takes you through the definitions and formulas that you need to calculate the various types of arithmetic averages, deviation analyses, and times series trends. You will find simple definitions, clear examples, and listings of advantages and disadvantages.

The chapter concludes by focusing on the uses and potential misuses of statistical ratios in financial analysis. You will also be made aware of the cautions necessary for making your presentation and interpretation of the data validity and usefulness.

For periodic and summary reporting, the primary tools of a business entity are its financial statements. Outside the business, financial information is made available to stockholders, creditors, credit agencies, government, SEC, and other users who are involved in the firm's financial status and progress. Reports for external use typically include an income statement, balance sheet, changes in financial position, and possible statements of retained earnings and capitalization. Quarterly, semiannual, or annual periods are generally compared in these reports.

By comparison, the reports for use within an organization contain much more detailed and varied data on specific performance results, organizational progress, financial position, and problem situations. This information is used for in-depth analysis, interpretation, control, decision making, and planning.

THE VITAL ROLE OF STATISTICAL ANALYSIS
IN THE BUSINESS ENVIRONMENT

The statistical analysis approach plays a vital role in the everyday financial environment. This important technique enables a business to:

- Handle its growth, operational complexities, and information needs.
- Compete in the marketplace to achieve its sales goals, control costs, generate sources of capital, and increase profitability.
- Lay down reliable guidelines for decision making.
- Aggressively pursue operational growth and financial stability.
- Establish the basic criteria for sound and achievable operational objectives—and control performance within the plan's limits.
- Evaluate and interpret the accomplishment of performance goals.
- Cope with the increasing intervention of government in the business economy, with its attendant influence on operations.
- Introduce more and better scientific methods into the operation and administration of the business.

For the business to enjoy these benefits, you the financial manager must use statistical analysis to selectively assemble, analyze, interpret, and present the relevant quantitative data. Specifically, you must:

- Collect, assemble, and collate the data.
- Classify the data appropriately and condense it into a related data series.
- Present the resultant information in a comprehensive form—text, tables, graphics, or some combination of the three—to meet the user's particular requirements.
- Analyze and interpret the reported data.

As you can see, the statistical approach is normally characterized as objective in nature. As a scientific tool, it falls into the realm of classification. The technique applies not only to data that can be reduced to quantitative form, but it can accommodate large masses of specific data items. Reliable data, therefore, must always be utilized.

This is not to say that your subjective interpretation will not affect results. To understand, interpret, and assess the quantitative results properly, you often have to supplement reports with nonquantitative data.

WHAT TO DO WITH THE RAW DATA

Before all else, you must have reliable data to work with. Most businesses, in their transaction documentation, collect the data needed for use in the statistical approach. Remember, however, that the technique assumes that the data are reliable.

Once the data are on hand and proven to be reliable, you must take the following steps:

STEPS IN HANDLING RAW DATA

1. Classify the data.
2. Condense and summarize them.
3. Correlate them.

Classification

First, categorize the data into expense, cost, and general ledger accounts as delineated in your firm's chart of accounts. This step ensures reliability and consistency in classification and summation. Initially, some of the data may have been collected, classified, and reported by subaccounts that are subservient to the prime or control accounts.

Condensation and Summation

Total the pertinent subaccount data for prime or control account summations that are reported in the appropriate registers or ledgers. Data from these summary sources are then used to prepare a *trial balance*, which represents an aggregate debit and credit summation of all transactions during a given period. Prior-period ending balances are considered, if appropriate, in the development of balance sheet values. Operational data (sales, costs, and the like) are reported for both the current period and year to date.

Correlation

After summarizing the financial data into the trial balance from the updated general ledger, structure the information to meet the reporting requirements of the financial statements.

When analyzing data over time periods, your objective is to isolate, wherever possible, adverse data situation recurrences and trends. In other words, concern yourself with such influencing factors as the seasonality of operations, irregularities (fluctuations in sales volume and cost, along with their possible long-term tendencies), the need for borrowing due to cash flow problems, delays in receivables collection, changes in work flow scheduling, and so on.

APPLYING STATISTICAL ANALYSIS TO FINANCIAL DATA

Inasmuch as the statistical approach is concerned with data relationships and variations, it entails a familiarity with various statistical applications. The objectives and reasoning of the technique are expressed in terms of "averages," "estimates," and "probabilities." In this chapter, we will look at some of the common statistical applications to financial data analysis and assessment. In particular, you will see how to use

1. averaging
2. deviation analyses
3. time series trends (including the least squares method)
4. ratios

HOW TO EMPLOY DATA SERIES AVERAGING

An average represents a measure for "central tendency"—that is, a typical value around which other figures congregate or which divides their number in half. An average describes a whole series of figures involving magnitudes of the same data set; it represents an overall value. This data measurement permits you to compare either individual items in the grouping or different series of figures with regard to the central tendencies.

There are different types of averages, each with its own particular characteristics. The four most common averages include the

- arithmetic mean
- median
- mode
- geometric mean

Calculating the Arithmetic Mean ($\bar{X}$)

The *mean* is the resultant quotient when the sum of all the items in the series is divided by the number of items. This process is algebraically expressed as:

THE MEAN FORMULA

$$\bar{X} = \frac{\Sigma(X)}{N}$$

where $\bar{X}$ = the mean.

$\Sigma X =$ the total of the item values.

$N =$ number of items in the series.

Example: Here is how an arithmetic mean is developed for sales volume:

Period	Period Sales (in $000s)
1	520
2	530
3	525
4	535
	2,110

$$\overline{X} = \frac{\$2,110}{4}$$

$$= \$527.50$$

Another approach to finding the mean is the *deviation method*, which is based on the selection of an arbitrary midpoint value. This method yields what is called an *estimated mean*, and the formula is as follows:

**THE ESTIMATED
MEAN FORMULA**

$$\overline{Z} = \frac{\Sigma(fd)}{N}$$

where $\overline{Z} =$ the estimated mean.

$\Sigma(fd) =$ the sum of the frequency deviations.

$N =$ the frequency.

The average can then be calculated by means of the above formula.

Example: What is the average ratio of current assets to current liabilities, given the following information? The estimated mean, in this case, is 3.00. Since the combined sum of the deviations equals zero, the average ratio is a determinable value.

Ratios (Class Interval)	Midpoint (M.P.)	Number of Organizations' Frequency	Deviation*	Frequency Deviation
0–1.99	1	20	−2	−40
2–3.99	2	50	−1	−50
3–4.99 ⟶	3	40	0	0
4–5.99	4	30	+1	30
Totals		140		−60

*Midpoint differences from an estimated mean of 3 (arbitrary starting point).

$$\overline{Z} = \frac{\Sigma(fd)}{N}$$

$$\frac{-60}{140} = -.43$$

$$\overline{X} = \overline{Z} + \frac{\Sigma(fd)}{N}$$

$$\overline{X} = 3.00 - .43 = 2.57 \text{ (average ratio)}$$

The *advantages* of this method are as follows:

1. It is the most commonly used and recognized.
2. It is easily understood.
3. The computation is simple.
4. Only the total values and number of items are necessary for the computation.
5. The procedure may be treated algebraically.

The *prime disadvantage* is that the arithmetic mean is determined by every item included in the distribution series and is affected by extreme values in the series. The resultant value may therefore be distorted and not representative.

This method can be used in analyzing sales, overhead expenses, cash, receivables, and payables, among other types of accounting data.

Calculating the Median

Whereas the arithmetic mean is a *calculated* average, the median is a *position* average. It refers to the location of a value in a series. The median represents the value of the middle item when the items are arranged according to their relative sizes or magnitudes. As the average of position, the median average is referred to as *probable value* because the selected value may be located above or below the median value. The sum of the deviations about the median will be less than the total about any other point.

While the median divides the distribution into two parts, quartiles divide it into four parts and deciles divide it into ten parts. These position averages make possible a more detailed analysis of a distribution.

To determine the median for *ungrouped data* with an *odd number* of data sets:

1. Make an array of raw data arranged by magnitude.
2. Count the items and select the middle one.
3. Evaluate the middle item or *median*.

If the array has an *even number* of items, there is no actual value in the middle of the series. For example, if a series contains 12 items, the median position is *6.5,* or the value between items 6 and 7.

THE MEDIAN FORMULA

The median formula is:

$$\overline{X} = l_1 + \left(\frac{\frac{N}{2} - \Sigma f_1}{f \text{ med}} \right) i$$

where $\overline{X}$ = median.

l_1 = lower limit of medium class.

Σf_1 = sum of all frequency cumulations before entering the median class.

$f \text{ med}$ = frequency in median class.

i = size of class interval.

N = number or organizations.

Example: Calculate the sales median for the following organizations:

Sales (in $000s)	Number of Organizations Involved	Cumulative Frequencies
0–199.0	40	40
200.0–299.0	60	100
300.0–399.0	100	200
400.0–499.0	100	300
500.0–599.0	100	400
600.0 and over	80	480
Median class	480	

To solve the equation:

$$\overline{X} = 400 + \left(\frac{\frac{480 - 200}{2}}{100} \right) 100$$

$$= 400 + \left(\frac{40}{100} \right) \times 100$$

$$= 400 + 40 \text{ or } 440.0 \text{ median sales}$$

where N = 480 organizations

l_1 = 400.0

Σf = 200

$f \text{ med}$ = 100

i = 100

The *advantages* of the median average are:

1. It is easily calculated.

2. It is not distorted in value by unusual items.

3. The calculation is possible even when distribution is open-ended.

4. It is more typical of a data series due to its independence of unusual values.

The *disadvantages* of the median approach are:

1. It is not as common or as familiar as the arithmetic mean.
2. Items must be arranged according to magnitude before the median can be computed.
3. It has larger standard and probable errors than the arithmetic mean.
4. It cannot be manipulated algebraically.

Using the Mode

The *mode* represents the value that occurs most frequently in a data series; it assumes that enough data items are available for a smooth distribution. If a frequency distribution is smooth or *ideal,* the *modal value* corresponds to the value of the maximum point of the distribution; it is the value in a series that is most likely to occur. The *midpoint* of a modal class may not be used as the value of the mode since its value will change if the size of the class interval is changed.

The modal can be calculated as follows:

THE MODAL FORMULA

$$\overline{X} = l_1 + \frac{\Delta_i}{\Delta_1 + \Delta_2} l$$

where $\overline{X}$ = the modal value.

l_1 = the lower limit of class.

Δ_1 = difference between frequencies in modal class.

Δ_2 = the difference between frequencies in the modal class and the *postmodal* class.

i = the size of the class interval.

Example: Calculate the mode for income versus sales:

Period Income ($) (Class)	Sales Volume (in $000s)
2,000–2,500	100.0
3,000–3,500	120.0
3,000–3,500	150.0
2,500–3,000	130.0
2,200–2,700	100.0

$$\text{Modal value} = 3,000 + \left(\frac{30.0}{30.0 + 20.0}\right)500$$
$$= 3,000 + (3/5 \times 500)$$
$$= 3,000 + 300 = 3,300$$
income dollar
average

where $l_1 = \$3,000$
$\Delta_1 = 150.0 - 120.0 = 30.0$
$\Delta_2 = 150.0 - 130.0 = 20.0$
$i = 500$

The *advantages* of mode are that:

1. As an average of position, its value is entirely independent of extreme values.
2. It is the most typical and therefore the most descriptive of averages.
3. The mode is simple to approximate by observation with a small number of data items.

The *disadvantages* include:

1. The mode can only be approximated when limited data are available.
2. Its significance is limited with a large number of values.

Using the Geometric Mean

This type of mean is used primarily for *averaging ratios* and computing average rates of increase or decrease among data sets. The logarithm of the geometric mean is equal to the average of the data items' logarithms. The geometric mean is a calculated value that depends on the sizes of all the values. It is therefore less affected by extreme items than the arithmetic mean. The formula is:

THE GEOMETRIC MEAN FORMULA

$$Gm = \sqrt{x_1 \cdot x_2 \cdot x_3 \ldots \ldots x_n} \text{ (product of } x\text{'s)}$$
$$Gm = \sqrt{140\% \cdot 150\%}$$
$$= \sqrt{21,000\%}$$
$$= 144.9\% \text{ or an average increase of } 44.9\%$$

Example: In 19X3, one plant increased its sales volume by 40% as compared to another plant's increase during the same period. Estimate the *average percent increase* in 19X3 as compared to 19X2. For the first plant, sales in 19X3 over 19X2 are 140%; for the second plant, they are 150%. If equal importance is given to each plant irrespective of the absolute sales volume figures, then the geometric mean is used.

The *advantages* of the geometric mean are:

1. It is a more typical average than the arithmetic mean.
2. It can be manipulated algebraically.

The prime *disadvantages* are:

1. It is not widely known or used.
2. It is relatively more difficult to compute.
3. The average layperson does not easily understand the principles involved.

Applying the Various Types of Averaging

Let's summarize what we know about averages:

- Whereas the arithmetic mean is a computed average, the median and the mode are positional averages.
- As a computed average, the mean cannot be determined graphically.
- In a symmetrical frequency distribution, the mean, median, and mode are located at the same point.
- Extreme values in a data series affect the usefulness of the mean average but not that of the median or mode.
- Varying class intervals usually make the mean unreliable but do not affect the median.
- The mean average can be combined, but not the median or mode.
- The mean average can be obtained from raw data, but the median and mode cannot be determined without an array or frequency distribution.

Each averaging method has its own usefulness in statistical analysis. Your selection of the appropriate method depends on:

- how much data you have and how it is distributed
- how the data are classified
- the type of problem you are trying to solve

HOW TO USE DEVIATION ANALYSIS

Calculating Mean Deviation

Graphically, the data points in a series are scattered, or dispersed, around the arithmetic mean or median. The measure of dispersion—how far a point is from that point—is the *mean deviation,* or the average of the deviations of the points from the mean or median. The mean deviation (dispersion) range can be computed about either the arithmetic mean or the median because it depends on every value in the series.

To determine the mean deviation of a data series, take the average of data points and divide it into the total deviation value: the smaller the average deviation about the point, then the smaller the scatter, or dispersion, of the values. Since the sum of the deviations about the arithmetic mean is zero, ignore signs in determining the average.

The deviation of sales by period averaged $74, a very small dispersion or scatter among periods.

Example: Compute the mean deviation from monthly sales volume.

Monthly Periods	Sales Volume (in $000s)	Deviation from Monthly Average ($000s)
January	500.0	7.25
February	496.0	11.25
March	508.0	.75
April	510.0	2.75
May	512.0	4.75
June	507.0	.25
July	515.0	7.75
August	510.0	2.75
Totals	4,058.0	37.50

Calculation of average volume:

$$\frac{\$4,058}{8 \text{ months}} = \$507.25 \text{ average volume}$$

Each entry in the right-hand column reflects the difference between the actual volume for the month and the average for eight months. For example

$$7.25 \rightarrow 500.00 \ \& \ 507.25$$
$$11.25 \rightarrow 496.0 \ \ \& \ 507.25$$

Remember, signs are ignored.

Calculation of mean deviation:
$$\frac{\$37.50}{\$507.25} = .074 \text{ or } \$74 \text{ mean deviation}$$

The same process of analysis can be applied to cash flow, receivables, payables, costs, and the like.

Determining Standard Deviation

The *standard deviation* is a special kind of average deviation from the mean. It is computed by taking the quadratic mean of deviations from arithmetic mean of the values (root—mean square of the deviations from the arithmetic mean). The computation (long method) formula is:

THE STANDARD DEVIATION FORMULA

$$\sigma = \sqrt{\frac{\Sigma(x^2)}{N}}$$

σ = the standard deviation.
x = the deviations from the arithmetic mean.
N = the total number of data sets or items.

A more convenient (short method) calculation formula for ungrouped data is:

THE SHORT METHOD FORMULA

$$\sigma = \sqrt{\frac{\Sigma X^2}{N} - \left(\frac{\Sigma X}{N}\right)^2}$$

By the long method, the computation for ungrouped data is as follows:

- Compute the difference between each actual value and the arithmetic mean.
- Square the resultant values and calculate the average of the squares.
- Find the square root of the resultant value or total.

Example: Let's illustrate the short and long methods for calculating the standard deviation for period net income.

Period	Net Income (in $000s)	Deviations from Average	Net Income (Squared in $000s)	Deviations Squared
	X	x	X^2	x^2
1	25	−3	625	9
2	28	—	784	—
3	29	+1	841	1
4	26	−2	676	4
5	29	+1	841	1
6	31	+3	961	9
	168 ÷ 6 = 28		4,728	24

Long method formula:

$$\sigma = \sqrt{\frac{\Sigma x^2}{N}}$$

$$= \sqrt{\frac{24}{6}}$$

$$= \sqrt{4}$$

$$= 2 \text{ or } \$2,000 \text{ standard deviation}$$

Short method formula:

$$\sigma = \sqrt{\frac{\Sigma X^2}{N}} - \sqrt{\left(\frac{\Sigma X}{N}\right)^2}$$

$$= \sqrt{\frac{4,728}{6} - \left(\frac{168}{6}\right)^2}$$

$$= \sqrt{788 - (28)^2}$$

$$= \sqrt{788 - 784}$$

$$= \sqrt{4}$$

$$= 2 \text{ or } \$2,000 \text{ standard deviation}$$

The Uses of Mean and Standard Deviations

Deviations, or variations, indicate how well an average represents the data. Measures of variation therefore supplement your description of the data. Variations can be measured on an absolute basis (mean deviation) or on a relative basis (standard deviation). Both methods, however, are based on the deviation of each item in a data series from an average. In the average or mean deviation, the mean of the deviation is taken irrespective of sign (+ or −), but in the standard deviation the square root of the mean of the squared deviations is used.

The standard deviation is the more important measure in absolute variation or dispersion. You can analyze the normal curve in terms of standard deviation and apply these findings to data series tending toward normality. This method is normally employed in sampling and correlation techniques. In as much as the value of every item in the data series affects the standard deviation, this method places greater emphasis on extremes than does mean deviation. The reason is that, in the calculation of the standard deviation, all values are squared.

HOW TO PUT TIME SERIES TREND ANALYSIS TO WORK

A *time series* is a sequential arrangement of selected statistical data according to its occurrence in time. The objective of time series trend analysis is to measure the variation of a data set about the measures of central tendency, typically for the purpose of data comparisons. Comparisons may be made with comparable organizations in the same industry or related overall industrial averages. Current data may be compared with past data in the same series, such as sales volume or product costs. Using this approach, you can generally project what can be expected in the future.

Projecting the time series can be classified as *statistical forecasting*. Time series analysis is therefore very important to analysts who apply statistics to business activity and economics. An economy's dynamic nature makes the time factor a vital element in analyzing sales, product costs, income, production, and so on. A time series represents economic data moving through time, and its analysis provides the basis for reviewing the statistics in motion.

The impacting considerations in time series analysis are:

1. trend
2. seasonal variation
3. cyclical changes
4. irregular data series fluctuations

THINGS TO WATCH FOR IN THE SERIES ANALYSIS

A *trend* is a long-term movement, either upward or downward. It may develop in production, sales, costs, and other areas of a business. Time series trends can be attributed to a number of factors, such as the introduction of mass production, technological changes, variations in population growth, development of new products, revisions in product production mix, war, inflation, and so on.

Seasonal variations represent period movements that occur at regular time intervals, particularly during the calendar year. For example, consumer expenditures in retail stores increase at Christmas and Easter, and costs for utilities go up during the winter season. Similarly, employment fluctuates during the year in certain industries, such as agriculture. In essence, the two major causes for seasonal variations are: weather changes (winter, summer) and customs (holidays, vacations, personal habits).

Cyclical variations are usually influenced by prosperity, recession, and depression. In periods of prosperity, sales, production, income, and employment are accelerated, whereas the opposite effect is predominant in periods of depression. The cycles of economic activity show no regularity with respect to their occurrence or duration. History has proven that predicting future cycles with any degree of accepted accuracy is extremely difficult, if not impossible.

Irregular variations represent movements with no apparent pattern or regularity. Unlike cyclical economic conditions, irregular variations, such as strikes, floods, fires, wars, and the like, may occur once or a number of times. Their effects may last for a day, two weeks, two months, or much longer. Both the occurrence and the duration of this type of variation are very difficult to predict.

Steps in the Preliminary Data Series Review

For the sake of *realistic measurement,* you must take certain preliminary steps to ensure the relative comparability of the time series data. The point of preliminary review is to put data on a comparable basis before the actual analysis. Adjustments may be required due to

- Variations in the time periods
- Price changes or units sold
- Product mix
- Industrial comparisons

IMPORTANT ADJUSTMENTS IN DATA FOR REALISTIC ASSESSMENT

Time period. Production and sales volume may vary among periods due to the different number of workdays in a given period (February or "vacation" months versus months with no holidays). To eliminate this problem, divide production and sales volumes by the number of workdays, so that the data are comparable for activity analysis purposes. Do the same for receivable and payable balances, as well as for other financial data to be analyzed and measured.

In some organizations, a quarter consists of two four-week periods and one five-week period for accumulating and reporting purposes. In such cases, the four- and five-week periods are segregated and separately analyzed. Other organizations use a thirteen-month segregation of the annual time span.

Price and unit changes. The sales price is generally calculated by multiplying product sales quantities by price per unit. In the case of services, the sales value may be a lump sum or a cost rate per hour. Because units and prices change from time to time, you cannot make valid sales comparisons unless you make adjustments for price changes. To do so, divide the sales by the relevant unit price for the period(s). This gives you the actual units sold, because the unit quantities must be equal to the relevant sales divided by the appropriate price. If more than one product is involved, perform a separate calculation for each.

Product mix. A product mix entails different prices, quantities, and marginal or gross profits. To analyze the individual contribution and progress status of specific product data in the organization's overall operations, you have to segregate it. Further, this information must be known for future planning purposes.

Related industry comparisons. When making reliable and related inter-industry comparisons, you must know the composition and objective of what you are comparing. Ratios can play a significant role in these comparisons. For example, who is to say that inventories should always be maintained at an industry average. For some organizations, the average may be too high or too low, depending on their requirements. The same logic applies to comparing days of sales in receivables, bad debt average, capital asset requirements, working capital, extent of liability commitments, and the like with industrial averages.

These comparisons are often healthy and productive because they indicate that a problem might exist. You have a kind of signal that a situation should be thoroughly reviewed and evaluated, perhaps with some sort of corrective action taken.

Making Your Analysis Easy to Grasp

To make your time series analysis easy for others to comprehend, plot the comparable data on a graph, as is done effectively in many organizations. A graph makes trends and developments in a data series immediately visual. Arithmetic or semilogarithmic plotting may be appropriate. A graphic display may also present the basis and method for the actual conducting of a time series analysis.

Why Trend Analysis Is Used

If you were to graph raw, unanalyzed data, your presentation would be at best superficial. With trend analysis, you can determine the direction of a specific data series—growth or decline. You can further establish the

1. intensity of the growth or decline
2. consistency of the trend
3. basic causes for the directional trend or data fluctuations

In assessing trends, you can also make meaningful comparisons with organizations in the same industry, the general industrial economy, gross national product, population, and so on.

Comparing Trend Determination Methods

Because trend determination methods are predicated on estimates rather than on absolute precision, a trend is more realistically determined over a long time span. The short-term analysis may not be significant.

The continuation of past trends may provide an invaluable insight to future anticipations, which aids in assessing and planning an organization's operations. The process of *forecasting*, or extending the trend into the future, is generally known as *extrapolation* (the projection of known values). This process can be accomplished by

1. inspection or estimate (the freehand method)
2. calculation (semiaveraging, moving average, and least squares methods)

Inspection or freehand method. After plotting the data points on a graph, you can draw a line indicating the trend of data. This line reflects a very subjective decision since its direction depends on what the analyst perceives as the trend. In some instances, the line can be accurate if the data series trend is reasonably constant or the statistician is experienced and knowledgeable in the background of the data series. Model 1 presents a simplified illustration of this method.

MODEL 1. A Simple Example of a Sales Trend Line by Inspection (in $000s).

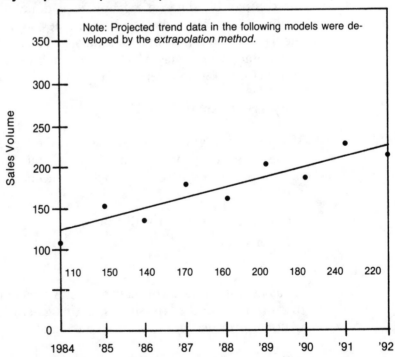

Note: Projected trend data in the following models were developed by the *extrapolation method.*

The *advantages* of this method are:

1. It is simple to accomplish.
2. It may be more representative and logical than a line drawn based on a mathematical equation.

The *disadvantages* include the fact that the results may vary among statisticians. Considerable practice and experience are required to make a realistic and representative trend line fit.

Semiaveraging process. In this method, you segregate the time series data into two equal parts and calculate the arithmetic mean for each part of the series. Plot two points and draw a connecting line that represents the trend.

The *advantages* of this method are its simplicity and its totally subjective results.

The *disadvantages* are:

1. The arithmetic mean, which is strongly influenced by extreme values, is used to locate the trend line.
2. This approach is limited primarily to fitting straight line trends.

Moving average procedure. You can use this procedure not only for establishing a trend line but also in connection with seasonal, cyclical, and irregular variations. This method tends to eliminate any type of fluctuations by smoothing them out and removing their influence.

To calculate the moving average, take a series of successive periods in which the first item in each group averaged is dropped and the next item in the series is included in the averaging process.

As shown in Model 2, no trend moving average (the dashed line) is reflected for the first and last periods. As viewed on the graph, the trend line is smoothed out in comparison to the line for the original plotted data.

The *advantages* of the moving average are:

1. Only simple computations are involved.
2. It may adequately replace the fitting of complex mathematical curves.

The *disadvantages* of the method are:

1. It cannot be brought up to date because the last point in the trend must occur several years (or periods) before the end of the data series. For example, a five-year moving average ends three years before the end of the data.

MODEL 2. Demonstration of the Moving Average Procedure.

Sales Volume Trend Computation
Using a 3-Year Moving Average

Year	Sales Volume (in $000s)	3-Year Moving Total	3-Year Moving Average
1985	150	—	—
1986	160	480	160
1987	170	490	163
1988	160	510	170
1989	180	530	177
1990	190	570	190
1991	200	580	193
1992	190	590	196
1993	200	—	—

Trend Line Graphic Display (in $000s)

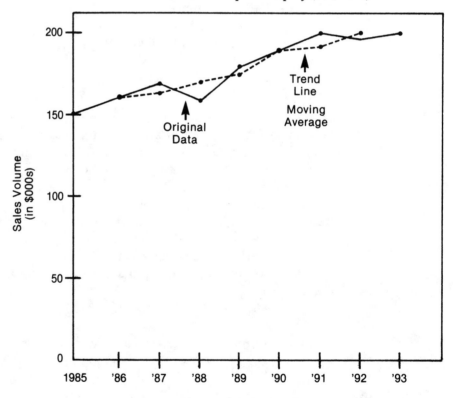

2. The moving average is computed by the use of the arithmetic mean, which is affected by extreme values.

3. The trend concept involves the presumption of a smooth growth or decline—the moving average is generally irregular in appearance.

Least squares approach. This method aids in determining the *line of best fit* to a series of values that describes the trend of the data sets. This method can also be employed in fitting curvilinear trends. If the trend is assumed to be a straight line, the trend line will be represented by the formula $Y = a + bX$. In this formula, the a and b values must be determined.

The prime logic of least squares is that the line of best fit is a line about which the sum of the squares of the deviations will be minimal. The deviations represent the differences or variances between the trend line (or theoretical) data and the actual values.

To determine the least squares line for a given data series, you must use a set of normal equations:

THE LEAST SQUARES METHOD EQUATIONS

$$(1)\ \Sigma Y\quad = Na + b\ \Sigma(X)$$
$$(2)\ \Sigma XY\quad = a\Sigma X + b\Sigma(X)^2$$

where Na = the number of data sets.

$\Sigma(Y)$ = dependent variable (Y).

$b\Sigma(X)$ = independent variable (X).

The coefficient of the second unknown (b) is X. Multiplying the equation $Y = a + bX$ by X, the result is $XY = aX + bX^2$. In summarizing the second equation, the result is:

$$\Sigma(XY) = a\ \Sigma\ (X) + b\ \Sigma\ (X^2)$$

Using these two equations, you can determine the values of the two unknowns and fit the line. Note that the sum of all the squared deviations of Y values from the Yc values must be at a minimum to be representative of a least squares trend. The result is a *dynamic average* path through the original data. (See Model 3.)

Applying the least squares method. The upper part of Model 4 shows how to determine the least squares trend line for annual sales volume, as well as how the equation values were computed. The year of origin is 1982, and the unit of measurement is sales volume in thousands of dollars. The sum (Σ) of X, or 55, was obtained by adding the numbers of each year. N represents the number of years, 11. In substituting the computed values in the equations, the trend line formula was calculated to be:

$$Y\ (Sales) = 109.5 + 3.95\ (X)$$

MODEL 3. An Illustration of Deviations of Original Values (Y) from Trend Values (Yc).

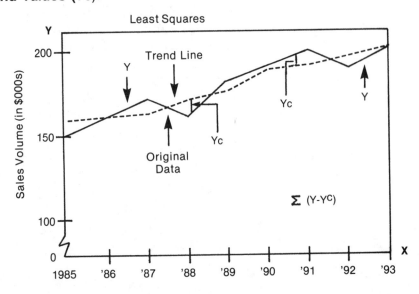

Displaying a mathematical trend line graphically. At the bottom of Model 4 is a graphic presentation of the trend line reflected in the analysis formula. To obtain the trend values, the various values of X by year are substituted in the equation. For 1984, for example, the X value is 2. The computation is:

$$Y = 109.5 + 3.95 \ (2)$$
$$= 109.5 + 7.9$$
$$= 117.4 \text{ for } 1984$$

The points located on the graph are for 1982, 1987, and 1991. In actual practice, two points are generally sufficient to draw a straight line trend.

Using the short method with an odd number of periods. For odd numbers of time periods, the mean of the X values coincides with one of the periods. The short method for computing trends can therefore be *simplified* with an odd number of years. Take the middle year as the origin year and assign it an X value which is equal to 0. A minus sign is given to the X values for the years previous to the origin year and a plus sign to the years following the origin year. The sum of the X values will therefore be zero since the values comprised two similar arithmetic progressions that are equal in amount but opposite in sign. The *normal* equations have to be modified since $\Sigma\ (X)$ is zero. Here is a comparison of the two sets of equations before and after the simplification:

MODEL 4. A Demonstration of the Least Squares Method.

Computation of Least Squares Trend Line
Annual Sales Volume (in $000s for 1982–1992)

Year	X	Annual Sales Volume (in $000s) Y	XY	X^2
1982	0	112.0	0	0
1983	1	115.0	115.0	1
1984	2	120.0	240.0	4
1985	3	125.0	375.0	9
1986	4	120.0	480.0	16
1987	5	130.0	650.0	25
1988	6	130.0	780.0	36
1989	7	125.0	875.0	49
1990	8	135.0	1,080.0	64
1991	9	150.0	1,350.0	81
1992	10	160.0	1,600.0	100
	$\Sigma(X) = 55$	$\Sigma(Y) = 1,422.0$	$\Sigma(XY) = 7,545.0$	$\Sigma(X^2) = 385$

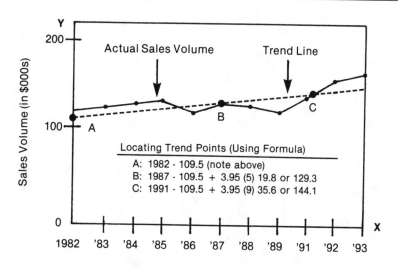

THE SHORT METHOD EQUATIONS

Normal Equations

(1) $\Sigma(Y) = Na + b\Sigma(X)$

(2) $\Sigma(XY) = a\Sigma(X) + b\Sigma(X^2)$

Simplified Equations

$\Sigma(Y) = Na$

$\Sigma(XY) = b\Sigma(X^2)$

Model 5 presents the computations involved in the least squares trend line using the *short method* and an odd number of years. Compare it to Model 4, noting that the total values for Σ (X), Σ (XY), and Σ (X^2) have

MODEL 5. A Demonstration of the Short Method.

Computation of Least Squares Trend Line
Annual Sales Volume (in $000s for 1982–1992)

Year	X	Annual Sales Volume (in $000s) Y	XY	X^2
1982	−5	112.0	−560.0	25
1983	−4	115.0	−460.0	16
1984	−3	120.0	−360.0	9
1985	−2	125.0	−250.0	4
1986	−1	120.0	−120.0	1
1987	0	130.0	.0	0
1988	1	130.0	130.0	1
1989	2	125.0	250.0	4
1990	3	135.0	405.0	9
1991	4	150.0	600.0	16
1992	5	160.0	800.0	25
	$\Sigma(X) = 0$	$\Sigma(Y) = 1{,}422.0$	$\Sigma(XY) = 435.0$	$\Sigma(X^2) = 110$

Simplified Equations   *Substituting Values*
(1) $\Sigma(Y) = Na$ $1{,}422.0 = 11a;\quad a = 129.27$
(2) $XY = b\Sigma(X^2)$ $435.0 = 110b;\quad b = 3.95$

Sales Volume Trend Equation:
$Y = 129.27 + 3.95(X)$

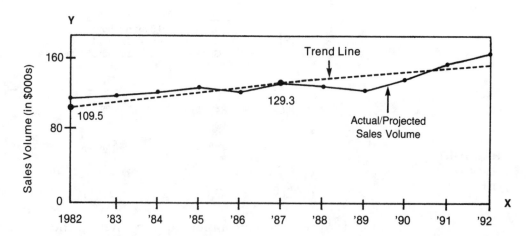

changed using the short method. In Model 5, the resultant equation for
the sales volume trend is calculated to be: $Y = 129.27 + 3.95\ (X)$. Note
that *b* retains the same value (3.95) as in the long method since the slope
of a straight line *does not vary*.

Using the short method with an even number of periods. If the time series has an even number of years, the mean falls between two years, thereby necessitating the use of decimals or fractions to measure the distance of any year from the original. To simplify the calculations, use half-year units instead of annual units. For the years 1982–1991 in Model 5, the origin is between the years 1986 and 1987. The X value of 1986 in half-year units is −1; in 1985, it's −3 and so on. The X value for 1987 is a +1; in 1988, it's +3 and so on. Under these circumstances, the sum of the X values for even-numbered years (time periods) also equals zero.

EXAMPLE OF SHORT METHOD WITH EVEN NUMBER OF PERIODS

Here is an illustration of how the X values in the least squares short method for finding the trend using an even number of years.

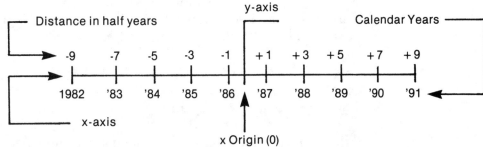

The following table shows you how to use the least squares short method (with an even number of years) to find the straight line trend for annual sales. The data are from Model 5, except only the years 1982–1991 are used:

Least Squares Short Method with Even Number of Years

Annual Sales

Year	Annual Sales (in $000s) Y	X	XY	X^2
1982	112.0	−9	−1008.0	81
1983	115.0	−7	−805.0	49
1984	120.0	−5	−600.0	25
1985	125.0	−3	−375.0	9
1986	120.0	−1	−120.0	1
1987	130.0	+1	+130.0	1
1988	130.0	+3	+390.0	9
1989	125.0	+5	+625.0	25
1990	135.0	+7	+945.0	49
1991	150.0	+9	+1,350.0	81
	1,262.0	0	532.0	330

$$\Sigma Y = 1,262.0 \quad \Sigma X = 0 \quad \Sigma XY = 532.0 \quad \Sigma X^2 = \underline{330}$$

$$a = \frac{\Sigma Y}{N}$$

$$a = \frac{1,262}{10} = 126.2$$

$$b = \frac{\Sigma XY}{X^2}$$

$$b = \frac{532}{330} = 1.61$$

Trend line: $Yc = 126.2 + 1.61 \ X$

Note: In this method, the slope increases or decreases by semiannual increments, and b therefore is one-half of what it would be in annual units. However, since the movement from one year to the next is $2x$ (half-year units), the trend values obtained from the trend equation are annual values. The trend value for year 1991 is:

$$Yc = 126.2 + 1.61 \ (+9) = 140.69$$

How to Use the Trend Equation

With the trend equation, you can obtain any trend value either *within* the range of time covered or analyzed or *beyond* the range in either direction. The latter capability permits you to project a time series into the future. In determining a trend value for a given time period, substitute the X value for a particular time period in the trend equation.

The trend line can be plotted by means of the following steps:

STEPS IN PLOTTING A STRAIGHT LINE TREND

1. Substitute for any two X values in the trend equation.
2. Plot the two trend values calculated for their respective time periods.
3. Connect a straight line through the two points.

It is preferable to use two time periods that are *some distance* from each other on the graph, such as the first and last periods. The wide spread lessens the possibility of inaccuracy in drawing the trend line.

Shifting the origin (or starting point). You can shift the data origin of a trend value. A shift in the origin does not affect the b value (the measure of the slope) because the trend line always has the same slope no matter where the starting point is taken. In both of the long and short methods, the b value was *3.95*.

The a value, however, does change, because it reflects the value of Y when X equals zero. Suppose you want to change the origin from 1982 to 1986. In Model 4, the derived equation was $Y = 109.5 + 3.95 \ (X)$. By substituting 4 for X, the value for Y becomes 125.3, and therefore $Yc = 125.3 + 3.95\ (X)$.

Why shift the origin? For refined data series analysis, especially for cycles, you may need to obtain cyclical turning points during a year; these would not be noticeable in annual data. Shifting the origin enables you to convert a trend equation from an annual to a monthly basis. To fit the trend line to original monthly data, you could use the same procedure as for annual data, but this method may be time-consuming. An alternate approach is to obtain the trend equation for the corresponding annual data, and then convert the equation to the monthly level by dividing b by 12; a remains unchanged.

Benefits of the Trend Method

The *advantages* of this method are:

1. It expresses trend in the form of a mathematical formula that is easily interpreted.
2. The results are definite and independent of any subjective estimate.
3. The form of the equation is convenient for extrapolation (projection into the future or past).

As for *disadvantages*, the technique assumes that the data follow a trend and that the trend can be expressed by a mathematical equation.

HOW TO USE RATIOS IN DATA ANALYSIS

Ratios compare one magnitude (a relative size) with another in the form of a multiple, such as 200:100. The multiple may also be a fraction, a percentage, or a rate. This is the basic principle of ratios.

Ratios simplify the numbers used in certain comparisons and analysis. With ratio analysis, a common financial technique, you can evaluate an organization's performance in terms of established or recognized standards based on historical experience.

Ratios highlight significant, abnormal, and changing trends as variations in the data being assessed. They involve the interpretation and explanation of the relationships between data sets at a given point in time or over a certain number of time periods.

Various types of ratios are used in business:

1. Ratios can compare a part or segment to its whole. In a given organization, for example, Product A sales are calculated to be 40% of total sales. Product B represents 35% and Product C represents 25%. Expressed as percentages their total equals 100%:

Product A	40%
Product B	35%
Product C	25%
Total	100%

2. One part or segment can be compared to another within the whole. For example, Product A amounted to $8 million as compared to Product B sales of $5 million. Expressed as a ratio, Product B sales are said to be 62.5% of Product A sales.

3. Another type of ratio compares one whole to another. For example, the sales volume of one organization can be compared to that of another organization. Sales for Organization A are 60% of the total sales in Organization B. This type of ratio reflects the relation of one magnitude to a similar magnitude at a comparable and compatible period in time.

Which type of ratio comparison you use depends on your purpose. Are you going to measure sales volume, profitability, an investment return, or a similar industry assessment?

What Financial Ratios Do

Financial ratios are important tools that are directly and indirectly useful in *managing* a business. Ratio indicators and comparisons provide relevant and important information, which become the basis for a sound decision-making process. Ratios help you to analyze an organization's operations, performance, and financial position—past and present. They serve as a planning basis to predict future trends, which provide management with a comparative means for assessing "what happened" when variances occur. Standard ratios are used to measure an organization's performance relative to other representative organizations in a particular industry. Although you have to be very cautious about the reliability of ratios, historical experience plays a significant role in validating the usefulness of ratio statistics, analysis, and measurement.

Whereas management is concerned with efficient performance, profitability, stability, and successful planning of future operations, ratio analysis is also important to investors who are concerned with an organization's operating and management performance and its financial stability. Creditors have a strong interest (the protection of their investment) in an organization's solvency and ability to meet its debts on schedule.

In financial reporting, the primary objective of ratio analysis is to *measure* an organization's return on sales, profitability relative to stockholders' equity, liquidity, operational efficiency, and so on. These applications are explained in detail in subsequent chapters. For now, let's point out a few things in general about ratios.

How You Can Misuse Ratios

Certain percentage ratios can be misleading or uninformative if not used properly.

MAGNITUDE TOO LARGE

As a rule, the magnitude to be measured should not be *much* larger than the base—perhaps you should question whether the base is too small for the intended comparison. In such cases, the high percentage factor obtained may be meaningless. For example, if an analyst were to state that an organization's profits increased by 1,000% in the past five years, the comparison would be difficult to comprehend and its implication hard to assess.

MAGNITUDE TOO SMALL

Conversely, the comparative magnitude should not be *too small* in relation to the base. For example, take the following statement: 1/40% of the consumers in Sales Territory A are prospective buyers of a product, as compared to 1/20% in Sales Territory B. This comparison is difficult to assess and understand realistically. Undoubtedly, the absolute comparative values would make more sense. Specifically, 1 person out of 20 in a sales territory population of 100,000 is a prospective product consumer. This comparison provides a magnitude that can be understood and evaluated.

RATIOS OR NUMBERS

This brings us to an important question: When should the management analyst report changes in data magnitude in terms of ratios or absolute numbers? The answer generally depends on the situation. Let's suppose that sales increased 50% over two years from $50 million to $75 million. That is a significant increase, and the percentage factor dramatically expresses its magnitude. What if an organization were to report that its profits increased 500% over the prior year's profits? The information appears to be significant. Yet the prior year's profits—let's say—were $1,000 on a $50,000 sales volume, and the 500% increase amounted to only $5,000. The "500%" increase is misleading.

Exercise caution when using ratio percentages for analyzing or reporting purposes. They may communicate an ambiguous and misleading message.

The Caution in Using Standard Ratios

A number of average ratios may serve as measuring tools of an organization's specific operations and performance. Yet to be useful and informative for data analysis, standard ratios should represent normal and comparable relationships among compatible items in the financial reporting of a business enterprise. Over the years, ratios have been developed that are common evaluation indicators, particularly among related organizations. The extreme precaution is this: to be relevantly comparative, ratios must use only data that are representative in context and composition. At best, average ratios provide only guidelines to existing proportions that are representative in a given industry. They permit an organization to compare its financial results with the averages in other organizations, thus ascertaining its relative standing or providing benchmarks for planning and attainment.

The Caution in Calculating Standard Ratios

The data elements used in the development of standard ratios should be homogeneous in terms of their degree and dimension. In other words, they should be comparable in nature and in the type of business being assessed. Yet sometimes specifically defining a similar industry and/or type of business is difficult, because many facets and subdivisions are involved. Comparisons can be misleading. Comparative questions have to be resolved regarding similarities in product(s), operational environment, relative size, financial structure, sales volume, and the type and number of customers. Major differences in these factors can influence the financial performance of the organization, as well as the character or composition of the data being assessed.

INFLUENCES ON COMPATIBILITY

Product. In a similar industry, one organization may be producing one product, whereas a comparable organization may be manufacturing a diversified line of products. Each product in the line can have its own gross margin, investment resource requirement and sales outlets, and each of these in turn can influence the financial performance and results of the organization.

Type of operation. Mass production techniques versus manual operations have a significant bearing on product price, profitability, manpower requirements, and investment in advanced machinery and equipment. Each of these factors can affect the comparative value of financial data and specific ratios.

Size of the organization. A business's asset investment value and/or sales volume can have an important effect on its data relationships. Net income to working capital and stockholders' equity may vary disproportionately. Inventory to working capital may have major variances, current ratio may be distorted, and receivable turnover may not be realistically comparable.

Customers, the type and number. Customers can have an impact on developing and assessing average ratio results. In one instance, credit policies may be too liberal, whereas in related organizations the extension of credit may be a very conservative approach. This factor could easily affect the collection time period, cash inflow, receivable turnover, incurrence of bad debts, the acid test, product price, profitability, loan requirements, and so on.

Uniformity of data. In computing average ratios for comparative purposes, the correspondence of accounting procedures is relevant and important. The guidelines for uniform financial reporting have been set forth by SEC and AICPA (American Institute of Certified Public Accountants). In the audit of an organization's financial statements, the auditing firm will always include a statement to the effect that, in their opinion, the financial statements are "in conformity with the generally accepted accounting principles applied on a consistent basis." This is an assurance to the reader that "accepted principles and practices have been followed." Uniformity in accounting principles ensures that the composition of the reported data is comparable in nature and conducive to average ratio development and analysis.

Uniformity of accounting periods. Organizations included in standard ratio development and assessment should have compatible accounting periods. Some organizations use a calendar month, while others employ four weeks or a four-, four-, five-week quarter. On an annual basis, this disparity in period length poses no problem unless the month of closing is different. For example, in the automobile industry the annual closing period occurs at the end of October since their new models are generally introduced in November. The differences in the annual closing date has an important impact on the validity of the data to be used in establishing reliable standard ratios.

THE NEED FOR A STANDARD OF MEASUREMENT

When making comparisons and analyzing results in terms of *variances*, you need an adequate standard of measurement. In the financial environment, quantitative measurement takes the form of relative dollar values at points in time, measured increases or decreases over time periods, and the use of percentages and ratios. The income statement reflects period and year-to-date operating result values, while the balance sheet measures the assets, liabilities, and capital at a point in time.

Two primary comparative tools in data measurement are categorized as "horizontal" and "vertical." Both approaches use dollars and percentages as the units of measurement.

Applying Horizontal Analysis

In the income statement analysis, the horizontal approach reveals the rate of change in the factors affecting income. In balance sheet analysis, it provides a dynamic approach to reviewing the increases and decreases that occurred over time periods.

Applying Vertical Analysis

For the income statement, the vertical method indicates how sales income is distributed among the factors involved in producing it, such as the relationships of cost of sales, G&A, and selling expenses. For the balance sheet, the vertical approach indicates the quantitative relationships among the data items at a particular point in time. For example, accounts receivable may be expressed as a percentage of current or total assets, or accounts payable as a percentage of current or total liabilities. This type of analysis can also be used in comparing one relevant organization against another.

COMMON MISTAKES IN COLLECTING, ANALYZING, AND INTERPRETING DATA

COLLECTION

The *collection of statistical data* must be complete. The data must be consistent and comparable if it is to be representative and valid for analysis and measurement. It must coincide with the objectives for its accumulation and collection. As a data collector, you must thoroughly review the data and eliminate anything that is extraneous or irrelevant. The careful selection and collection of data goes a long way toward precluding the misuse and misinterpretation of the resultant ratio analyses.

ANALYSIS

In the *analysis of the data,* using absolute values rather than percentages may be more practical, enlightening, and valid. Percentages can be misleading if relative weight is not applied. Improper or invalid analyses can result from the misuse of correlations, from the irrelevant or noncomparable use of ratios, from faulty interpretation of trends, from the inappropriate use of the arithmetic mean, and so on.

INTERPRE-TATION

The *interpretation* of statistical data entails problems. Faulty misuses include a superficial assessment of one or two related facts as opposed to the presentation of the underlying total background of the data (appropriate basics must be understood). Seasonal variations, when interpreted as cyclical, have a valid bearing in decision making; if interpreted as future trends, these variations may not reflect the actual situation. Assumptions may be misleading when they are based on averages rather than on individual cases, and vice versa. Data interpretation is extremely vital to successful data analysis and understanding.

PRESENTATION   The *presentation of statistical data* must be suited to the communication objective. Highlighting variances in comparative data presentations permits rapid assimilation of pertinent facts for further investigation. Excessive detail—such as a large array of data with irrelevant data inclusions—tends to confuse rather than enlighten. Exercise extreme care when presenting statistical data so that worthwhile assessments can be achieved.

These are only some of the misuses of statistics. If you establish appropriate procedural guidelines in the use, analysis, and presentation of statistics, you can prevent the improper use and interpretation of statistical presentations.

2

How to Measure Operational Effectiveness and Control in Resource Utilization

CHAPTER HIGHLIGHTS

Receivables, inventory, and payables all play a vital role in an organization's operational performance and in capital utilization planning and control. Management can use data from each of these areas to measure, plan, and control performance efficiency.

The primary sources of this data are two major financial reports: the income statement (called the summary of operations in some organizations) and the balance sheet (also called the statement of financial position). This chapter discusses pertinent data from both reports as they apply to performance measurement and control. Covered are ratios for:

- Measuring and interpreting the accounts receivable position for purposes of collection estimating, cash flow planning, and assessing an organization's credit policy.

- Analyzing the relationship among purchases, payables, and disbursements as an aid to business planning. This chapter explains how to measure an organization's debt-paying ability and determine whether trade payable commitments can be met.

- Assessing inventory controls to measure their effectiveness, projecting inventory levels, and implementing inventory classification to cut costs and free up working capital.

- Manpower planning for projecting costs and sales forecasts. Also, indirect-to-direct personnel ratios are developed to measure and control the effectivity of manpower utilization and cost.

Model 6 provides the basic information that will be used to develop ratios and trend analyses.

MODEL 6. Basic Information for Developing Ratios and Trend Analyses.

Financial Statement Data for Analysis
December 31, 19X4
(in $000,000s)

Income Statement	First Quarter Values	%	Second Quarter Values	%	Third Quarter Values	%	Fourth Quarter Values	%	Annual Period Values	%
Sales	$ 252.8	100.0	$ 274.9	100.0	$ 276.2	100.0	$ 273.1	100.0	$ 1,077.0	100.0
Cost of sales	223.9	88.6	243.3	88.5	248.1	89.8	247.7	90.7	963.0	89.4
Gross profit	$ 28.9	11.4	$ 31.6	11.5	$ 28.1	10.2	$ 25.4	9.3	$ 114.0	10.6
G&A	11.8	4.7	12.0	4.4	11.6	4.2	12.6	4.6	48.0	4.5
Income from operations	$ 17.1	6.7	$ 19.6	7.1	$ 16.5	6.0	$ 12.8	4.7	$ 66.0	6.1
Interest ($42.6M × 8%)	(.8)	(.3)	(.8)	(.3)	(.9)	(.3)	(.9)	(.3)	(3.4)	(.3)
Net other income/deductions	(1.3)	(.5)	(1.5)	(.5)	(1.2)	(.5)	(1.1)	(.4)	(5.1)	(.5)
Income before taxes	$ 15.0	5.9	$ 17.3	6.3	$ 14.4	5.2	$ 10.8	4.0	$ 57.5	5.3
Provision for income taxes	7.5	2.9	8.6	3.1	7.2	2.6	5.4	2.0	28.7	2.6
Net income	$ 7.5	3.0	$ 8.7	3.2	$ 7.2	2.6	$ 5.4	2.0	$ 28.8	2.7

Pertinent Balance Sheet Data

	First Quarter Values	Second Quarter Values	Third Quarter Values	Fourth Quarter Values	Average
Cash	$ 38.0	$ 32.9	$ 36.6	$ 35.5	$ 35.8
Receivables	110.4	111.5	102.3	105.1	107.3
Inventory	260.0	268.5	256.9	243.4	257.2
Other	22.1	21.3	27.4	21.1	23.0
Current assets	$ 430.5	$ 434.2	$ 423.2	$ 405.1	$ 423.3
Net fixed assets	64.9	66.3	67.0	68.2	66.6
Other noncurrent assets	11.7	11.5	12.4	12.5	12.0
Total assets	$ 507.1	$ 512.0	$ 502.6	$ 485.8	$ 501.9
Current liabilities	$ 310.5	$ 308.7	$ 294.1	$ 273.9	$ 296.8
Funded debt	42.6	42.6	42.6	42.6	42.6
Total liabilities	$ 353.1	$ 351.3	$ 336.7	$ 316.5	$ 339.4
Owners' equity	154.0	160.7	165.9	169.3	162.5
Total liabilities/equity	$ 507.1	$ 512.0	$ 502.6	$ 485.8	$ 501.9
Annualized sales	$ 1,011.2	$ 1,099.6	$ 1,104.8	$ 1,092.4	$ 1,077.0
Indirect manpower (No.)	16,522	16,508	16,595	16,910	16,634
Direct personnel (No.)	34,737	34,550	34,824	35,779	34,972

HOW TO INTERPRET AND MEASURE THE RECEIVABLE POSITION

To analyze, plan, and control a desirable receivable position thoroughly, you should consider a number of factors. The more important factors involve data relationship ratios, trends, and assessment of certain variables.

Using the Ratio of Sales to Receivables to Assess the Receivables Position

MAKING THE CALCULATION

Example: The following *quarterly ratios* were developed from the information in Model 6. (Although the more precise procedure is to use annualized sales and average receivable balances for comparative purposes, monthly values may also be used.)

Sales and Receivable Balances (in $000,000s)

	First Quarter	Second Quarter	Third Quarter	Fourth Quarter	Annual
Sales	$252.8	$274.9	$276.2	$273.1	$1,077.0
Receivable balances	110.4	111.5	102.3	105.1	107.3
Receivable turnover	2.29 (or 229%)	2.47 (or 247%)	2.70 (or 270%)	2.60 (or 260%)	10.04 (or 1004%)
Annualized turnover	9.16	9.86	10.80	10.39	

These data results indicate that the relationship was more favorable in the last two quarters compared to the first two periods. In the last two periods, the receivables were below the average of $107.3 million, whereas the sales were above the quarterly average of $269.2 million.

INTERPRETING THE RESULTS

Generally, changes in the sales ratios can be attributed to disproportionate increases and decreases in sales volume or in receivables, which cause fluctuations in the ratio values. When measuring the proportions among various related items in the financial statements, note the data variations that may indicate problem situations requiring investigative analysis. You may find that the variations are due to circumstances that do not require any action. Instead, they may be the result of situations either common to all business entities or characteristic to the operating environment.

Using Trend Ratios to Measure the
Sales/Receivable Position

**MAKING THE
CALCULATION**

You can also measure the sales/receivable position by means of trend ratios among periods of time. This approach is more effectively employed by annual periods.

Example: Quarterly data from Model 6 is used.

Sales and Receivables (in $000,000s)

Quarters	Sales Values	Sales Trend Ratio	Receivable Values	Receivables Trend Ratio	Sales/Receivable Ratio
1	$252.8	100%	$110.4	100%	229%
2	274.9	109	111.5	101	247
3	276.2	109	102.3	93	270
4	273.1	108	105.1	95	260

The sales volume clearly increased in the last three quarters compared to the first-quarter base. Conversely, the receivables decreased in the last two quarters but slightly increased in the second quarter (101%). The ratio trend is favorable in the example because the increases in sales did not materialize in higher receivables, which would necessitate a greater capital investment in outstanding customer accounts.

Sales Trend Ratios:
Two Key Factors That Affect the
Sales Position

**INTERPRETING
THE RESULTS**

The next step is to specifically assess the cause(s) for the variations in the sales and receivable values. Although the sales data in the example do not appear to be of major significance—since the last quarter's dollar amounts are fairly comparable—the factors affecting sales dollars should be ascertained as a basis for analytical assessment of more extreme situations.

Generally, the two major factors affecting the sales position are sales volume and price. Behind these factors are other relevant considerations, such as the general economy (rising, falling, static), seasonal situations associated with particular industries (automotive manufacturers' problems in 1982–1983), and factors affecting specific organizations in their operating environment.

Sales volume. Situations that affect product and service sales volume involve such common circumstances as

- product/service demands by the customer
- product/service quality
- the efficiency and aggressiveness of the marketing organization
- favorable markets due to a rising/recovering economy
- an organization's reputation with regard to the products or services it markets

Business cycles definitely influence an organization's marketing results. The upswings create demand, whereas the downsides make customers cautious and conservative in their buying activities.

Prices. The factors governing sales prices include the

- scope and aggressiveness of the competition
- unique features and quality of the product or service
- organization's ability to meet customer requirements on schedule
- efficiency of the organization in controlling costs effectively
- "state of the art" progress an organization reflects in enhancing its product usefulness and capabilities

Factors That Influence the Receivable Position

The extent and collection of outstanding receivables are primarily contingent on the customers' ability to pay its obligations. In turn, their ability depends much on the same factors as those discussed for sales above—prevailing market conditions, business cycles, and the problems associated with specific industries and individual customers.

Customers' inability to pay can result from such circumstances as

- sellers' overextension of credit
- inadequate investigation and verification of a customer's credit ratings (past and current)
- generous concessions in the form of liberal terms to favorite customers to increase their purchases

Certain customers may also be experiencing internal problems, such as operational inefficiencies and costs, poor sales volume, labor relations and elemental catastrophes (flooding, fires, snow storms, and the like).

The collection of receivables may therefore be delayed or impaired. The selling organization may be forced to bank borrowing with its attendant interest costs (drain on profits), and/or it may have to depend more on greater creditor financing to meet its own obligations. Neither alternative is conducive to sound financial operations.

SOLUTION

The solution may be to exercise constant surveillance, analysis, and control of receivables. The goal would be to take corrective action when customer account balances increase too rapidly in relation to sales. This may mean a thorough review of the organization's collection policy, more stringent control of customer credit, and a discerning assessment of the prevailing policies on credit terms.

Using the Receivables to Sales Ratio to Measure Financial Performance

HOW TO MAKE THE CALCULATION

When measuring the financial stability and performance of an organization relative to its receivable position, determine the average age or level of its customer accounts outstanding at given points in time. To do so, calculate the *receivable to sales ratio*. Divide the average receivables by the total credit sales. For example, the average receivables on an annual basis would be the sum of the beginning and ending balances divided by two.

Example: Quarterly end balances for receivables and relevant periods for sales were used to calculate the trends in the following table. The annual ending balance and total sales are also provided.

(in $000,000s)

	First Quarter	Second Quarter	Third Quarter	Fourth Quarter	Annual Values
Sales	$ 252.8	$ 274.9	$ 276.2	$ 273.1	$1077.0
Annualized sales	1011.2	1099.6	1104.8	1092.4	—
Receivables	110.4	111.5	102.3	105.1	107.3
Receivables to sales ratio	43.7%	40.6%	37.0%	38.5%	10.0%
Using Annualized Sales and Quarterly Receivable Balances					
Receivables to sales ratio	10.9%	10.1%	9.3%	9.6%	10.0%

Receivable Turnover Ratio

This ratio measures the average number of times that receivables *turned over* during a reported time period. In general, it reflects the relationship between operating results (in this case, sales) and the capital employed (receivables). These ratios quarterly and annual were presented under "Using the Ratio of Sales to Receivables to Assess Receivable Position." The ratio is calculated as follows:

$$\text{Receivable turnover ratio} = \frac{\text{Total credit sales}}{\text{Average receivables}}$$

**Average Collection Period:
One Way to Size Up an
Organization's Credit Policy**

**HOW TO
MAKE THE
CALCULATION**

The collection period represents the average number of days between the day that the invoice is sent out and the day the customer pays the bill. The formula for calculating this average is:

$$\text{Average collection period} = \text{Sales ratio} \times \text{Number of days in period}$$

Example: Calculate the average collection period using the receivable to sales ratio from the preceding example:

$$\text{Average collection period} = 10\% \times 365 \text{ (days in year)} = 36.5 \text{ days}$$

**ALTERNATIVE
APPROACH**

Another approach is to

1. Divide the *annual credit sales* by 365 to obtain the average daily credit sales.
2. Divide the average accounts receivable (include trade notes if appropriate) by the average daily credit sales.

Example:

(in $000,000s)

Step 1:

$$\frac{\$1,077.0 \text{ (credit sales)}}{365} = 2.95$$

Step 2:

$$\frac{\$107.3 \text{ (average receivables)}}{2.95 \text{ (sales/day)}} = 36.4 \text{ days}$$

**INTERPRETING
THE RATIO**

The collection period measures an organization's efficiency in enforcing its credit policy in terms of controlling the receivable position within desirable limits. Directly related to the credit terms, the collection period generally can be readily compared to related industry average ratios. If a 30-day payment cycle is used, then the collection period should not

exceed $1\frac{1}{3}$ times the established payment period. (This is the situation
in the preceding example—36.4 days.)

Usually, changes in the collection ratio (particularly, if significant)
result from revisions in the organization's credit policy (greater or lesser
liberal terms) or from inability to collect its receivables on the scheduled
due dates.

**Using the Planning Aging
Receivables Procedure
in Collections Estimating and Cash
Flow**

Another method of assessing the receivable position is to analyze the
individual receivable balances at year-end. This can also be done on a
monthly or quarterly basis, particularly if the system is mechanized. If
significant collection changes are occurring from one time period to another, then the aging process can assist in highlighting specific problem
situations.

**MAKING THE
CALCULATION**

In the aging procedure, the receivable accounts are classified according
to their billing dates. Generally, the time periods are under 30 days, 30–
60 days, and 61–90 days. Accounts may be over 90 days in some situations.

Example: The annual periods in the following table end on December 31 of
19X3 and 19X4.

Aging Procedure (in $000,000s)

Age of Billings	Billed 12/31/X3	% of Total	Billed 12/31/X4	% of Total	% Variance
Under 30 Days	$77.7	80	$ 89.3	85	+5
30–60 Days	14.6	15	12.6	12	−3
61–90 Days	4.9	5	3.2	3	−2
Totals	$97.2	100	$105.1	100	

**INTERPRETING
THE RATIO**

The billing age of the receivables seems to indicate a favorable trend in
the collection activity. Outstanding receivables, as of 12/31/X4, show a
5% increase in the billing category under 30 days, in spite of a 15%
increase ($89.3 million − $77.7 = $11.6 ÷ $77.7 = 15%) in customer
billings. In the 30–60 Days classification, the billings outstanding decreased 3% in 19X4, and 2% lower uncollected billings were scheduled
in the 61–90 Days category. The trends are basically favorable relative
to the anticipated collection process.

The aging receivables approach can be very useful in cash flow planning as well as in estimating possibly doubtful collections. If unfavorable trends occur, then it may be necessary to output a detailed report of the specific past due accounts for investigation and corrective action with the customer.

Days of Sales in Receivables Ratio

MAKING THE CALCULATION

To ascertain the trend of days of uncollected sales in receivables:

1. Convert the quarterly sales to a sales per day factor.
2. Divide the resultant value into the ending receivable balance.

This process can be performed on a monthly basis (which is more precise for trends) or annually (for comparative purposes).

Example: A 90-day factor is used for the quarterly periods and 360 days on an annual basis for purposes of consistency. The receivable balance annual average is $107.3 million.

(in $000,000s)

	First Quarter	Second Quarter	Third Quarter	Fourth Quarter	Annual Quarter
Sales/period	$252.8	$274.9	$276.2	$273.1	$1,077.0
Receivable balances	110.4	111.5	102.3	105.1	107.3
Days/period	90	90	90	90	360
Sales/day	$ 2.81	$ 3.05	$ 3.07	$ 3.03	$ 2.99
Days sales in receivables	39.3	36.5	33.3	34.7	35.9

The first two quarters had the highest days of sales in receivables, primarily because of the higher-than-average receivable balances. First quarter sales were the lowest of the periods, which accounted for the high 39.3 days factor of sales in that period.

HOW TO ESTIMATE ENDING RECEIVABLE BALANCES

These results, if proven consistent over time periods, can provide at least a preliminary basis for *estimating ending receivable balances* predicated on sales projections. The calculating process is as follows:

$$(1) \quad \text{Daily sales} = \frac{\text{Credit sales}}{\text{Days/period}}$$

$$(2) \quad \begin{array}{l}\text{Ending} \\ \text{receivable} \\ \text{balance}\end{array} = \text{Days of sales factor} \times \text{Sales/day}$$

Further, days of sales in receivables provides *trends among periods* for analysis and assessment relative to future anticipations.

CALCULATING DAYS OF SALES IN BACKLOG TO MEASURE BACKLOG EFFECTIVENESS

The success and growth of any organization depends upon its ability to sustain its current business volume and acquire new business. This task is accomplished by zealous sales promotion, in connection with the development of new products and/or services. Therefore, sales bookings (new business) clearly represent one of the most sensitive areas that command management's attention when evaluating operational trends. Management must continually monitor progress because of its importance in operating and planning decisions.

To compute the ending backlog balance:

1. Combine the period's beginning balance with new orders booked.
2. Deduct period sales/deliveries.

Also consider adjustments for canceled or additional quantities, price changes, and possible errors in data entry or computations.

How to Measure Backlog Position Effectiveness

Management and their planning/marketing staffs spend considerable time and effort developing realistic sales goal plans. Their projections are based on:

1. past performance
2. market intelligence
3. anticipated sales predicated on customer objectives and feedback
4. production capability
5. adequate and skilled manpower
6. facility/equipment requirements
7. availability of financial resources

MAKING THE CALCULATION   To measure backlog effectiveness, you must analyze the historical performance of the *days of sales factor in backlog*. To do so, convert period sales into days of sales, and divide this factor into the backlog balance. The equation is as follows:

$$\text{Days of sales in backlog} = \frac{\text{Backlog balance}}{\text{Sales volume} \div \text{Days in period}}$$

Example: The following data are for the years 19X3 and 19X4:

(in $000s)*

	Backlog Balance	Total Sales	Days in Period	Sales/ Day	Days sales in Backlog
19X3	$1,300.0	$1,070.0	360	$2,972	43.7
19X4	1,600.0	1,250.0	360	3,472	46.1

*Excluding sales/day

A WORD OF CAUTION WHEN INTERPRETING THE RESULTS

Note that the backlog position may be misleading because some sales may be for long-range delivery. These may not help in the current period's operational activity, where the objective is to maintain a stabilized work force on a scheduled plan of operations. Therefore, a detailed analysis must be made of the backlog position to ensure a continuing level of activity on a sustained and scheduled basis. The volume of backlog affects all organizations' operations either directly or indirectly and has a decided effect on financial resources, profitability, and return on investment.

HOW TO ANALYZE THE RELATIONSHIP AMONG PURCHASES, PAYABLES, AND DISBURSEMENTS AS AN AID IN BUSINESS PLANNING

A definite and constant relationship exists among the purchasing activity, trade payable commitments, and their payment. Model 7 illustrates an assessment of the 19X4 quarterly and annual actuals, along with the *resultant statistics and ratios* that evolved from the analysis of the data.

The information presented in Model 7 has no major or significant implications. Among quarterly periods, the dollar values were fairly consistent, indicating that seasonal fluctuations were minimal and that there were no radical changes in the operating environment. The beginning and ending payable balances were practically identical ($42.0 million versus $41.9 million). The same holds true for both the annual purchases and disbursements.

How to Interpret the Data

APPLICATIONS

The *days purchases in payables* averaged 48.1 days or approximately 1½ months of purchases in the payable balance. This factor, if proven valid

MODEL 7. Analyzing Purchases, Disbursements, and Payables: Quarterly Assessment of Relationships.

(in $000,000s)

	First Quarter	Second Quarter	Third Quarter	Fourth Quarter	Annual Period
Accounts payable, BB	$ 42.0	$ 40.7	$ 41.8	$ 43.3	$ 42.0
Period purchases	78.3	79.2	78.9	77.1	313.5
Total	$120.3	$119.9	$120.7	$120.4	$355.5
Cash disbursements	79.6	78.1	77.4	78.5	313.6
Accounts payables, EB	$ 40.7	$ 41.8	$ 43.3	$ 41.9	$ 41.9

Averages per day (90 days in quarter; 360 annual)

	First Quarter	Second Quarter	Third Quarter	Fourth Quarter	Annual Period
Purchases ($000s)	$870	$880	$877	$856	$871 avg.
Disbursements ($000s)	884	868	860	872	871 avg.
Days purchases in payables ($40,700 ÷ 870)	46.8	47.5	49.4	48.9	48.1
Days purchases in disbursements ($79,600 ÷ 870)	91.5	88.8	88.3	91.7	90.1

Ratios

	First Quarter	Second Quarter	Third Quarter	Fourth Quarter	Annual Period
Accounts payable turnover	1.9	1.9	1.8	1.8	7.5
Disbursements to purchases + Beginning balance ($79.6 ÷ $120.3)	66%	65%	64%	65%	—

Trends in % using first quarter as base period:

	First Quarter	Second Quarter	Third Quarter	Fourth Quarter	Annual Period
Purchases	100	101	101	98.5	—
Disbursements	100	98.1	97.2	98.6	—
Ending payables	100	103	106	103	—

over future periods, would be of importance in the projection of payable balances based on the purchasing activity. If nothing else, the days factor can be used as a guideline in verifying payables' integrity developed by more detailed conventional methods.

Average daily purchases versus daily disbursements were practically on a *one-to-one* basis for the year. On a quarterly assessment review, the average days purchases in disbursement payouts were approximately 90 days. This factor may be used for planning material/supplies payable disbursements based on their purchase values.

The *accounts payable turnover ratio* was approximately 1.8–1.9 times per quarterly period, with the annual rate being 7.5. This ratio indicates the number of times the payables turned over within a time period (quarterly and annual periods were used). Multiplying the quarterly factor by four will yield the annual turnover, indicating payment cycle results.

This ratio can be used not only for comparative purposes among periods but also for estimating purchases based on a given account's *payable ending balance.* Generally, however, purchases are estimated before payable balances are projected. Yet the factor approach may be useful in projecting ending payable balances by dividing the estimated purchases by the turnover rate.

Disbursements as a percent of beginning payable balance plus purchases averaged 65% per quarter. This statistic can be used for comparative purposes among time periods. It might also be used for estimating disbursements based on the combined total of the beginning payable balance plus the period's purchases.

How to Use Financial Data Trend Ratios

At the bottom of Model 7 are the *calculated trends* for purchases, disbursements, and ending payable balances. They were developed by dividing the first quarter values into the other three quarter amounts. The trend variations among periods were minor, except the third quarter ending payable balance of 106%. This figure resulted from a decrease in cash disbursements compared to disbursements in the other periods.

A series of *trend ratios* is designed to show an increase or decrease in an item, as well as the rate of increase or decrease. The trend ratios do not in themselves indicate whether movement is favorable or unfavorable but rather reveal the behavior of the items as time passes. Further, they provide a horizontal analysis of comparable data among periods.

HOW TO EMPLOY THE VELOCITY PROCEDURE TO ASSESS AN ORGANIZATION'S DEBT-PAYING CAPABILITY

Historically, this method of analyzing an organization's debt-paying ability was used primarily for liquidation assessment—that is, for determining whether a business could pay its debts in the extreme event that it liquidated its operations. However, an organization can also use this procedure to analyze its ongoing operations relative to its financial position in terms of its debt-paying ability.

This method compares the *velocity* (the rapidity of debt-paying status change) of the current assets and current liabilities. The data involve the *maturity and aging* primarily of the receivables, payables, and inventory. Further, they present the current position on an estimated time-cash-realizable (timing of cash availability inflow versus outflow) basis.

Analyzing the Current Financial Position

Model 8 illustrates the computation process and results, using basic and generalized data. The estimated results indicate that the accounts receivable represents 41.5% of the total current asset collections and that the inventory is 51.6%. The aged payable commitments represent 85.5% of the total current liabilities listed.

With respect to the *maturity of the receivables,* 69.5% are anticipated to be collected within 30 days with the balance due in 31 to 90 days. Relative to inventory, 15.5% of the cash sales will be collected within 30 days, and the balance is to be received in 31–60 days. Credit sales, representing 72.3% of the inventory sales, will be collected in 90 days.

In the *accounts payable* section, 52.1% of the payables are scheduled for payment within 30 days, and the balance is due in 31–90 days.

The current position (the ratio of current assets to current liabilities) reflects a 2.6 rate, which appears to be adequate in light of industry averages. The *working capital ratio* (that is, working capital to liabilities) is calculated to be 1.6, indicating that the owners' equity in the current assets is 1.6 times the current creditors' contribution to capital.

INTERPRETING THE RESULTS

The sum of the estimated cash receipts within 30 days and the cash balance exceeds ($62.9 million − $28.0 = $34.9 ÷ 28) payables due in 30 days by 125%. These estimates indicate that the organization is in a favorable position to meet its immediate debt commitments. Model 8's data do not represent a cash budget because they do not reflect estimated expenses, tax provisions, and miscellaneous commitments.

APPLICATION

This type of current position assessment affords management an opportunity to review its debt-paying ability. It can also be used as a basis to support future debt commitments and creditor confidence in the organization's ability to pay its debts on schedule.

HOW TO USE THE DAYS PURCHASES OUTSTANDING RATIO TO DETERMINE WHETHER YOU ARE MEETING YOUR TRADE PAYABLE COMMITMENTS

MAKING THE CALCULATION

The primary objective of this ratio is to review an organization's trade payable commitments and to determine whether it is meeting them on schedule. The equation for the calculation is as follows:

$$\text{Days purchases outstanding} = \frac{\text{Trade payables}}{\text{Period purchases} \div \text{Days in period}}$$

MODEL 8. Current Position of Debt-Paying Ability: Velocity Method.
($000s)

Current Assets			Current Liabilities		
Cash		$ 10,000	Notes Payable in 30 days		$ 8,000
Aged Receivables (Estimated)		*% of A/R*	*Aged Payables (Estimated)*		*% of A/P*
Due in 30 days	$41,400	69.5	Due in 30 days	$28,000	58.1
31–60 days	15,000	25.1	31–60 days	14,700	30.5
61–90 days	3,200	5.4	61–90 days	5,500	11.4
	59,600			48,200	
Aged Inventory (Estimated)		*% of Inv.*			
Cash Sales					
In 30 days	$11,500	15.5			
31–60 days	9,000	12.2			
Credit sales in 90 days	53,600	72.3			
	74,100				
Totals	$143,700			$56,200	

49

Example: Using the following data, calculate the days purchases outstanding. Although the information is on an annual basis, the same calculation can be used for monthly and quarterly periods.

($000s)

	Average Trade Payables	Total Purchases	Days in Period	Days Purchases Outstanding
19X3	$10,150	$ 90,100	360	40.6
19X4	12,400	113,500	360	39.3

Calculations: *19X3*   *19X4*

$$\frac{\$10,150}{\$90,100 \div 360 = 250.3} = 40.6 \text{ days} \qquad \frac{\$12,400}{\$113,500 \div 360 = 315.3} = 39.3 \text{ days}$$

INTERPRETING THE RESULTS

As you can see, the fewer days of purchases in the payable balance, the more favorable the debts paying ability. Further, from a vendor viewpoint, the ratio is one measure of an organization's ability to pay its debts on schedule.

This illustration indicates that there were 1.3 days fewer purchases in the 19X4 payable balance as compared to 19X3. In 19X4, purchases increased by 26% ($113,500 − $90,100 = $23,400 ÷ $90,100), whereas the payable balance increased by only 22%, which accounts for the fewer days purchases outstanding.

USING THE NUMBER OF TIMES INTEREST EARNED TO ASSESS DEBTS PAYING

Another ratio that focuses on debt-paying ability is the *number of times interest is covered by operating profits.*

MAKING THE CALCULATION

Example: The following computations are based on the data in Model 6 by quarterly periods. The equation employed is:

$$\text{Times interest earned} = \frac{\text{Income from operations}}{\text{Interest expense}}$$

($000s)

	First Quarter	Second Quarter	Third Quarter	Fourth Quarter	Annual Period
Income from operations	$17,100	$19,600	$16,500	$12,800	$66,000
Interest earned	800	800	900	900	3,400
Times interest earned	21.4	24.5	18.3	14.2	19.4

Income from operations represents the amount of earnings available to meet the fixed interest obligations on the funded debt of $42.6 million. The times interest earned ratio ranged from *14.2 times* in the fourth quarter to a high of *24.5 times* in the second quarter, with an annual average of *19.4 times*.

The primary cause for the fluctuations in the times interest earned ratio is due to the changes in the income from operations (a high of $19.6 million to a low of $12.8). Interest expense remained relatively stable. This ratio *signifies* that there is an average of $19.40 of operating income earned for each dollar of interest expense.

INTERPRETING THE RESULTS

The high ratios in the example are favorable to the organization's financial position. Conversely, the lower ratios may indicate adverse financial situations if the operating income were to decline substantially, since interest expense is a basic commitment that must be paid on schedule.

In the example, the low times interest earned ratio of 14.2 is due primarily to the reduced income from operations of $12.8 million. The decline was 34.7% below the second quarter high of $19.6 million operating income. As shown in Model 6, the operating income decline was due to reduced gross profit and higher G&A expenses.

APPLICATION

This ratio is used to measure the level to which operating income can decline without adversely affecting the organization's ability to meet interest payments on its fixed funded debt. Note that the income from operations values is used because, if income decreased, income taxes would decline proportionately. Note too that an organization may have fixed commitments other than interest expense in the form of rental obligations on leased property. In such situations, the fixed costs are added to the interest expense, and the *ratio* would properly be classified as the *number of time fixed costs earned*. The addition of other significant fixed charges to interest expense may have a decided impact on operating income results.

HOW TO USE THE INTEREST PLUS FUNDED DEBT PAYMENT RATIO TO DETERMINE WHETHER AN ORGANIZATION CAN MEET DEBT COMMITMENTS

MAKING THE CALCULATION

This ratio assesses an organization's position in meeting interest plus debt payments on a scheduled basis. The portion of the long-term debt due for payment within the current annual period is classified as a current liability in the balance sheet. The equation used to derive this ratio is as follows:

$$\text{Debt coverage} = \frac{\text{Pretax earnings}}{\text{Interest} + \left(\dfrac{\text{Funded debt payment}}{1 - \text{Tax rate}}\right)}$$

Example:

Ratio Calculation
(in $000s)

	First Quarter	Second Quarter	Third Quarter	Fourth Quarter
Interest expense	$ 800	$ 800	$ 900	$ 900
Funded debt payments	1,000	1,000	1,000	1,000
Pretax earnings	15,000	17,300	14,400	10,800
Tax rate	52%	52%	52%	52%
Times ratio	5.2	6.0	4.8	3.6

Illustrating computation for first quarter:

$$\text{Debt coverage} = \frac{\$15,000}{\$800 + \dfrac{\$1,000}{.48}} = \frac{15,000}{2,883} = 5.2 \text{ times}$$

INTERPRETING THE RESULTS

The decline in the ratio is attributed to the decrease in pretax earnings. Interest expense was relatively stable and the funded debt payments were fixed. This is an unfavorable trend because the ratio is decreasing from a high of *6.0 times* in the second quarter to a low of *3.6 times* in the fourth quarter.

APPLICATION

The ratio decline should serve as a warning to the organization (particularly if other debt-paying ratios are following a similar pattern), that it may encounter problems in borrowing more money and meeting debt commitments on a scheduled basis. Trade vendors would also be concerned, since this situation may lead to deferred payments and even default. The organization must make a detailed assessment of prevailing circumstances for possible corrective action.

HOW TO ASSESS INVENTORY CONTROLS

General management policy is to carry enough inventory to support the actual and/or anticipated sales volume. In addition to the inventory investment, management must consider the expense incurred to support activities related to inventory management, such as procurement, inspection, handling, storage, and record keeping (a computerized process).

Control of inventory is probably one of the most difficult management problems. The dilemma is that inventory must be large enough to meet customer demands and, at the same time, conservative enough to minimize

1. support expenses
2. possible interest on borrowed funds
3. deterioration or obsolescence losses
4. the negative impact on cash flow from sales

To measure inventory efficiency and monitor significant changes, you must employ some form of performance measurement and planning. Three approaches used by most organizations are the

1. ratio of inventory to cost of sales
2. turnover factor
3. average age of inventories in terms of days

Using the Ratio of Inventory to Cost of Sales to Assess and Project Inventory Levels

MAKING THE CALCULATION

To calculate this ratio, divide the average inventory by the cost of sales.

Example: In the following table, the annual inventory average was derived by combining the quarterly balances and dividing the total by four. Normally, the average would be obtained by combining the beginning and ending balances and dividing by two.

(in $000,000s)

Inventory values	$260.0	$268.5	$256.9	$243.4	$257.2
Cost of sales	223.9	243.3	248.1	247.7	*963.0*
Ratio of inventory to cost of sales	116%	110%	104%	98%	27%
Annualized basis	27%	28%	26%	25%	

INTERPRETING THE RESULTS

Note that the inventory ratio to cost of sales declined from 116% to 98% in the fourth quarter. This is a favorable trend in that the inventory balances on hand were decreasing whereas the cost of sales by period were increasing. The situation indicates that the inventory levels were being used more effectively over the course of the year. The *annual average* of 27% means that the inventory balance represents about 25% of the cost of sales.

APPLICATION

If these ratios are proven to be valid historically, they can be used to estimate (at least, preliminarily) inventory levels based on cost of sales projections. They may also be useful in checking projected inventory levels that were developed by more conventional methods.

Using Turnover of Average Inventories to Measure Inventory Effectiveness

Turnover ratios express the relationship between operating results and the capital resources employed. Inventory turnover can be expressed on the basis of sales or cost of sales. A number of organizations use sales because this element is commonly employed for other types of turnover calculations, such as expense and profit margins. Consensus, however, among professionals is that the most appropriate basis is *cost of sales*. The more acceptable turnover ratio is therefore the *cost of sales relationship to average inventory*.

Generally, the sales ratios reflect similar trends as cost of sales, but they are *less accurate* due to the variations in profit margin. Sales can be used as a substitute when cost of sales data is unavailable. Note that, in the retail environment, the ratio of sales to inventory at *sales prices* provides the same turnover ratio as cost of sales to inventory at *cost prices*.

MAKING THE CALCULATION   *Example:*

Quarterly Turnover Ratios and Annual Average
(in $000s)

	First Quarter	Second Quarter	Third Quarter	Fourth Quarter	Annual Period
Cost of sales (C/S)	$223.9	$243.3	$248.1	$247.7	$963.0
Average inventory	260.0	268.5	256.9	243.4	257.2
Annualized C/S	895.6	973.2	992.4	990.8	
Turnover Ratios					
Number of times	.86	.91	.96	1.0	3.7
Annualized	3.4	3.6	3.9	4.1	3.7

INTERPRETING THE RESULTS   The aggregate average annual turnover rate is 3.7. Quarterly period ratios varied from .86 to 1.0, which signifies an improved inventory utilization effectivity—indicating more inventory is being absorbed into the cost of sales.

The Preferred Approach: Turnover of Inventories by Classification

The turnover ratios in the preceding example represent the aggregate inventory. Another approach is to ascertain the turnover ratios by inventory categories. This approach is more informative because you can more thoroughly assess capital resource efficiency and highlight specific problems or inventory management achievements.

MAKING THE CALCULATION

The ratio classifications are as follows:

Turnover of	Calculating Equations
1. Finished goods	= *Cost of sales ÷ Average finished products inventory
2. Work in process	= *Cost of products manufactured ÷ Work in process average inventory
3. Raw materials	= *Cost of materials used ÷ Raw material average inventory

*Costs could be annualized.

APPLICATION

Determining the turnover ratios by inventory classifications provides data relative to the magnitude of excessive or depleted inventory levels; it also highlights the slow-moving and/or potentially obsolete inventory. Further, this process permits the assessment of (1) the degree of coordination between the production and sales of the various products and (2) the balance maintained in the raw materials used in production. You can also ascertain which materials are overstocked and which are insufficient.

A WORD OF CAUTION

Advantageous purchasing resulting in surplus stock may be justified under certain circumstances. Yet you should carefully consider the disadvantages of possible obsolescence, increased carrying costs, expenditure of resources, and future price declines.

Drawbacks to Physical Turnover Ratios

To determine the turnover of inventory, compare the average monthly volume in units of inventory with the volume of units sold or issued. The results represent a *physical turnover ratio,* which is often used as a *measure of operating performance.*

Certain negative aspects are associated with the use of the physical turnover ratios:

The assumption that all units of inventory are homogeneous is generally not the case. You therefore have no means for comparing the experience of one period with another.

The available inventory units fluctuate between minimum and maximum. As a result, the ratio improves as the minimum is approached and becomes more negative when receipts increase the available inventory.

The selection of the base affects the turnover ratio—namely, beginning, ending, and average balances. Business cycles and seasonal fluctuations will further complicate the selection of a basis.

IMPLEMENTING INVENTORY CLASSIFICATION RATIOS TO CUT COSTS AND FREE UP WORKING CAPITAL

Inventories provide material items for various product/function activities. Some items are used immediately and others turn over slowly. Items that you consider inactive or obsolete only increase costs and absorb working capital needlessly. This type of inventory should be minimized.

Since material handling costs can be expensive, their impact can affect net profit—especially in the case of slow-moving inventory. Storage costs can be reduced and control simplified if such inventory is handled and moved only infrequently. Rapidly moving items can then be stored for immediate accessibility and movement at minimal effort and cost.

With inventory classified into activity (or usage) categories, you can establish periodic inventory cycles so that slow-moving and inactive inventory items will be counted less frequently. The segregation of inventory offers a number of advantages, particularly in organizations with a substantial working capital investment in inventories. Adopting this procedure will result in a reduction of materials handling, storage, and obsolescence costs; it also makes more working capital available for priority operational requirements.

Inventory segregation has another distinct advantage as a decision-making tool because it gives management an index of associated activity for each stock item carried in inventory. This index should substantially improve the purchasing and inventory control functions. For the procurement cycle system, you can use a series of *control ratios* to classify the inventory and provide realistic inventory balances.

COMPUTING THE AVERAGE AGE OF INVENTORIES IN DAYS TO MEASURE INVENTORY EFFECTIVENESS

MAKING THE CALCULATION   The average days of inventories is computed by using the following equation:

$$\text{Average days} \atop \text{of inventories} = \left(\text{Number of days} \atop \text{in period}\right) \times \left(\frac{\text{Period-end inventory balances}}{\text{Total cost of sales}}\right)$$

Example: For simplicity, a 90-day quarter and a 360-day annual calculation were used in the following table:

	(in $000,000s)				
	First Quarter	*Second Quarter*	*Third Quarter*	*Fourth Quarter*	*Annual Period*
Inventory balances	$260.0	$268.5	$256.9	$243.4	$243.4
Cost of sales	223.9	243.4	248.1	247.7	963.0
Days in period	90	90	90	90	360
Inventory divided by cost of sales	1.16	1.10	1.04	.98	.253
Average Age of Inventories (in days)	104	99	94	88	91

INTERPRETING THE RESULTS

The average age of inventories declined in each quarter, with an annual average of 91 days. This result indicates a favorable trend, particularly if it continues. The cause for the declining trend is a decreasing inventory balance, whereas the cost of sales was increasing, apparently as the result of a more effective utilization of inventory.

How to Estimate Inventory Balances Based on Projected Cost of Sales

MAKING THE CALCULATION

If your age factors and trends prove to be valid over time, you may be able, at least on a preliminary basis, to estimate inventory balances based on projected cost of sales. The following procedure assumes an annual basis, but it can apply to other time periods:

Steps	*Refer to Preceding Example*	*Annual Basis*
1.	Select average age of inventory factor to be used.	91 days
2.	Indicate number of days in period.	360 days
3.	Divide results in Step 1 by Step 2 (91 ÷ 360).	.253
4.	Multiply projected cost of sales by factor in Step 3.	$963.0 × .253
5.	Result is an estimated inventory balance.	$243.6

USING THE SALES-TO-INVENTORY RATIO TO MEASURE SALES EFFICIENCY

This ratio measures the relationship of inventory to sales volume, indicating whether there is too much or too little inventory to support a given level of sales. (Again, cost of sales is generally used for this ratio, but sales can substitute for it.)

The relation of inventory to sales volume is a general measure of sales efficiency. The major objective is to have the smallest possible inventory to meet sales requirements efficiently. As a rule, an organization that conducts a large volume of business on a comparatively small inventory has a high degree of merchandising effectiveness.

When you compare the dollar amount of sales with the dollar value of the inventory, note that these two amounts are on different bases. The inventory is valued conventionally at cost or market, whichever is lower. On the other hand, sales are valued at selling price (cost plus gross margin). Further, to compare two or more periods, you must know the prevailing business conditions. As an example, a change in the price level at which new stock is acquired would change the relationship between sales and inventory. The dollar relationship could vary markedly without any actual change in the physical volume of sales or inventory.

A WORD OF CAUTION

The ratio of sales to inventory is generally considered to be a very rough measure of performance. Moreover, most businesses have seasonal fluctuations, and the inventory on a balance sheet date may therefore represent a very high or a very low point.

MAKING THE COMPUTATION

To compute this ratio, divide sales by the inventory balance (preferably an averaged value).

Example:

(in $000,000s)

	First Quarter	Second Quarter	Third Quarter	Fourth Quarter	Annual Period
Sales volume	$ 252.8	$ 274.9	$ 276.2	$ 273.1	$1,077.0
Annualized sales	1,011.2	1,099.6	1,104.8	1,092.4	1,077.0
Inventory balances	260.0	268.5	256.9	243.4	257.2 Avg
Sales-to-inventory ratio	.97	1.0	1.1	1.1	4.2
Annualized sales to inventory	3.9	4.1	4.3	4.5	4.2

INTERPRETING THE RESULTS

On a quarterly basis, the sales to inventory ratio ranged from .97 to 1.1, with an annual average of 4.2. Based on annualized sales, the ratios ranged from a low of 3.9 to a high of 4.5; in essence, sales were approximately four times inventory. The variations among periods are primarily attributed to an increasing sales base. The decline in inventory, on the other hand, represents a favorable situation if it does not hinder operational objectives.

HOW TO USE INDIRECT TO DIRECT PERSONNEL RATIOS FOR MANPOWER PLANNING AND CONTROL

One of the essentials in all organizations regardless of size is a pool of competent human resources, both direct and indirect, to perform the tasks and services necessary to achieve operational goals and objectives. Manpower planning and control are vital functions to all levels of supervision in order to produce a competitive product or to perform services that can be sold profitably. Management should give indirect personnel requirements particularly close scrutiny because of their impact on profitable operations and overhead costs.

MAKING THE CALCULATION

To monitor indirect manpower planning and control, you can use the *indirect to direct personnel ratio*. To calculate this ratio, *divide the indirect personnel level by the direct.*

Example: The following quarter-end ratios were developed using the data from Model 6.

	19X4				
	March	*June*	*September*	*December*	*Annual*
Indirect to direct ratio	47.6% (16,522 ÷ 34,737)	47.8%	47.7%	47.3%	47.6%

INTERPRETING THE RESULTS

The ratios are relatively consistent throughout the year with an average of 47.6%. Between the end of March and the end of December, direct personnel increased 3.0% and the indirect manpower increased by 388 or 2.3%. This represents a favorable trend, indicating that management has maintained a desirable relationship between direct and indirect personnel.

How to Project Indirect Manpower

As part of the organization's preliminary operating plan, indirect manpower projections can be made in two ways: (1) by multiplying direct manpower requirements by the average ratio (such as 47.6%) or (2) by a management-controlled objective ratio if historical experience supports the validity of this approach. However, indirect manpower—like direct—is planned in the final analysis by individual organizational units according to their variable activities and needs. Justification of the forecast must be based on the overall operating plan's objectives.

USING THE SALES-TO-DIRECT-PERSONNEL RATIO TO PROJECT SALES

MAKING THE CALCULATION

Projecting preliminary sales data, if properly validated, may be appropriate, based on a direct manpower forecast. You can use the relationship of sales to direct manpower to check the reasonableness not only of sales projections based on historical experience but also of future expectations developed by more conventional procedures. The factors are developed using the following equation:

$$\text{Sales to direct manpower} = \frac{\text{Sales volume}}{\text{Direct manpower}}$$

Example: Based on the data in Model 6, these quarterly period and annual average factors were developed:

19X8

	March	June	September	December	Quarterly Average
Sales to direct manpower (per one direct person)	$7,278	$7,957	$7,931	$7,633	$7,698

For the March ending period, sales of $252.8 million were divided by the average direct manpower of 34,737 to obtain the $7,278 figure. The quarterly average was obtained by using the period average sales of $269.2 million divided by the quarterly direct manpower average of 34,972. The total sales for the year per direct headcount is approximately $30,796 ($1,077.0 million sales divided by the average direct manpower of 34,972).

INTERPRETING THE RESULTS

The primary cause for the low sales factor in March is below-average quarterly sales. The higher factors for June and September resulted from a larger sales volume, while the direct manpower strength remained below the annual quarterly average.

SALES TO TOTAL MANPOWER FACTOR: ONE APPROACH TO SALES ASSESSMENT AND PLANNING

MAKING THE CALCULATION

Although this relationship is not usually helpful to most organizations, it is a possible approach to sales assessment and planning. The equation for its development follows:

$$\text{Sales to total manpower} = \frac{\text{Sales volume}}{\text{Total manpower}}$$

Example: Using the data in Model 6, the following factors were calculated:

	March	June	September	December	Quarterly Average
Sales to total manpower	$4,932 (per employee)	$5,384	$5,372	$5,183	$5,218

INTERPRETING THE RESULTS

The below-average ratio in March is primarily attributed to below-average quarterly sales. The above-average factors for the June and September quarters resulted from higher sales without an attendant increase in total manpower.

A WORD OF CAUTION

The drawback to this ratio is that indirect headcount is included in the factor. Indirect manpower is not, of course, directly involved in producing or performing customer services. The ratio may be skewed as a result. An organization may be top-heavy in administrative, clerical, and support activities due to either inadequate controls or the nature of the business. Only historical experience can verify the usefulness of this factor for performance assessment and planning.

3

How to Use Direct Cost and G&A Expenditure Ratios to Avoid Diluting Profits

CHAPTER HIGHLIGHTS

Cost ratios are commonly employed in analyzing operational cost activity. With these ratios in hand, the analyst is well equipped to control and plan costs with the object of establishing a competitive yet profitable product price.

To supply the data for analysis, objective setting, and program control, an effective cost accumulation system is indispensable. The requirements and phases of such a system make up the first section of the chapter.

Next you will become acquainted with what you must consider when making use of cost ratio analyses, specifically the relative merits of cost of sales versus sales data.

Overhead is then the focus of the discussion, particularly how to equitably allocate factory overhead expense to direct labor dollars and hours, prime cost, sales and cost of sales, machine hour rates, product units, and weighting factors.

Unit cost rates, in relation to product cost methods, are described and explained, with special attention given to G&A* and selling expense ratios to product units, sales, and total costs.

You will then see how a manpower plan is put together and how direct manpower is converted to labor hours by means of a computer program or manual calculations. The final section deals with the reporting of manpower actuals for assessment and planning.

Direct cost expenditures are costs directly associated with and identifiable to a tangible product, service, and/or project. Direct costs involve direct labor, direct material, plant (factory) overhead, and other direct costs such as computer usage, direct travel, production outside the plant, and possibly consultants. Costs are considered "direct" if they meet the following major criteria:

---

*General and Administrative expenses

Authorization to expend resources comes through approved product/ project work order guidelines.

Costs are properly *identified* as direct within the scope of the labor and organizational classification codes.

There must be appropriate *consistency in cost classification* and application throughout the organization.

Cost measurement must be in terms of specific units (direct hours, dollars, or other quantities) that are both practical and economical to use.

Direct costs must fulfill product/project requirements for production, service, and/or end item needs through either or all of the following:

    —R & D, engineering, or other related technical effort.
    —Material contribution to the product or the physical alteration to material.
    —Direct manpower utilization and performance.
    —Preparation of end item or services rendered documentation.

HOW TO ESTABLISH A COST ACCUMULATION SYSTEM

APPLICATIONS   A cost accumulation system enables you to identify the direct elements of cost in accordance with the established organizational procedures and specifically relate them to a product, service, project, contract, or sales order as required. Indirect costs are generally identified to organizational levels and/or through an overhead rate application.

Costs are charged to the organization performing the task or to the responsible organization for which the work is being performed. The cost charging justification is based on an approved budget authorization notice. The cost charge assignment is resolved by the responsible management before the work activity actually commences and resources (in the form of labor, material, etc.) are expended. This is a cost control procedure for ensuring appropriate organization identification and responsibility for proper and specific cost charging and accumulation before effort is initiated.

The collected information must be accurate and timely for all organizational levels of reporting as required, such as cost center, section, department, project budget center, functional (manufacturing, engineering) and division summaries.

In most organizations, particularly those dealing with high volume transactions and diversified activities, the cost accumulation process is computerized for ease in extensive record keeping, summations, and multiple-user reports on a timely basis for analysis, corrective task direction, and planning.

REQUIREMENTS To establish a rewarding and efficient cost accumulation system, you must be certain of the following prerequisites:

1. Approved work authorization documents.
2. Integrity in and disciplined adherence to cost system processing requirements.
3. To the extent possible, all relevant direct cost elements should be related to the basic labor charge.
4. Supervision incurring the cost expenditure must be responsible for cost assignment.
5. The appropriate and responsible financial operations organization should provide the users with the account structure, the system for cost accumulation, and surveillance guidelines at pre-established control points.

The Cost Accumulation Process, Step by Step

Control points are linked to the phases of the cost accumulation process. The pertinent steps are as follows:

- *Project:* To initiate a project, there must be a request (with cost justification) for management approval and authorization, which would include overhead expenditure requirements.
- *Budget Assignment and Control Responsibility:* The approved project authorization is forwarded to the concerned budgeting organization, which assigns the dollar budget and the responsibility for control.
- *Authority to Expend Resources:* The budget expenditure authorization requires that source documents (such as time cards or requests to purchase materials and supplies) be properly approved during the progression of the work activity.
- *Cost Expenditures:* Expenditures are to comply with the governing organizational policies and procedures so that they can be identified and classified as either direct or indirect.
- *Cost Classification:* The assigned cost classifications are validated in the mechanical master file through a matching process of input versus file established data content guidelines. If incorrect or non-existent in the file, they are returned to the responsible organization for correction and reentry.
- *Industrial or Cost Accounting Responsibilities:* The responsibility for maintaining the master audit file includes its composition and up-

dating. Their task is to develop, maintain, and monitor the cost accumulation system with respect to the following:

—Validating the work order and work authorization.
—Verifying the responsible source of cost incurrence.
—Comparing relevant estimates and budgets.
—Monitoring project inventories and open commitments.
—Accepting responsibility for required cost distributions.
—Maintaining such system surveillance activities as: Verifying direct/indirect cost classification, proper account distribution, labor charging by organization, request to purchase documentation and compatibility of labor charges with travel expenses, computer utilization audits, material disbursement documentation, and so on.

- *System Reporting:* This system produces various reports both for management review and for reasonable budget and cost control organizational units. The primary reports include cost data ledgers by contract/sales order, accounting work order, cost elements, and the work in process trial balance, which includes the cost of sales and expense information by contract. Special analytical reports are provided to meet organizational needs in terms of cost data assessment.

The cost accumulation system is the source for estimating, pricing, and other accounting statistics required for analysis and reporting. System mechanization enables you to capture such information at its basic source. Further, it permits you to update simultaneously more than one file to meet varied organization reporting requirements. Most important, the cost accumulation system provides the actual cost information needed to develop, use, and interpret direct cost expenditure *ratios* as well as their relationship to

1. cost of sales
2. sales
3. direct labor hours
4. cost per product unit

WHAT TO CONSIDER WHEN USING COST RATIO ANALYSES

CAUTION   Before looking at specific ratios, remember one thing about them: Although ratios are used as indexes of performance measurement, data analysis, and planning guidelines, your utilization of them must be tempered with discretion and judgment. Because most ratios attempt to reflect a great deal of information in a single figure, they can be misleading if you do not consider additional assessed data, such as

- ratio trends in successive periods of activity
- a detailed analysis of events that affected an organization's operations during the year
- ascertaining and evaluating the behavior of the related industry as a whole as it pertains to the organization

Comparing the Cost of Sales to Sales

Model 9 displays the relationship of cost of sales to sales for a six-month period plus the average of 88.0% for the combined periods. The lowest ratios of 86.5% and 86.8% in February and March are attributed to the relatively lower accumulated direct costs. The highest ratio 90.2% in the month of June reflects the largest cost by element, which was 43.8% greater than the lowest month. The increase was partially offset by a 37.8% higher sales volume for the same comparable periods.

When the cost of sales is compared to sales, the lowest ratio is only 1.8% below the average, and the highest monthly period ratio is 2.4% above the average. The average cost of sales ratio indicates a fairly reliable planning statistic to "ballpark" a total cost of sales value based on sales volume.

**Comparing Individual Cost
Elements to the Cost of Sales**

Note in Model 9 the period ratios by direct cost element, as well as the six-month averages.

Direct labor. The ratio of direct labor dollar to cost of sales averaged 26.2% for the six-month period. The *lowest ratio* of 24.6% occurred in the month of March, while labor costs increased 1.3% over February, yet the cost of sales were 3.1% higher, and thus the reduced ratio. The *highest ratio* of 27.8% occurred in May. While direct labor dollars exceeded April's by 11.0%, the total cost of sales increased by 10.8%, thereby accounting for the higher ratio.

Let's analyze the direct labor dollar ratio further. If the lowest ratio of 24.6% were applied to the six-month total of cost of sales ($225,500), the direct labor dollar estimate would be $55,500, instead of an actual of $59,000, with a negative difference of $3,500, or a 5.9% lower direct labor figure.

If we were to apply the largest ratio of 27.8% to the total cost of sales, the result would be $62,700, which is a plus $3,700 or 6.3% over

MODEL 9. Sales and Cost of Sales Ratio Analyses.
(in $000,000s)

Description	Jan.	Feb.	Mar.	Apr.	May	Jun.	Six-Month Period
Sales	$ 44.0	$ 37.0	$ 38.0	$ 41.0	$ 45.0	$ 51.0	$256.0
Direct labor	9.6	8.0	8.1	10.0	11.1	12.2	59.0
Overhead	13.0	10.9	11.0	13.5	14.8	16.4	79.6
Material and other direct costs (ODC)	15.8	13.1	13.9	12.6	14.1	17.4	86.9
Cost of sales	$ 38.4	$ 32.0	$ 33.0	$ 36.1	$ 40.0	$ 46.0	$225.5
Gross profit	5.6	5.0	5.0	4.9	5.0	5.0	30.5
G & A/selling expenses	2.7	2.1	2.2	2.7	2.1	2.0	13.8
Income from operations	$ 2.9	$ 2.9	$ 2.8	$ 2.2	$ 2.9	$ 3.0	$ 16.7
Operational Income to Sales Ratio	6.6	7.8	7.4	5.4	6.4	5.9	6.5
Direct Cost Ratios to Sales	%	%	%	%	%	%	%
Labor	21.8	21.6	21.3	24.4	24.7	23.9	23.1
Overhead expense	29.6	29.5	28.9	32.9	32.9	32.2	31.1
Material and ODC	35.9	35.4	36.6	30.7	31.3	34.1	33.9
Cost of sales	87.3	86.5	86.8	88.0	88.9	90.2	88.1
G&A/selling expense ratios	6.1	5.7	5.8	6.6	4.7	3.9	5.4
Total cost ratios	93.4	92.2	92.6	94.6	93.6	94.1	93.5
Direct Cost Ratios to Cost of Sales							
Labor	25.0	25.0	24.6	27.7	27.8	26.5	26.2
Overhead expenses	33.9	34.1	33.3	37.4	37.0	35.7	35.3
Material and ODC	41.1	40.9	42.1	34.9	35.2	37.8	38.5
Total	100.0	100.0	100.0	100.0	100.0	100.0	100.0

the actual cost of sales of $59,000. This indicates that the lowest estimated ratio would be under 5.9% and the highest ratio would result in a plus 6.3% in the cost of sales. These factors represent the maximum margin of difference in using the calculated ratios in the estimating/planning process based on the presented data.

Overhead expenses. As shown in Model 9, the average overhead expense ratio to cost of sales was 35.3% for the six-month period. The lowest period ratio of 33.3%, occurring in March, is primarily attributed to a 3.1% increase in cost of sales over February, whereas the overhead was only .9% higher for the same period.

The highest period ratio of 37.4% occurred in the month of April.

The primary cause is that overhead increased 22.7% over March, whereas the cost of sales was only 9.4% greater for the same period.

The lowest ratio was 2.0% under the six-month average, and the highest ratio was 2.1% over the average. Based on these factors, the maximum range of error of the calculated period ratios approximates a plus or minus 2.0%. Note that the overhead costs fluctuate by period with direct labor dollars but not in the same relative proportion.

Implications of the overhead expense ratios to cost of sales. In the above discussion, an analysis was made of the relationship of overhead expense incurred for a six-month period to the relevant time-period total cost of sales. This information provides management with a basis to project overhead expense as (1) a percent of cost of sales if that value is preliminarily forecasted in total as a *percent of sales;* (2) if overhead expenses are budgeted in detail (which they are before the budget is finalized), then the total overhead budget can be compared to historical experience as a percent of cost of sales to determine reasonableness based on the past. Predicated on the above two points, an *overhead rate* can be developed that will indicate to management:

a. Rate is too high in the competitive market (or possibly too low)
b. Usefulness in product/contract estimating and pricing
c. Highlights of revisions required to the overhead budget plan
d. Controls are necessary for specific overhead expenses
e. Overhead projections valid within the scope of operational objectives

The objectives in developing overhead expense ratios are to establish their usefulness in expense data analysis, determine and assess variations from the planned overhead budget and their cause, and to provide a realistic basis for planning future overhead expenses. The potential usage and value of overhead expense ratios are emphasized throughout this chapter.

Material and other direct costs. The six-month average ratio of material and other direct cost to cost of sales is 38.5%. The lowest ratio of 34.9% occurred in April. The primary reason for the low ratio is a 9.4% increase in cost of sales over the March period, whereas the direct material costs were 10.4% lower.

The highest period material cost ratio of 42.1% occurred in March. This situation resulted from a 6.1% increase in material and other costs over February, whereas the cost of sales increased only 3.1% over the comparable period.

The low April ratio of 34.9% was 3.6% under the six-month average of 38.5%, and the high ratio of 42.1% was 3.6% greater than the average. This indicates that the maximum error in estimating material costs based on cost of sales would be a plus or minus 3.6% for the high and low ratio periods.

Putting cost ratio analyses to work. Let's assume that your organization bases its preliminary cost planning data on the historical relationship of cost of sales to sales. To obtain the direct cost element values, simply apply the past experience ratios (if proven valid over time periods) to the cost of sales, as discussed. If this approach serves no other purpose you can use it to compare and assess planning data that are developed by more detailed and conventional procedures in the planning process. The approach represents an expedient means for finalizing the organization's operating plan relative to direct costs.

Comparing Individual Cost Elements to Sales

As shown in Model 9, the six-month average of direct labor costs to sales was 23%. On that basis, $1.00 in direct labor costs represents $4.34 ($256 million sales ÷ $59.0 million labor) in sales. If, however, you were to apply this factor to direct labor dollars from period to period, it would not truly represent the specific sales results. The differences ranged from 4% to 7% in sales values, both pluses and minuses, but the dollar value variances are not considered to be of major significance.

The overhead dollars to sales ratio averaged 31.1% for the six-month period. The fluctuations between periods ranged from 28.9% in March to 32.9% in both April and May. The higher overhead ratios are attributed to the greater percentage increases in overhead dollars for April and May (22.7% and 24.4% respectively over March), as compared to the higher sales volumes of 7.9% and 18.4% for the same periods.

The ratio of material and other direct cost dollars to sales averaged 33.9% for the six-month period. The differences between periods ranged from 30.7% in April to 36.6% in March. The low ratio is attributed to a 2.7% increase in sales over February, whereas overhead increased only .6% for the same comparable periods.

CAUTION

Any major fluctuations in the ratios of cost elements to sales from one period to another requires further analysis. You must determine the specific causes for the fluctuations before you can realistically use them for estimating and planning guidelines. As a form of performance measurement and analysis, the ratio approach is appropriate only if proven to be valid based on historical experience.

ALLOCATING OVERHEAD EXPENSES EQUITABLY

Direct labor costs, material costs, and other direct costs associated with manufacturing, either in total or per unit of production, are accumulated from basic source documentation. Timecards/reports, computer terminal input, bills of material, stores requisitions, work orders, and vendor invoices are all examples of such documentation. Manufacturing overhead, however, cannot be related specifically to any particular item of output. Yet burden or overhead application for overhead costing is essential to pricing policies, estimating, budgeting, inventory pricing, cost of sales determination, and so on. So you need methods to spread overhead over the production activity on an equitable basis.

Comparing Actual Versus Predetermined Overhead Rates

MAKING THE CALCULATION

Overhead may be applied to the product on the basis of rates or ratios, either before or after you actually ascertain the expenditures. If the overhead rate is based on actual costs for the period, then the *application rate* is obtained by dividing the overhead expenses by the *actual* production in terms of units, direct labor hours, or dollars:

$$\text{Application rate} = \frac{\text{Overhead expenses}}{\text{Production}}$$

To calculate a *predetermined rate*, divide the estimated overhead by the estimated production in units, direct labor hours, or dollars:

$$\text{Predetermined rate} = \frac{\text{Estimated overhead}}{\text{Estimated production}}$$

PROS AND CONS

When you use the actual overhead, however, you cannot complete the costing procedure until the close of the accounting period. This delay is often disadvantageous because you don't know the final costs on completed work until some time after the production order is filled, thereby delaying the accounting function also. When the overhead expenses are realistically *estimated in advance*, you can determine product costs immediately and smooth seasonal fluctuating activity. On the other hand, using estimates can lead to under- or overabsorbed overhead variances that must be adjusted periodically through accounting journals.

How to Apply Overhead to Products

Some of the common overhead applications are as follows:

ratio of overhead expenses to direct labor dollars

rate per direct labor hour

ratio of overhead expenses to prime costs (direct labor + material and ODC)

percentage of sales and cost of sales

rate per machine hour

product unit cost rate

Ratio of overhead expenses to direct labor dollars. As shown in Model 10, the average ratio for the six-month period is 1.349. To obtain this value, the overhead dollars of $79,600 were divided by the direct labor dollars of $59,000. The ratio indicates that every $1.00 of direct labor activity generates an average of $1.349 of overhead expense.

The lowest ratio of 1.333 is primarily attributed to the direct labor dollars being 12.9% above the six-month average, whereas the overhead expenses were only 11.3% higher than the average. The highest ratio of 1.363 in February represents a 1.0% increase over the six-month average.

APPLICATIONS   As long as the overhead ratio factors developed in Model 10 are reasonably consistent from one period to another, you can use the ratios to estimate the overhead expenses based on direct labor dollar projections.

The *advantages* of the direct labor dollar method are:

1. It is simple to use.
2. It is economical in that the information is readily available. Direct labor costs are derived from the labor distribution system and/or payroll summary, and the actual overhead expenses can be obtained from the expense ledger by organization, account, and total.

The *disadvantages* include:

1. The labor dollar expenditure bases are not necessarily adequate measures of the expense value contribution, as many overhead expenses (such as taxes, depreciation, and the like) do not depend on fluctuations of labor dollars.
2. The application ignores other factors in the cost of production, such as the use of expensive machinery that can exceed straight labor costs in some departments.
3. The method charges operations performed by high rate operators with proportionately more overhead than those performed by low rate operators.

MODEL 10. Miscellaneous Ratios and Rates.
Costs, Hours/Dollars, and Product Units
(Hours, Units, and Cost Values in $000s)

Data Description	Jan.	Feb.	Mar.	Apr.	May	Jun.	Six-Month Period
Direct Hour Rates							
Direct Labor Hours	3,500	3,000	3,000	3,600	3,300	3,700	20,100
Rates							
Direct labor dollars	$ 2.743	$ 2.667	$ 2.700	$ 2.778	$ 3.364	$ 3.297	$ 2.935
Overhead expense	3.714	3.633	3.667	3.750	4.485	4.432	3.960
Material and ODC	4.514	4.367	4.633	3.500	4.273	4.703	4.323
Cost of sales	$10.971	$10.667	$11.000	$10.028	$12.122	$12.432	$ 11.218
Cost Ratios							
Prime Costs (DL + DM + ODC)	$25,400	$21,100	$22,000	$22,600	$25,200	$29,600	$145,900
Overhead to prime costs	51.2	51.7	50.0	59.7	58.7	55.4	54.6
Overhead to DL dollars	1.354	1.363	1.358	1.350	1.333	1.344	1.349
Material to DL dollars	1.646	1.638	1.716	1.260	1.210	1.426	1.473
G&A/Selling Expense Ratio							
To sales	.061	.057	.058	.066	.047	.039	.054
To total costs	.066	.062	.063	.070	.050	.042	.058
Total Labor Cost Rate							
Cost of sales	$38,400	$32,000	$33,000	$36,100	$40,000	$46,000	$225,500
G&A/selling	2,700	2,100	2,200	2,700	2,100	2,000	13,800
Total costs	$41,100	$34,100	$35,200	$38,800	$42,100	$48,000	$239,300
Labor cost rate	$11.743	$11.367	$11.733	$10.778	$12.758	$12.973	$ 11.806
Cost Rates Per Unit							
Production Units	8,800	7,400	7,600	8,200	9,000	10,200	51,200
Rates							
Direct labor	$1.091	$1.081	$1.066	$1.220	$1.233	$1.196	$1.152
Overhead	1.477	1.473	1.447	1.646	1.644	1.608	1.555
Material/ODC	1.795	1.770	1.829	1.536	1.567	1.706	1.697
Sales costs to							
Units	$4.363	$4.324	$4.342	$4.402	$4.444	$4.510	$4.404
G&A/selling	.307	.284	.289	.329	.233	.196	.269
Total cost ratio to units	$4.670	$4.608	$4.631	$4.731	$4.677	$4.706	$4.673

Direct labor hour formula. To obtain the rate per direct labor hour, divide the overhead expense dollars by direct labor hours. Before applying overhead, you must determine the relationship (or ratio) between the amount of overhead expenses to be applied and the number of direct labor hours involved. The expense application can be by cost center, department, product, service, or total plant, as appropriate and required by the organization.

In Model 10, the six-month average direct labor hour rate is $3.96 per hour. The *lowest* expense rate of $3.63 occurred in February. This rate is attributed to a 16.2% reduction in overhead expenses, as compared to January, while direct labor hours were 14.3% lower in comparison.

The *highest* expense rate per hour of $4.485 occurred in May. The primary cause is that the May overhead increased by 9.6% over April, whereas the direct labor hours decreased by 8.3% for the same period. The simultaneous increase in expenses and decrease in labor hours accounted for the higher rate.

The *advantages* of the direct labor hour procedure are:

1. It is simple to use.
2. It represents a realistic application base when labor operations are the central factor in production.
3. By employing a time factor, the method overcomes a major objection to the direct labor dollar application because time is costed at the same overhead rate in spite of varying pay scales.

The *disadvantage* of the direct labor hour procedure is similar to that of direct labor dollars: it ignores the value contribution to the product by factors (expense) other than direct labor. For example, let's say that a machine shop is composed of drill presses, lathes, automatic screw machines, and the like. It is unrealistic and inaccurate to apply overhead on a departmental direct labor hour basis for such a department.

Overhead expense ratio to prime costs. Some organizations use a ratio of overhead to prime costs, if proven valid, as a factor for planning and performance measurement. Model 10 displays the ratios developed for the six-month period with a resultant average of 54.6%. The lowest ratio of 50.0% occurred in March (although January and February were close seconds). This ratio is primarily attributed to a relatively greater fluctuation in prime costs as compared to the overhead dollar values.

The highest ratio was in April, when the prime costs were 2.7% higher than March *but* the overhead expenses were 22.7% greater. The result of the higher overhead expenses was an increased ratio.

APPLICATIONS To use the ratio of overhead to prime costs effectively, you have to make a detailed analysis of the specific causes for cost data changes. You must also determine if this type of situation will continue to occur or if unusual circumstances caused the fluctuations.

PROS AND CONS   The *advantages* of the prime cost method are:

1. It is simple to use.
2. All the required data values are immediately available from the accounting records.

The *disadvantages* include:

1. It does not make use of the time factor in applying overhead.
2. There is no logical relationship between the major part of overhead costs and the dollar value of raw materials.
3. It is unlikely that accurate overhead costing can result from using both direct labor (due to varying direct labor calculation methods) and potential errors in time-projected material costs. These prime cost values are on a gross estimated value basis that would distort a valid relationship or ratio of overhead expense to prime costs for application purposes.
4. Use of this ratio is restricted to situations in which there are no extreme variations in product processing.
5. This method may prove to be more useful in certain departments rather than in the overall plant operations.

Percentage of sales and cost of sales. The ratio of overhead to sales and to cost of sales is displayed in Model 9. The analytical implications were discussed earlier in this chapter.

Machine hour rate method. To apply overhead as a rate per machine hour, first determine the *ratio* between the amount of overhead expense to be applied and the number of machine hours. Overhead is then allocated to the job or process by multiplying the machine hours involved in a specific operation by your rate. To derive the machine hour rate, divide the overhead expenses for a specific machine (or for a group of machines if they are identical in operation and cost) by the relevant machine hours:

$$\frac{\text{Machine}}{\text{hour rate}} = \frac{\text{Overhead expenses}}{\text{Machine hours}}$$

Generally, the machine hour rate represents an estimate of the actual overhead cost per hour for operating each machine.

COMPUTING MACHINE HOUR RATES

The three steps in calculating machine hour rates are as follows:

1. The affected departments project the estimated overhead expenses for the period in the form of a budget plan.

2. You regroup expense items into three classifications, such as: (a) specific charges to each machine relative to power, maintenance, and depreciation; (b) heat, light, and building costs; and (c) all other general and service costs, including indirect supplies and miscellaneous labor, supervision, and engineering support.

3. Combine the direct and prorated machine costs to determine the total projected overhead expenses to operate each machine during the year. The machine rate would be the result of dividing this total by the number of operational hours. The estimated machine hours may include either setup time or separate rates developed for operating and setup time.

PROS AND CONS

When machinery is the major factor in production, the machine hour application has undoubtedly the greatest number of *advantages* in allocating overhead:

1. *Cost accounting:* It provides the most accurate means for applying overhead expense to each task or job. Since the machine hour rate application uses time as a base in allocating overhead expenses, the rate is realistic even when one operator has to operate several machines or when several operators are required for each machine. The procedure also combines the operator's pay rate with the machine's overhead to obtain the total cost center rate for labor and overhead.

2. *Marketing:* Machine hour rates permit the sales group to quote definitively the estimated selling prices for each specific job.

3. *Engineering:* It provides a realistic procedure for estimating the job cost on a product specification basis with a great degree of accuracy.

4. *Management:* The overhead costing method involved in this rate is both logical and scientific. Management can therefore depend on accurate cost reports and be secure in price quotations to the customer. With such assurance, management can avoid either operating losses or the failure to obtain jobs. Further, the machine rate method provides a sound basis for the measurement of the monthly cost of idle machines.

The primary disadvantages of the machine hour rate include:

1. The cost accounting procedure increases costs since additional records, which ordinarily would not be required, have to be generated and maintained for each operation's machine time.

2. The method may not be universally applicable because it can be used only for costing machine operations.

3. It increases the detailed cost accounting workload because a blanket rate cannot be used if individual or group machine rates are utilized.

4. As relatively few organizations can use only machine rates, other types of rates must be employed in conjunction with the machine hour method. On the other hand, a number of affected organizations can use direct labor rates more uniformly throughout the plant, thereby applying the procedure more widely.

Product unit cost method. The simplest and most direct method of over-head application is on the basis of the product unit quantities produced. To develop the rate, divide the overhead expense dollars by the product units produced. The calculations may involve actuals, estimated actuals, or normal activity data. Further, the rates may be for the total plant, department, or cost center.

Model 10 displays the rates for a six-month period with an average of $1.555. The results were obtained by *dividing the period overhead dollars* by the *related units produced* in that period (see Model 9 for the overhead dollar values). In January, for example, the overhead dollars were $13,000 and the unit quantities produced were 8,800 (Model 10). These values produced a rate of $1.477 per unit ($13,000 ÷ 8,800 units).

RATE ANALYSIS FOR SIX-MONTH PERIOD

The average rate for the first three months was calculated to be $1.466 versus a $1.633 for the second three months or an 11.4% increase. The difference in average rates for the two three-month periods seems to be that overhead expenses increased by 28% in the second three-month period, whereas the units produced were only 15% greater. This situation accounted for the higher average rate.

This is one of the basic approaches to the analysis of rate differences between periods. A more detailed analysis of the circumstances relating to the reported figures may uncover other factors to be considered.

PROS AND CONS

The product unit method has its advantages and disadvantages. The product rate application is the simplest to use in applying overhead. Yet its usefulness is limited to situations involving only one product or a few closely related products characterized by a common denominator, such as weight. If no common denominator exists, you must determine some other pertinent and reasonable weighting factor, such as the *relevant point or factor basis.*

WEIGHTING FACTORS FOR OVERHEAD APPLICATIONS

You must adapt relative weighting factors per unit for a given period to the character of the specific industry. For example, units can be expressed in terms of pounds, gallons, feet, or whatever. Overhead is then applied on the basis of the factors you decide on.

Example: The following data are on a *unit weight basis:*

Unit quantity produced	500	400	600	—
Product unit weight	3 lbs.	5 lbs.	2 lbs.	—
Total weight produced	1,500	2,000	1,200	4,700
Cost per pound	$.4567	$.4567	$.4567	$.4567
Overhead cost applied	685.05	$913.40	$548.04	$2146.49
Cost per unit	$ 1.37	$ 1.52	$ .91	—

APPLYING DIRECT COST RATES PER PRODUCT UNIT

Model 10 displays the ratios of direct cost of sales and total cost to the number of product units produced. The cost rate per unit in each type of ratio was developed by dividing the elements of cost dollars by the number of units.

Comparing the Cost of Sales to Product Units

In Model 10, the ratio of total cost of sales to product units ranges from a low of $4.324 (February) to a high of $4.51 (June), with a six-month average of $4.404. The percent difference between the low and high rates is 4.3%. When February's cost of sales data is compared to June's, note the 43.8% increase ($32,000 to $42,000) in June. At the same time, the product units increased only 37.8% (7,400 to 10,200), thus accounting for the increase in the June rate.

The *total cost ratio* to product units averages $4.673 for the six-month period. The highest rate, April, is primarily attributed to the higher G&A and selling rate (.329), which was 22.3% greater than the six-month average of .269.

Applying the Direct Labor Rate to Product Units

The direct labor rate (or ratio) per product unit averaged $1.152 for the six-month period. The highest rate of $1.233 occurred in May, and it was 7.0% above the six-month average. The cause is principally the relatively greater increase in direct labor costs as compared to the increase in units produced.

The lowest rate of $1.066 for the six-month period occurred in March; it was 7.5% below the six-month average. This low resulted from a relatively greater increase in units produced as compared to the increase in direct labor dollars.

Using the Overhead Expense Rate

These rates were already discussed (see "Product Unit Cost Method"). In Model 10, the overhead costs for the second three months exceeded costs for the first three months by 30.9% ($34,900 to $45,700), whereas the units produced (23,800 to 27,400) were only 15.5% higher for the period. This situation resulted in the higher rate for the second quarter.

Calculating the Material and Other Direct Cost (ODC) Rate

The material and ODC cost rate per product unit averaged $1.697 for the six-month period as displayed in Model 10. The lowest rate of $1.5677 occurred in April. April's rate was 9.5% below the six-month average, primarily due to a reduction in material/ODC costs versus an increase in the number of units produced.

March saw the highest material rate per production unit ($1.829), which was 7.2% below the six-month average. The reason was a relatively greater increase in material costs as compared to the increase in units produced.

Note that the product units increased 15.1% in the second quarter over the first quarter, whereas material costs were only 3.0% higher, thereby accounting for the increased material cost rates.

Applying G&A/Selling Expense to Product Units

The six-month average for the G&A/selling expense rate is $.269 per production unit. April had the highest expense rate of $.329, which is 22.3% above the average. Compared to those of March, expenses were 22.7% higher but the production units increased by only 7.9%. A detailed analysis is required to determine the cause(s) for the higher expenses.

In June the expense rate dropped to a low of $.196, which was 27.1% below the six-month average. This situation resulted from the lowest expenses in the six-month period in tandem with the highest units of production.

APPLICATION These period rates per unit help you to rapidly assess product unit costs and highlight unusual variances.

Calculating the Labor Hour Rate for Total Costs

To obtain the labor rates, divide the total costs by the direct labor hours. The rates in Model 10 vary from a low of $10.78 in April to a high of

$12.97 in June, with a six-month average of $11.81. The lowest rate is .2% below average and the highest is 1.4% greater. In the low rate situation, the April direct labor hours increased 20% over March, whereas the total costs were only 10.2% higher, thus creating the low cost rate.

Compared to the low rate in April, the high June rate of $12.97 is 20.4% greater. In reviewing the two periods' basic data, observe the cause for the high cost rate: The total costs in June were 23.7% higher, whereas the direct hours increased by only 2.8% (3,600 to 3,700).

The labor hour rate approach is a rapid means for estimating total costs based on the labor rate—assuming that historical experience proved to be both reasonable and reliable.

DETERMINING COST UNITS IN RELATION TO PRODUCT COSTS

A major objective of cost accounting is to determine product unit costs. Yet the product unit is not always used as a cost unit. Unit costs are considered to be average costs, which are accumulated by jobs and processes or by operations, and spread out over the units produced.

Cost Accumulation by the Job Method

In the job method, the production cost for a job or lot is collected on a job order and posted to a cost sheet. Labor and material are charged directly to the job. Factory overhead is added to these costs according to rates predetermined by organizational practices and procedures. The total job cost is then divided by the number of units produced to obtain the *average cost per product unit*.

Cost Accumulation by Process Costing

Under the *process costing* procedure, all the costs for a process function (week, month, and so on) are accumulated on a process cost sheet. These costs are then divided by the period production to obtain unit costs. All the units produced from a particular process during a period have the same average cost.

Putting Unit Costs to Work

APPLICATION   The ratio of cost elements to product units helps you to estimate costs, price products, and measure cost performance based on historical experience (if proven to be reliable). The component cost element ratios enable you to analyze cost data in detail. Further, you can use the cost ratios for budget development and planning. Period-to-period production cost results can be compared, readily assessed, and variances derived for corrective action and future planning changes. (See Model 10.)

COMPARING G&A/SELLING EXPENSE TO SALES

Although the G&A and selling expense ratios to sales are generally computed separately, Model 10 presents them as a composite total, with a six-month average of 5.4%.

During the six-month period, the lowest ratio of 3.9% occurred in June. The principal cause for this low was the large sales volume of $51,000, compared to the lowest expense results in June.

The largest percentage of 6.6% came about in April. The cause was that April's sales of $41,000 were 16.9% less than June's but G&A/selling expenses were 35% greater.

In view of these high and low ratios, you have to analyze the detail to determine the specific causes for the fluctuations in the expense values. The investigation may provide the clues for their behavior that can be very important in estimating more realistically and in planning for the future.

With the expense ratio to sales, you can derive the estimated costs for product pricing and customer quotations based on the sales and cost outlook. Direct cost ratios to sales can be useful in developing reasonable cost of sales, and, together with G&A/selling expenses, they provide the total cost projections and estimated income from operations.

COMPARING G&A/SELLING EXPENSE TO TOTAL COSTS

Model 10 displays the subject ratios for six periods plus the average of 5.8%. The lowest percentage of 4.2% occurred in June, and the highest ratio of 7.0% materialized in April.

When the April data are compared to that of March, the G&A/selling expenses increased 22.7%, whereas the total costs were only 7.4% greater ($35,200 versus $38,800). The changes in the April results were the contributing cause to the high percentage experienced.

In comparing April's high rate of 7.0% to June's low of 4.2%, observe that June's total costs *increased* 23.7% ($38,800 to $48,000), while the G&A/selling expenses *decreased* 25.9% ($2,700 to $2,000). This situation accounts for the decline in the rate to 4.2%, which was 27.6% below the six-month average of 5.8%.

APPLICATION   The G&A/selling expense ratio to total costs can be used to estimate these expenses by applying the developed monthly percentages shown in Model 10 or on an estimated semiannual average (5.8%) basis to the appropriate time-projected costs. Total costs may have been estimated on the basis of a labor rate per direct labor hour (see Model 10) or as a total cost ratio to projected sales volume.

PLANNING, CONTROLLING, AND ANALYZING MANPOWER

To be successful, a business entity must plan and control its manpower. Manpower projections are based not only on current and anticipated sales volume, but also on the number of employees and the skills required to generate the product. In the planning process, you must also consider indirect support needs for managing, administering, maintaining records, and otherwise assisting the direct production effort.

Each organizational unit develops a manpower operating plan on which labor costs and various payroll expenses are based. Manpower, generally the major cost in operating a business, involves all types of personnel in researching, engineering, manufacturing, administrating, and other activities.

Preparing the Division Manpower Plan

The division manpower projections represent a summary of the departments, wherein direct personnel planning may be at the cost or budget center levels. Labor needs are developed in detail by job classification, payroll category (direct or indirect), and unit functional organizations. Justification of the required headcount is based on current and anticipated workloads by job classification.

Major functional manpower projections are based on the following relevant considerations:

Engineering departments plan their manpower needs within the framework of their current authorized and projected engineering projects. The manning plan also includes the requirements for general research and development programs, as well as for specific customer engineering applications.

Manufacturing or production departments base their planning on the product unit sales requirements and projections, which reflect inventory levels and a time-phased schedule of needs. The manufacturing schedule generally includes product quality assurance and inspection, packing, receiving, and shipping. The functional structure may vary among organizations depending on their needs and organizational practices.

Administrative functions (accounting, budgeting, estimating, marketing) plan their manpower needs and departmental expenses according to management-approved headcount projections and unit budgets.

The approved manpower forecasts become a part of the operating plan, which is the basic blueprint for the organization's operation. Actual performance is analyzed and measured on the basis of this plan of operation.

Converting Direct Manpower to Labor Hours by Computer

Model 11 presents an overview of the conversion of direct manpower projections to hours and dollars. A brief description of the computerized process follows.

Primary input. The direct *manpower projections* are approved by the responsible members of management. The input is by cost center (if applicable) and identified to a department showing the projected headcount by period. The manpower is segregated into hourly, salaried, and possibly job classifications. The computer process summarizes the cost centers' planned headcounts to functional department and division totals.

A planned *overtime percent limit* is inputted. The percent constraint is at the designated cost center or department levels.

A planned overtime dollar *premium rate* is provided by the budgeting group in accordance with organizational policy. The rates consist of time and a half, double time, or a flat rate per hour over 40 hours per week.

The *straight time hours per day factor,* generally eight hours, is entered into the computerized system. Some organizations may use ten hours per day for a four-day week. The factor depends on the organization's policy and practices.

A *productive hours per day* factor may be entered into the system depending on an organization's needs. The objective is to let nonproductive time have its effect on the overhead expense budget. The factor of .925 is shown in Model 11, which represents the historical relationship (or ratio) of productive hours to straight time. To get the .925 factor, divide the productive hours of 7.4/day by the straight time hours of 8.0. The .6 hours difference represents the estimated time for sickness, training, meetings, idleness, and so on.

**MODEL 11. Direct Manpower Conversion to Direct Labor Hours and Dollars:
A Computerized Planning Process.**

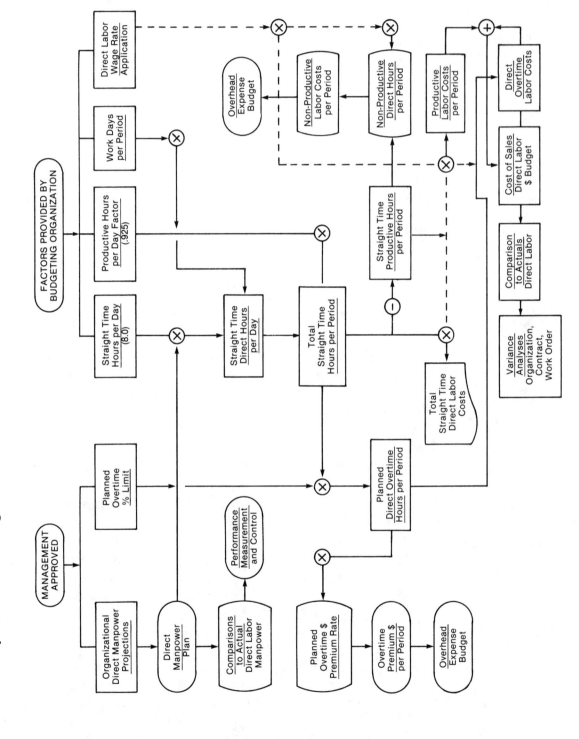

The *work days per accounting period* are provided as a direct input. This factor may vary among periods depending on their established accounting month periods, which take into consideration holidays, calendar month workdays, or cycles of five, four, and four weeks in a quarter.

Direct and indirect *labor rates* are direct input. The labor rates may be on an hourly basis by job classification, by average organizational rate, or possibly by cluster rates (more than one organization's average rate). The rates are based on actual historical experience. The projected rates undoubtedly anticipate merit increases within the upcoming twelve months.

Depending on the objectives of the computerized labor system, other relevant input may include:

—direct hour projections by contract, project, product and/or work order
—direct manpower, direct hour, and dollar actuals
—actual direct labor rates and averages by job classification

This type of input permits mechanical comparisons (actuals versus projections), varied variance analyses, and highlights of problem situations.

Computer Processing Functions

Direct manpower projections are converted into straight time labor hours per day and per period by organization and/or project.

The productive hours per day factor is applied to the period's straight time hours. This yields the productive hours per period, which, when subtracted from straight time hours, results in nonproductive hours per period.

The planned overtime percent limit is applied to straight time hours by period to obtain the planned direct overtime hours by period.

Nonproductive direct hours are multiplied by the appropriate wage rate(s) to obtain nonproductive labor costs by period. These are reflected in the overhead expense budget.

The period productive hours are multiplied by the appropriate wage rate(s) to derive the productive labor costs by period, which are reflected in the cost of sales.

The overtime premium dollar rate is applied to the planned direct overtime hours to obtain the overtime premium dollars by period, which are reflected in the overhead expense budget.

The appropriate rate is applied to the planned overtime hours to obtain the direct straight time labor costs for reflection in the cost of sales. To obtain the total cost for overtime activities, combine the overtime premium dollars with the overtime straight time labor costs.

Computerized reporting

- The actual headcount by organization is compared with the planned manning to provide the deviations by period for analysis, assessment of performance, and initiation of controls when feasible and appropriate.
- The actual direct labor hours and dollars are compared to the planned projections to ascertain variances for corrective action. The labor hour and dollar reporting can be by organization, contract, project, product, and/or work order.
- The developed overhead expense budget items (overtime premium dollars and nonproductive costs) are compared to actuals to determine variances.

Automated processing and reporting in the manpower system, as shown in Model 11, enables you to develop a direct manpower plan with the associated labor hours and costs. The data are segregated to achieve varied reporting objectives, particularly performance analysis, measurement, and control. Variance development and isolating problem situations highlight the system.

REPORTING MANPOWER ACTUALS FOR ASSESSMENT AND PLANNING

Model 12 displays a format for reporting manpower actuals. You can readily compare manpower projections, in terms of headcounts and ratios, to the actuals to ascertain variations and causes when significant.

Establishing Ratios of Indirect to Direct Manpower

Model 12 presents the actual direct factory and engineering manpower, although other direct functional classifications can be included for consideration in ratio analyses. The factory direct manpower approximates two-thirds of the total direct headcount. The ratio between periods for the factory direct ranged from a low of 64.5% to a high of 65.7%. The engineering percentages varied accordingly from a low of 34.3% to 35.5%.

The *factory indirect to direct ratio* varied among the reported periods from a low of 41.5% (May and June) to a high of 43.4% (February). The

MODEL 12. Reporting Manpower Actuals for Assessment and Planning.

Direct Manpower

Period	Factory	% of Total Direct	Engineering	% of Total Direct	Total Direct
Jan.	14,410	64.6	7,902	35.4	22,312
Feb.	14,322	64.5	7,887	35.5	22,209
Mar.	14,712	64.5	7,959	35.5	22,671
Apr.	14,645	64.8	7,943	35.2	22,588
May	15,268	65.6	8,003	34.4	23,271
Jun.	15,274	65.7	7,987	34.3	23,261
Jul.	15,255	65.7	7,958	34.3	23,213
Aug.	15,190	65.5	7,997	34.5	23,187
Sep.	14,972	65.2	7,989	34.8	22,961
Oct.	14,789	65.1	7,916	34.9	22,705
Nov.	14,576	64.8	7,922	35.2	22,498
Dec.	14,482	64.7	7,910	35.3	22,392

Indirect Manpower

Period	Factory	% Factory Direct	Engineering	% Engineering Direct	G&A Selling	% Total Direct	Total Indirect	Total Headcount	% Indirect to Direct
Jan.	6,218	43.2	992	12.6	3,387	15.2	10,597	32,909	47.5
Feb.	6,211	43.4	978	12.4	3,384	15.2	10,573	32,782	47.6
Mar.	6,287	42.7	988	12.4	3,398	15.0	10,673	33,344	47.1
Apr.	6,278	42.9	981	12.4	3,392	15.0	10,651	33,239	47.2
May	6,334	41.5	908	11.3	3,411	14.7	10,653	33,924	45.8
Jun.	6,341	41.5	903	11.3	3,408	14.7	10,652	33,913	45.8
Jul.	6,349	41.6	894	11.2	3,396	14.6	10,639	33,852	45.8
Aug.	6,352	41.8	898	11.2	3,409	14.7	10,659	33,846	46.0
Sep.	6,301	42.1	902	11.3	3,401	14.8	10,604	33,565	46.2
Oct.	6,292	42.5	891	11.3	3,397	15.0	10,580	33,285	46.6
Nov.	6,271	43.0	893	11.3	3,399	15.1	10,563	33,061	47.0
Dec.	6,196	42.8	887	11.2	3,391	15.1	10,474	32,866	46.8

engineering indirect to direct period ratios ranged from 11.2% to 12.6%, with an average of approximately 11.6%.

The *G&A and selling indirect to total direct* headcount averaged 15% by period. Because the ratio is fairly consistent among periods, it provides a reasonable ratio for preliminary G&A and selling organization's headcount planning. The ratio may also be used as a validity check when the indirect manpower is developed by more detailed processes (such as unit organization and job classification).

IMPORTANCE OF INDIRECT TO DIRECT HEADCOUNT

The most important overall ratio statistic is the percentage of *total indirect to direct headcount* (provided by period at the extreme right of Model 12). Most organizations establish an indirect to direct ratio goal for the total organization, particularly if the operation is substantially oriented toward manufacturing and engineering. Generally, a low ratio is assumed to be a prime indicator of more productive and effective utilization of indirect personnel. Further, if indirect manpower is reasonably reduced and controlled, the effect on total overhead expenses and rate (relative to product cost and competitive sales price) can be significant.

In Model 12 the lowest calculated ratio percentage of 45.8% occurred in the May, June, and July periods, whereas the highest percentage of 47.6% was in February. In comparing May's low percentage to February's ratio, note the following differences:

	Total Direct Manpower	*Total Indirect*
May	23,271	10,653
February	22,209	10,573
Difference	1,062 ÷ 22,209 = +4.8%	80 ÷ 10,573 = +.8%

The primary cause for the lower ratio in May is a combined effect of 1,062 higher direct manpower base (or 4.8%) and only .8% increase in the indirect headcount. This is a desirable situation from the standpoint of cost control and manpower management, as long as the lower indirect support does not penalize the direct operational environment.

FINAL CAUTION

Although ratios offer a succinct method for analyzing operational results, you must use them with caution: They can misdirect your interpretation and use of them. Be sure to assess thoroughly the historical experience and trends to establish their validity. As a financial analyst, you must be aware of the underlying principles and circumstances that influence ratio fluctuations and, as a result, their appropriate use.

4

How to Monitor and Control Those Elusive Overhead Costs

CHAPTER HIGHLIGHTS

Monitoring, planning, and contolling overhead expenses can be particularly difficult. Yet they need not present a problem if you make use of the overhead expense ratios explained in this chapter.

As any ratios, these depend on an effective accumulation system for their accuracy. The chapter therefore begins by describing a computerized expense processing system. Also shown is how the overhead data flow interfaces with the balance sheet and cash flow. The models here illustrate factory overhead and G&A/selling expense comparisons, as well as the expense ratios for sound analysis and planning guidelines. Other models help you to assess advertising and sales promotion expenses, with special emphasis on their budgeting and effect on sales volume.

Overhead expenses are then correlated to direct labor dollars. The focus is on period expense ratios to direct labor dollars, expense category ratios to direct labor dollars, and, finally, the correlation of indirect to direct labor dollars.

Ultimately, you will see how to assess comparisons of factory overhead budgets and actual expenses, as well as how to use these analyses in budget planning.

Overhead expenses represent indirect services and support for operational activities. These expenses generally do not contribute directly—nor are they readily identified—to the manufacture of a product, performing direct services or to achieving direct project requirements. Instead, overhead expenses are accumulated in detailed accounts, budgeted, and reported by each organization. The expenses are then summarized into primary control accounts (as specified by the chart of accounts), such as manufacturing (factory), engineering, quality assurance, administrative, selling, research and development (if applicable), plus other categories depending on organizational requirements.

Certain expense ratios can help you to assess these indirect costs and control excessive expenditures. The key factors in monitoring these expenses are ongoing surveillance, control measures, and performance measurement.

HOW TO PROCESS OVERHEAD ACCUMULATION

Model 13 displays a basic mechanical system for processing overhead expense. In many organizations, computerized expense processing is cost-effective, providing a timely vehicle for expense accumulation, surveillance, and control. Periodic data are compared to the budget, significant variances are analyzed to determine causes, and corrective action is taken. In developing the overhead budget plan, the possibility of invalid assumptions always exists, so the assumptions may have to be revised to reflect existing realities in overhead expense projections.

Utilizing Input from the Source Documents

In an automated system, expense data from source documents is input by means of a station transactor device, as shown in Model 13. The basic documentation consists of indirect labor timecards, vendor invoices, petty cash vouchers, travel expense reports, inventory expense requisitions, repair and maintenance work orders, miscellaneous journals, and so on. The inputted information, including the date and the amount involved in the transaction, is identified and charged to a document number, a valid expense account, and an organizational number.

The various categories of the inputted expenses are then identified. The classifications of the model are only general examples; their type and detail may vary among organizations depending on their respective needs and control objectives.

Inputting Additional Information for Processing

INFORMATION FROM THE MASTER FILES

In addition to the source data, the automated system needs other information before it can perform processing and meet its requirements. This information is fed into the computer from other master files (see Model 13).

The *actual direct labor master file* provides direct labor hours and dollar data to develop an overhead rate per direct hour and/or overhead expense percent of direct labor dollars. This computation can be

MODEL 13. How to Process Overhead Expense Accumulation by Computer.

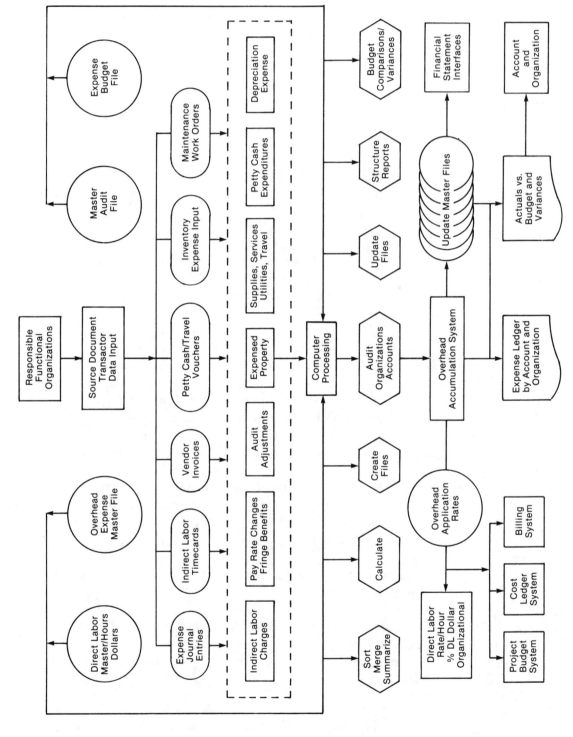

done for an individual organizational unit (cost center, department, burden center) and for the overall organization. Rates can be developed by contract or by sales order—whichever the established needs are.

The *overhead expense file* provides prior periods' expense information, arranged by account and organization and summarized year to date. As new period actuals become available, the computer program adds the data to the file and summarizes them. The program can generate rates by direct labor hour and as a percent of direct labor dollars, which are compared with the overhead expense budget and variances calculated for reporting purposes.

The *expense budget file* contains the annual budget by period and by year to date totals for comparison with actuals and calculating variances.

How the Computer Processes the Data

Before accepting data into the system, the computer program audits the input to verify the validity of expense and organizational identifier numbers. It rejects invalid information, which is returned to the inputting organization for corrective action and re-input.

Computer processing involves a number of routines that clerks would perform in a manual system. The program segregates account information by appropriate organization, merges it, and summarizes it in the overhead ledger. It also performs the required calculation, such as adding subaccounts to their control totals and organization levels.

It creates file records when necessary to accommodate new information and/or to make changes in existing file information.

It updates the appropriate master files and structures data into preestablished report formats.

Identifying the Elements of System Output

As displayed in Model 13, the results of the overhead expense accumulation are as follows:

An updated expense ledger by account and organization with appropriate subtotal and total summations.

Development of overhead application rates per direct hour or a percent of direct labor dollars, which can be used in the cost ledger system, project budget reporting, and the customer billing process.

Updating of master files as appropriate to feed other system requirements—general ledger and financial statement interfaces (income statement, cash flow, and balance sheet).

Actuals versus budget comparison (period and year to date) with variances.

Although not shown in Model 13 but in subsequent displays, the percent of each account to the total overhead (both actuals and budget) would be calculated, indicating the variance percentage increase or decrease among period increments and/or annual totals. This type of report provides a comprehensive review of changes that occurred. Various ratios are also developed from this system which will be described in this chapter.

Putting the Automated System to Work

The computerized overhead expense accumulation system provides you with a number of useful outputs:

Timely accumulating and processing of expense information with minimal manual effort.

Expense ledger by organization.

Overhead application rates for the cost ledger and billing systems.

Reporting of a budget versus actuals.

Various ratios for performance evaluation and operational control and planning.

It is a cost-effective process.

INTERFACING OVERHEAD EXPENSE DATA FLOW

CLASSIFYING THE EXPENSES

Model 14 displays the overhead data flow interfaces that occur after the expenses have been accumulated and processed. At the top of the exhibit are the major expense classifications. In the bottom part of each of these boxes is a listing of the more detailed account identifiers within the categories. Through journalization, the expense accounts are set up as liabilities in the general ledger. The exceptions are prepaid expenses (current asset) and reserve for depreciation/amortization (reduction to property, plant, and equipment—a noncurrent asset).

Expenses are classified and segregated as either factory overhead (cost of sales item) or G&A and selling expenses (period costs and reduction to gross profit). These items are reflected in the income statement.

MODEL 14. Overhead Expense Data Flow Interfaces: A Computerized Approach.

Indirect Labor	Accounts Payable	Insurance	Prepaid Taxes	Other Taxes	Depreciation Expense
Salaries/Wages	Supplies	Compensation	Real and	Social Security	Buildings
Management Incentive	Utilities	Group	Personal Property	Sales and Use	Machinery
Repair/Maintenance	Dues/Donations	Retirement	State Franchise	Other	Equipment
Labor	Travel	Plan			Furniture
	Telephone/Telegraph	Other			
	Professional/Outside Services				
	Rentals				
	Advertising/Sales Promotion				
	Repair/Maintenance				

Overhead Accumulation System

Expense Ledger Factory O/H GA and Selling

General Ledger/ Trail Balance

Income Statement

Reserve for Depreciation

Other Taxes

Prepaid Expense

Other Liabilities

Accounts Payable

Accrued Salaries/Wages

Cash Flow Reporting System

Direct Cash Outflow or Lag for Payment

Cash Balance

Balance Sheet

Analyzing the Balance Sheet

The automated general ledger/balance sheet system provides the account balances for the balance sheet statement (that is accrued salaries and wages, accounts payable, and the like). When the liabilities become due for payment, they are paid and become reductions to the outstanding balances. As prepaid expenses are expired over time, they are reduced accordingly.

The depreciation reserve account reflects the period accumulation of depreciation expense, which represents a reduction to gross fixed asset costs. In some organizations, depreciation expense is reflected as a source of funds from operations. This expense is not reflected in the cash flow system as it is *not an actual cash receipt* or expenditure, but rather a contingency fund for fixed asset replacements.

Analyzing Cash Flow

As direct cash payments are made, the amounts are classified as cash disbursements. The same is done to other liabilities as they are paid over a longer time span.

Model 14 shows how the overhead system interfaces with other segments of the overall financial reporting system. It provides an insight as to how the expense data are classified, collected, and reported from the overhead accumulation to the creation of liabilities and subsequently their payment. Some expenses are paid at the time of their occurrence and entered directly in the cash disbursement register.

COMPARING INDIVIDUAL EXPENSES TO TOTAL EXPENSE

The rates and ratios in Model 15 are the types used in analyzing overhead expenses and in planning operational budgets, and its numerical data will augment our discussion. Comparisons and illustrations are provided for two annual time periods. Specifically, the model compares the *ratio relationships* among the individual expense accounts and the total for 19X4 and 19X3. Also presented are the variance amounts for the two years of actuals, along with the percent change of increase or decrease among the accounts. The model's reporting format summarizes the pertinent factors involved in a thorough expense analysis of overhead expense performance. Highlights of the upper portion of the model are as follows:

ANALYZING INDIVIDUAL EXPENSES

- The total expense variance between the two years was $16,000, which represented a 6.3% increase in 19X4 over 19X3. In dollar magni-

MODEL 15. Factory Overhead Expense Comparisons and Ratio Analyses.

(in $000s)

Expense Classification	19X4 Actuals	% Ratio to Total Expense	19X3 Actuals	% Ratio to Total Expense	19X4 Variances Over (Under)	19X4 % Variance Over (Under)
Indirect labor	$125,000	46.3	$120,000	47.3	$ 5,000	4.2
Miscellaneous labor benefits	50,000	18.5	45,000	17.7	5,000	11.1
Retirement plan	12,500	4.6	11,000	4.3	1,500	13.6
Management incentive	2,500	.9	2,200	.9	300	13.6
Supplies	18,500	6.9	18,000	7.1	500	2.8
Taxes and insurance	14,200	5.3	13,800	5.4	400	2.9
Repair and maintenance	12,500	4.6	11,800	4.7	700	5.9
Depreciation	13,200	4.9	12,500	4.9	700	5.6
Equipment rentals	2,400	.9	1,900	.7	500	26.3
Utilities	4,200	1.6	3,800	1.5	400	10.5
Telephone and telegraph	4,000	1.5	3,900	1.5	100	2.6
Travel	3,800	1.4	3,700	1.5	100	2.7
Professional/outside services	4,700	1.8	4,200	1.7	500	11.9
Entertainment	900	.3	800	.3	100	12.5
Dues and donations	800	.3	700	.3	100	14.3
Miscellaneous expense	600	.2	500	.2	100	20.0
Totals	$269,800	100.0	$253,800	100.0	$16,000	6.3

Overview of Relationships

Values						
Direct labor (DL) hours	39,400		37,300		2,100	5.6
Direct labor (DL) dollars	$ 198,000		$181,650		16,350	9.0
Sales volume	1,100,000		995,000		105,000	10.6
Cost of sales	945,000		865,000		80,000	9.2
Fringe benefits	65,000		58,200		6,800	11.7
Rates & Ratios						
Expense rate/DL hour	$ 6.85		$ 6.80		$ .05	.7
Expense ratio to DL dollars	136.2		139.7		(3.5)	(2.6)
Expense ratio to sales	24.5		25.5		(1.0)	(4.1)
Expense ratio to cost of sales	28.6		29.3		(.7)	(2.4)
Indirect to DL dollar ratio	63.1		66.1		(3.0)	(4.8)
DL dollars to cost of sales	21.0		21.0		—	—
Fringe benefit rate/DL hour	$ 1.65		$ 1.59		$ .06	3.6
Fringe benefit ratio to DL $	20.1		19.3		.8	4.0

tude, the largest variances occurred in indirect labor, retirement plan, and other labor benefits, which accounted for approximately 72% of the total variance.

- In the other expense accounts, the relatively modest dollar increases can be primarily attributed to a 5.6% increase in direct labor hours and a 10.6% greater sales activity, which indicates a higher production activity.

- The *ratio* of the individual expense accounts to their totals in both years were modestly consistent, indicating that the actual performance results were in accord with operational plan activity requirements.

- The comparative analysis data in Model 15, if reasonably consistent over time, provides a sound basis for developing an expense budget— or at least a preliminary assessment of budget data later to be developed by more detailed procedures. Budget to actuals comparisons can highlight significant variances for further analysis and possible corrective action.

These analyses, as well as monthly comparisons and timely performance assessments, can be readily accomplished through a computerized program.

How to Use Expense Relationships

The expense relationships in the lower portion of Model 15 highlight the aggregate analysis of the actual overhead expenses:

- The *factory expense rate per direct hour* was $6.85 in 19X4 versus $6.80 in 19X3. This is a .74% increase. Although there was an overall increase of 6.3% in total overhead expenses, the effect of higher expenses was offset by the increased direct labor hour base of 5.6%.

    The expense rate statistic can be useful when you are estimating product costs per direct labor hour. It may also serve as a planning guide for developing factory overhead budgets on an aggregate basis.

- The *expense ratio to direct labor dollars* was calculated to be 136.2% in 19X4 versus 139.7% in 19X3, for a variance of 3.5% or a 2.6% decrease. The rate reduction is primarily attributed to a 9.0% increase in direct labor dollars versus an offsetting increase of only 6.3% in total expenses.

    This ratio may be useful in bidding and estimating contract costs.

- Factory overhead is one of the direct cost elements in the product cost of sales composition, along with direct labor and material and other direct costs. In Model 15, the *overhead ratio to cost of sales* was 28.6% and 29.3% for 19X4 and 19X3, respectively. The small decrease was due to the higher cost of sales, which was only partially offset by a smaller increase in the factory overhead.

- The *overhead expense ratios to sales* for 19X4 and 19X3 were 24.5% and 25.5%, respectively. The decrease resulted from a 10.6% increase in sales revenue versus a relatively smaller increase in overhead expenses. Look at the upper part of Model 15 to see which expense accounts declined as a ratio to total overhead.

- A frequently used control ratio assessment is the indirect to direct manpower and/or dollars. In Model 15, the indirect to direct labor dollar ratios were 63.1% and 66.1% for 19X4 and 19X3, respectively. The 3.0% decrease in 19X4 represents a 4.8% decline factor—a favorable trend in overhead expense control. As indirect labor generally represents the largest expenditure in overhead, reductions can become significant in both dollar values and in the overhead rate.

  The lower indirect ratio in 19X4 resulted from the relatively greater increase in the direct labor dollar base of 9.0%, as compared to the lower 4.2% increase in indirect labor dollars.

- The fringe benefit rates per direct labor hour for 19X4 and 19X3 were $1.65 and $1.59, respectively, with a difference of $.06 per direct hour. The increase in 19X4 benefits (retirement plan, management incentive, and other labor benefits) were relatively higher than the increase in direct labor hours of 5.6%, as shown in Model 15.

  These statistics are used to assess actual result performance and to plan overhead expense.

- The *ratios of fringe benefits to total labor dollars* were 20.1% and 19.3%, respectively, for 19X4 and 19X3. The 19X4 ratio increased by 0.8%, which resulted from a 9.0% increase in direct labor dollars. *Total labor dollars* are used in the calculations because both direct and indirect personnel share in the retirement and other labor benefits (vacations, sick leave, insurance, and the like).

  This ratio highlights the proportion of fringe benefit expenditures in relation to total labor dollars. These expenses are generally classified as noncontrollable since the guidelines for expense allocation are governed by organizational policy and procedures. Results of union negotiations may also be a major consideration in unionized organizations.

HOW TO ANALYZE G&A/SELLING EXPENSES

G&A/selling and R&D expenses (if applicable) are generally accumulated and budgeted under their separate categories, particularly if they are of significant values. With this procedure, you can establish detailed controls and provide for detailed analyses.

- *G&A organizations* include general management, controller's suborganizations, and procurement.
- *Selling organizations* include marketing and contract administration.

In Model 16, however, G&A and selling expenses are combined in the expense accumulation and reporting format. Like the factory overhead comparison in Model 15, the ratios in this model compare individual expenses to the total expenses, show over (under) variances for 19X4 and 19X3, and display the percent of increase (decrease). This type of information provides a basis for detailed account analysis of the two time periods' results, and it may also be helpful in planning.

Let's look more closely at Model 16.

ANALYZING MODEL 16

- *Total G&A and selling expenses increased* by $3,650.0 in 19X4 over 19X3, representing a modest increase in view of a 10.6% growth in sales volume and a 5.6% higher direct labor hour activity. The primary expense increases were in indirect labor, miscellaneous labor benefits, and the supplies account.

  The increase of $200.0 in advertising and sales promotion expense was offset by a similar decrease in sales commissions. Since the exact details are unknown for the displayed data, the probability is that current customers increased their product purchase volumes.

- The *ratios of individual expenses to the total* in 19X4 and 19X3 are fairly consistent in the two time periods. The major exceptions were indirect labor and benefits, equipment rentals, and professional/outside services.

- The expense accounts increased or decreased considerably in 19X4 over 19X3, from a 50% increase in miscellaneous expense to a 14.3% decrease in sales commissions. Although most of the variances' dollar amounts appear to be significant for G&A and selling expenses, the 19X3 base figures were low compared to the factory overhead, as shown in Model 15.

Analyzing Expense Relationships

In the lower portion of Model 16, pertinent rates and ratios are provided for the G&A and selling expense analysis. A few ratios are common to many organizations and others are rarely used, their usefulness depending on their applicability and the organization's practices.

Let's see how they are used:

MODEL 16. G&A/Selling Expense Comparisons and Ratio Analyses.

(in $000s)

Expense Classification	19x4 Actuals	% Ratio to Total Expense	19x3 Actuals	% Ratio to Total Expense	19x4 Variances Over (Under)	19x4 % Variance Over (Under)
Indirect labor	$27,000	47.4	$25,000	46.9	$2,000	8.0
Miscellaneous labor benefits	3,700	6.5	3,200	6.0	500	15.6
Retirement plan	1,300	2.3	1,200	2.3	100	8.3
Management incentive	700	1.2	600	1.1	100	16.7
Supplies	5,400	9.5	5,000	9.4	400	8.0
Taxes and insurance	2,700	4.7	2,400	4.5	300	12.5
Repair and maintenance	350	.6	300	.6	50	16.7
Depreciation	800	1.4	700	1.3	100	14.3
Equipment rentals	2,200	3.9	2,500	4.7	(300)	(12.0)
Utilities	800	1.4	700	1.3	100	14.3
Telephone and telegraph	2,700	4.7	2,600	4.9	100	3.8
Travel	1,400	2.5	1,100	1.9	300	27.3
Professional/outside services	2,000	3.5	2,300	4.4	(300)	(13.0)
Entertainment	600	1.0	500	.9	100	20.0
Dues and donations	500	.9	600	1.1	(100)	(16.7)
Miscellaneous	600	1.1	400	.8	200	50.0
Advertising/promotion	3,000	5.3	2,800	5.3	200	7.1
Sales commissions	1,200	2.1	1,400	2.6	(200)	(14.3)
Total G&A and selling	$56,950	100.0	$53,300	100.0	$3,650	6.8

Overview of Relationships					
Values					
Direct labor (DL) hours	39,400		37,300		2,100	5.6
Direct labor (DL) dollars	$ 198,000		$181,650		$ 16,350	9.0
Sales dollars	1,100,000		995,000		105,000	10.6
Gross profit dollars	155,000		130,000		25,000	19.2
Rates & Ratios					
Expense rate/DL hour	$ 1.45		$ 1.43		$ .02	1.4
Expense ratio to DL dollars	28.8%		29.3%		(.5)	(1.7)
Expense ratio to sales	5.2%		5.4%		(.2)	(3.7)
Sales to expense ratio	19.3		18.7		.6	3.2
Expense ratio to gross profit	36.7		41.0%		(4.3)	(10.5)

- The *expense rate per direct hour* was calculated to be $1.45 for 19X4 as compared to $1.43 for 19X3. This trend appears to be consistent. The difference of $.02 can be attributed to the relatively higher increase in expenses as compared to the direct labor hour base. As direct labor hour activity and sales volume increase, they affect G&A and selling expenses but not to the same degrees. The expense rate, if proven consistent, can be used as a control and planning factor.

- The *G&A and selling expense ratios* to direct labor dollars were 28.8% and 29.3%, respectively, for 19x4 and 19X3.

  If you were to project direct labor dollars and apply these ratios, you could derive approximate G&A and selling expense values for use as a check against their detailed expense development. Further, you could utilize the information for preliminary budget guidelines.

  The ratio for 19X4 of 28.8% in Model 16 represents 1.7% decrease compared to 19X3. The cause for the decrease is a relatively greater increase in 19X4 direct labor dollars (resulting from increased hours and higher labor rate) as compared to the expenses. Actually, the expense rate *per hour* is more commonly used as a factor because an increasing labor rate per hour does not distort the increased labor activity.

- For the sake of expediency in preliminary planning, you might sometimes project G&A and selling expense based on gross profit anticipations. In Model 16, the *expense ratios to gross profit* were 36.7% and 41.0%, respectively, for 19X4 and 19X3. If the expense ratio to gross profit is proven valid over time, you may apply it to the profit for preliminary values that can be used until other data become available. Periodic analyses will either verify this method's validity (and usefulness) or indicate inaccuracies.

  The 10.5% decrease in the expense ratio for 19X4, as compared to 19x3, is attributed to the 19.2% increase in gross profit in 19X4 with only a 6.8% increase in expenses. The increase in the 19X4 gross profit is primarily due to the higher sales revenue with only a partial offset by the higher cost of sales.

- The *G&A and selling expense ratio to sales dollar* was 5.2% in 19X4 versus 5.4% in 19X3. The expense variance difference in 19X4 was a minus (.2%), which resulted from a higher sales volume.

  This ratio, if validated, can be very useful as a guideline in projecting G&A and selling expenses based on sales even before you develop the details by more conventional methods. If you determine that the expenses will approximate $.052 on each sales dollar, then applying the factor to sales gives you the minimum amount of expenditures that will be incurred. Management controls must be exercised to reduce the expenses or constrain them within preestablished limits.

ANALYZING ADVERTISING AND SALES PROMOTION EXPENSE

The cost for advertising and sales promotion can be significant, particularly if the organization's product is consumer-oriented. The public is deluged daily by advertisements about the merits of automobiles, medications, foodstuffs, tires, and so on. Television, radio, newspapers, direct mail, and magazines all seek the consumer's attention.

Specifically and accurately measuring the sales growth and net income resulting from any sales campaign is often difficult. Unless the campaign is restricted to one type of advertising, the problem is to ascertain which media accounted for the sales gain and which contributed little to the effort. Even a detailed analysis of the varied advertising expenses may not reveal the answers to this question.

Budgeting for Advertising and Sales Promotion

The budget represents an important tool in planning and controlling these expenses. Generally, organizations with substantial advertising budgets segregate and accumulate advertising expenses into detailed account classifications that can be compared to the budget plan on an analytical basis.

When establishing the budget, consider the organization's overall planning objectives relative to sales goals, marketing strategies, and projections. Historical experience codes may be developed in order that charges can be identified to specific product or product lines. Segregate major categories into expenditures for television, radio, newspapers, and so on as appropriate so that you can assess results.

Carefully consider the timing of the actual expenditures because of seasonal influences and also as a basis for projecting actual cash outflow.

IN SUMMARY   Model 16 presents ways to analyze G&A and selling expenses, as well as to measure performance and anticipate future results by means of applicable expense rates and ratios. The ratio of G&A and selling expenses to sales expresses the surveillance and control measures that an organization exercises in relation to sales volume. These expenses have the primary lien on gross profit results. Changes in the ratio over time result from changes in business conditions and in the business environment, specifically changes in product demands and sales strategies.

If proven valid, the developed factors help you to establish expenditure controls. You can readily prepare the comparisons, rates, and ratios through rather simple mechanical routines. Exception reporting can highlight significant variances for corrective action and/or revised planning.

ASSESSING SALES ACTIVITY EXPENDITURES

As in other areas of analysis, you can develop factors, such as the ratio to sales and net income, based on historical experience. These ratios then help you to limit and control advertising, promotion, and commission spending.

MODEL 17. Illustrative Approach in Assessing and Controlling Sales Activity Expenditures.

(in $000s)

Values	19X4	19X3	Variance	% Change
Sales	$1,100,000	$995,000	$105,000	+10.6
Net income	49,025	38,350	10,675	+27.8
Advertising and promotion	3,000	2,800	200	+ 7.1
Commissions	1,200	1,400	(200)	−14.3
	Ratio to Sales			
Advertising and promotion	.27%	.28%	−.01%	− 3.5%
Commissions	.11%	.14%	−.03%	−21.4%
	Ratio to Net Income			
Advertising and promotion	6.1%	7.3%	−1.2%	−16.4%
Commissions	2.4%	3.7%	−1.3%	−35.1%

Assessing the Data

In Model 17, note that the 19X4 advertising and sales promotion expenses increased 7.1% versus a 10.6% increase in sales. These expenses apparently have a decided influence on sales volume increases but not in the same proportions. (Conclusion has to be further supported by historical experience.) Generally, the effort and expense contributed to product/ market exploitation result in higher sales volumes and increased profit-

As shown in Model 17, the 19X4 profits increased by 27.8%, but other factors may have also contributed to the increase, such as higher product prices, lower costs, more efficient operation, or improved cost control measures.

Why the 19X4 sales commission expenses declined by 14.3%, however, is difficult to explain. The answer might have to do with reduced commissions on sales, direct customer purchases with no sales representative involvement, error in cost accumulation, or other circumstances.

Ratio to sales. The advertising and sales promotion ratio in 19X4 decreased by 3.6%. This may be the result of a greater proportional increase in sales as compared to the expenses.

The 19X4 commission expense ratio declined by 21.4%. Although the dollar decrease was only $200,000, the greater 19X4 sales base volume undoubtedly accounted for the reduced ratio.

Ratio to net income. The net income decreased by 16.4% in 19X4, primarily because of the 27.8% increase in income with only a 7.1% increase in those expenses.

The cause for the 35.1% decrease in the 19X4 sales commissions ratio is attributed to the 27.8% increase in net income versus a 14.3% decline in commissions.

This type of analysis enables you to assess selling expenses in relation to the trends in sales volume and net income. It might also help you to establish expense limitations and controls. Further, the data provide guidelines based on historical experience for expense surveillance and for planning a realistic selling expense budget. The proviso, of course, is that the ratio relationships prove to be valid over time.

HOW TO CORRELATE OVERHEAD EXPENSE TO DIRECT LABOR DOLLARS

Model 18 is a scattergraph correlation chart of overhead expenses related to direct labor dollars using monthly data based on five-, four-, four-week quarters. The values used in plotting the graph are provided below the chart. Note the following:

1. This is a common procedure used in establishing a correlation formula. The plotted points represent the x and y intersections of overhead at varying direct labor dollar values as experienced in 19X4 (note the Model 15 totals).

2. The equations used to develop the formula are shown in Model 18. By substituting the dollar values shown for X, Y, and XY into the equations, the a and b factors are calculated as illustrated.

3. The resultant formula is

   Y (overhead) = 2.683 (2.7 rounded) + 1.2 × X (direct labor dollars)

Example: Assuming projected labor dollars of $17 million, what is the projected overhead dollars?

$$Y = 2.683 + 1.2 (\$17.0)$$
$$= 2.683 + 20.4$$
$$= \$23.083 \text{ million}$$

Refer to the graph: The $17 million intersection on the regression line indicates an approximate $23 million expense value.

4. The four plotted points at the extreme right of the chart indicate the five-week monthly periods, which reflect higher monthly values for direct labor and overhead. The four-week periods are represented by the plot points at the lower left in the graph.

MODEL 18. Correlating Overhead Expense to Direct Labor Dollars.

*Least Squares Calculations**

	X(DL)	Y(OH)	XY	X²	Y²	Formula Equations
J	18.6	25.7	478.0	346.0	660.5	$Y = Na + b\Sigma X$
F	15.6	21.6	337.0	243.4	466.6	$XY = a\Sigma X + b\Sigma X^2$
M	16.1	22.0	354.2	259.2	484.0	*Calculations*
A	19.8	25.9	512.8	392.0	670.8	$270.0 = 12a + 198.0b$
M	15.3	21.9	335.1	234.1	479.6	$4,503.6 = 198.0a + 3,307.8b$
J	15.9	20.9	332.3	252.8	436.8	$4,455.0 = 198.0a + 3,267.0b$
J	18.0	25.3	455.4	324.0	640.1	$48.6 = \qquad\qquad 40.8b$
A	15.5	20.5	317.8	240.3	420.3	$b = \underline{1.2}$
S	14.5	20.1	291.5	210.3	404.0	$270.0 = 12a + (198 \times 1.2)$ or 237.6
O	19.4	25.5	494.7	376.4	650.3	$12a = 32.4; \quad a = 2.7$
N	14.7	20.1	295.5	216.1	404.0	*Formula*
D	14.6	20.5	219.3	213.2	420.3	$Y = 2.7 + 1.2 (X)$
Totals	198.0	270.0	4,503.6	3,307.8	6,137.3	Point A: 2.7 + 1.2 (15.5) or 18.6; Y = 21.3 ←
						Point B: 2.7 + 1.2 (19.0) or 22.8; Y = 25.5 ←

*Values based on five-, four-, four-week quarters

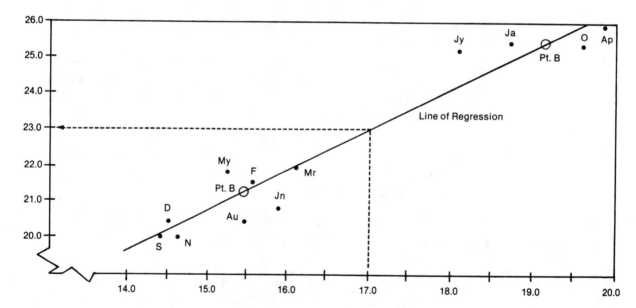

5. If you draw the slope of the regression line, you can either make an "eye" inspection or use the formula at two labor base values. The labor values used are $15.5 million and $19.0 million. The calculation is illustrated in Model 18, with the results for Points A and B $21.3 million and $25.5 million, respectively. A connecting line drawn between these two points represents the median among all of the plotted points.

RELATING PERIOD EXPENSE RATIOS TO DIRECT LABOR DOLLARS

Model 19 is a graphic overview of total expense ratios to direct labor dollars by period. By highlighting the changes in ratios, it pinpoints the deviations from the average, either for analysis and corrective action in the future or for establishing and revising planning criteria. In this chart, note that the largest *plus* deviation (.07, in May) was due primarily to the increase in expenses for that period, but the direct labor dollars remained relatively stable.

On the downside, the ratios for April and June are *negative* due to high level of direct labor dollars as compared to the expense values.

Commencing in April, every other month's ratio was either above or below the average for the year. This pattern follows the fluctuations in the direct labor dollar base, while the period expense dollars remained fairly constant. In a case like this, you might look for the causes of the changes in direct labor dollars and of the constancy of expenses. The answers could form a basis for future planning.

RELATING OVERHEAD EXPENSES TO DIRECT LABOR HOUR ACTIVITY

Model 20 displays the relationship between weekly average of direct labor hours and overhead expenses by accounting period. The average rate per direct labor hour was $6.85, as shown in the data below the display. Note that for six months the expense rate was below the average and for six months it was above-average. As a general observation, period expenses followed the increase and decrease in direct labor hours except in a couple of instances; this is considered to be a normal trend. As direct labor hour activity increases, the variable expenses tend to edge higher but not in the same relative proportion.

The objective of Model 20 is to show the relationship of expenses to the changes in the labor hour activity. This information provides a basis for measuring expense performance, initiating controls, and budgeting for future periods.

COMPARING EXPENSE CATEGORIES TO DIRECT LABOR DOLLARS

Model 21 displays in graphic form the ratios of individual expense categories to direct labor dollars by time period. It shows the proportion and changes of the expense categories to the total overhead expense ratio

MODEL 19. Comparing Total Overhead Expense to Direct Labor Dollars (by Time Periods).

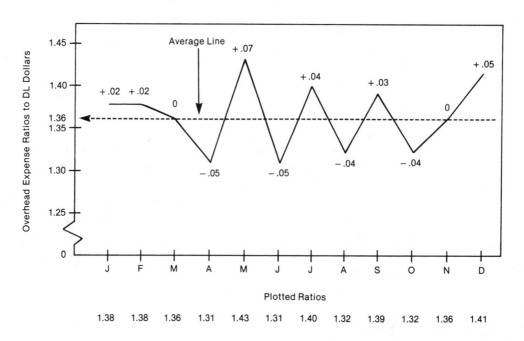

Plotted Ratios

1.38	1.38	1.36	1.31	1.43	1.31	1.40	1.32	1.39	1.32	1.36	1.41

MODEL 20. Correlating Overhead Expense to Direct Labor Hour Activity (Year Ended 19X4).

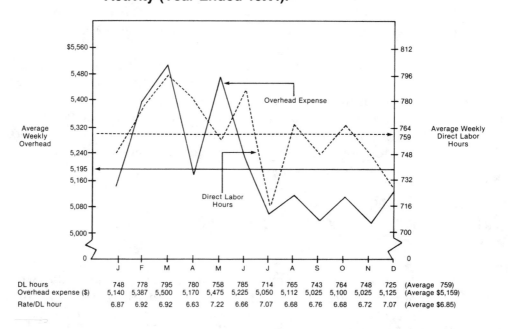

	J	F	M	A	M	J	J	A	S	O	N	D	
DL hours	748	778	795	780	758	785	714	765	743	764	748	725	(Average 759)
Overhead expense ($)	5,140	5,387	5,500	5,170	5,475	5,225	5,050	5,112	5,025	5,100	5,025	5,125	(Average $5,159)
Rate/DL hour	6.87	6.92	6.92	6.63	7.22	6.66	7.07	6.68	6.76	6.68	6.72	7.07	(Average $6.85)

MODEL 21. Comparing Expense Categories to Direct Labor Dollars.

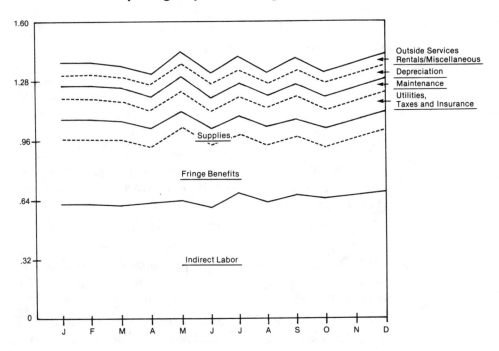

						Plotting Data by Period							
Ind. L.	.62	.62	.61	.61	.63	.60	.67	.62	.66	.64	.65	.67	
Fringes	.34	.35	.36	.32	.40	.33	.32	.31	.31	.28	.31	.32	
S/T	.96	.97	.97	.93	1.03	.93	.99	.93	.97	.92	.96	.99	
Supplies	.11	.11	.10	.09	.09	.08	.09	.09	.09	.09	.09	.09	
S/T	1.07	1.08	1.07	1.02	1.12	1.01	1.08	1.02	1.06	1.01	1.05	1.08	
Util./Txs.	.12	.11	.11	.11	.11	.11	.12	.11	.12	.11	.12	.12	
S/T	1.19	1.19	1.18	1.13	1.23	1.12	1.20	1.13	1.18	1.12	1.17	1.20	
R&M	.06	.07	.07	.06	.07	.06	.06	.06	.07	.06	.06	.07	
S/T	1.25	1.26	1.25	1.19	1.30	1.18	1.26	1.19	1.25	1.18	1.23	1.27	
Deprec.	.06	.06	.06	.06	.06	.06	.07	.07	.07	.07	.07	.08	
S/T	1.31	1.32	1.31	1.25	1.36	1.24	1.33	1.26	1.32	1.25	1.30	1.35	
O/S Svcs	.07	.06	.05	.06	.07	.07	.07	.06	.07	.07	.06	.06	
Tot. Exp. Ratios	1.38	1.38	1.36	1.31	1.43	1.31	1.40	1.32	1.39	1.32	1.36	1.41	(to 1 DL$)

per direct labor dollar. The ratios were developed by dividing the period category expenses by direct labor dollars.

Below the graph is the numerical data used in plotting. An analysis of the data reveals the following observations:

- *Indirect labor:* The higher ratios occurred in July, September, November, and December, as reflected by the upward thrust of the ratio line for those periods. The ratio differences are due principally to labor dollar fluctuations.

- *Fringe benefits:* The highest ratio occurred in May, and the lowest ratios were experienced in August through November. The contributing causes for these changes were the fluctuations in fringe benefit expenses.

- *Supplies:* This expense ratio remained fairly constant by period, with the lowest ratio occurring in June.

- *Utilities, taxes, and insurance:* Approximately consistent for all periods, this expense ratio provides a reasonable factor for budgeting this category of expenses.

- *Repair and maintenance:* This ratio fluctuated between $.06 and $.07 per direct labor dollar. These factors will be useful in assessing future performance and in projecting these expenses.

- *Depreciation:* The ratio factors were 6% and 7% of direct labor dollars, with the exception of 8% in December. The situation is primarily due to the below-average direct labor dollars and above-average expense total.

- *Outside services, rentals, and miscellaneous:* These expenses remained relatively consistent throughout the periods. Modest fluctuations can be attributed primarily to the changes in the direct labor dollar base.

Model 21 presents an overview of category expense ratios to direct labor dollars with a proportionate analysis of period expense ratios. The display indicates how labor and expense changes affect the ratio from one period to another. If consistent and valid over subsequent time periods, the ratios enable you to monitor expenses and develop overhead budgets. They also aid in checking on planning data that is based on more detailed development procedures.

HOW TO CORRELATE INDIRECT TO DIRECT LABOR DOLLARS

Model 22 was developed to demonstrate the correlation between indirect and direct labor dollars. The data used for the calculations are shown below the plotted graph. The equations to derive the mathematical cor-

MODEL 22. Correlating Indirect to Direct Labor Dollars.

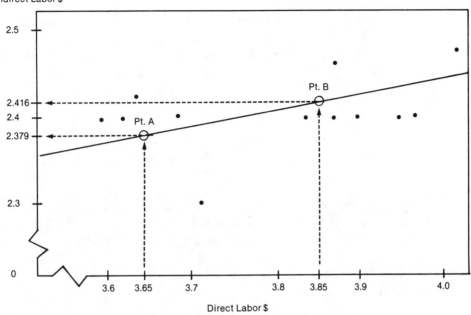

Indirect Labor $

Direct Labor $

Ratio % of Indirect to Direct Labor Dollars

J	F	M	A	M	J	J	A	S	O	N	D	
62.2	61.5	62.5	60.0	63.2	60.0	66.7	61.5	66.7	64.1	61.5	66.7	(Average 63.2)

Weekly Averages for Computing Correlation
(Dollar Values Rounded in $000,000s)

Periods	X	Y	XY	X²	Y²	Least Squares Equations
J	3.7	2.3	8.51	13.59	5.29	$Y = Na + b\Sigma X$
F	3.9	2.4	9.36	15.21	5.76	$XY = a\Sigma X + b\Sigma X^2$
M	4.0	2.5	10.00	16.00	6.25	
A	4.0	2.4	9.60	16.00	5.76	*Calculations*
M	3.8	2.4	9.12	14.44	5.76	$28.9 = 12a + 45.70b$
J	4.0	2.4	9.60	16.00	5.76	$110.10 = 45.7 + 174.30b$
J	3.6	2.4	8.64	12.96	5.76	$110.05 = 45.7 + 174.03b$
A	3.9	2.4	9.36	15.21	5.76	
S	3.6	2.4	8.64	12.96	5.76	$.05 = .27b$
O	3.9	2.5	9.75	15.21	6.25	$b = .185$
N	3.7	2.4	8.88	13.69	5.76	$28.9 = 12a + 8.45$
D	3.6	2.4	8.64	12.96	5.76	$12a = 20.45$
Totals	45.7	28.9	110.10	174.33	69.63	$a = 1.704$

Locating Points A and B for Regression Line

Point A: Y = 1.704 + .185 (3.650)
   Y = 1.704 + .675 or 2.379

Formula
   Y = 1.704 + .185 (X)

Point B: Y = 1.704 + .185 (3.85)
   Y = 1.704 + .712 or 2.416

relation formula, also shown in the model, represent the commonly used process in the least squares method approach.

The calculations displayed solve for a, which was $1.704 million, and the variable b factor of .185. The resultant equation is expressed as follows:

$$Y = \$1.704 + .185 \times X$$
where
Y = indirect labor
X = direct labor dollars

To locate the regression line, two labor values are used: point A, $3.650 and point B, $3.850 (both values in millions of dollars). A line connecting these two points represents the regression or trend line.

Verifying the Validity of the Trend Line

To validate the reasonableness of the trend line, select two or more labor values. Then, to determine the indirect labor value locations on the regression line, use the following formula:

$$Y = a + bX$$

Direct labor values of $3.8 and 3.95 million are selected, and the results ($2.407 and $2.435 million of indirect labor) are located on the trend line. As an overview assessment, this indicates that the trend line is reasonably representative of the data correlation.

As a rapid means of estimating indirect labor dollars based on direct labor, select any value for direct labor dollars and draw a vertical line from the labor value to the trend line. At this intersection, draw a horizontal line to the left margin of the display. The result is the estimated indirect labor dollar value.

Other methods used to test the validity of the correlation formula are to calculate the coefficient of correlation and the standard error of estimate.

CALCULATING THE INDIRECT TO DIRECT LABOR DOLLAR RATIO

Model 23 presents another approach to the indirect to direct labor dollar ratios, reflecting the time period deviations from the average. The display reveals that the ratios are below average in the first six months plus August

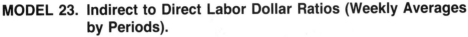

MODEL 23. Indirect to Direct Labor Dollar Ratios (Weekly Averages by Periods).

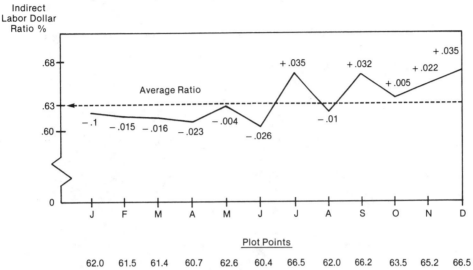

and above average in the remaining periods. The primary cause for the below-average variances is the higher direct labor dollar base combined with relatively consistent indirect labor dollar values. The above-average ratios resulted from the below-average direct labor dollars.

This type of presentation highlights at a glance the ratio fluctuations between periods. These fluctuations indicate problem situations requiring attention and control. Further, if the circumstances are valid, the factors may provide a basis for future planning.

ANALYZING THE SUPPLIES EXPENSE RATE PER DIRECT LABOR HOUR

Model 24 displays the period supplies expense rate trend per direct labor hour. The high rate of $.55 in February is attributed primarily to supply expenses being 20% higher than the annual average and direct labor hours being only 2.5% above average.

The lowest expense rate of $.41 occurred in June. An analysis reveals that direct labor hours were 3.4% above average, whereas supply expenses were 8.2% *below* the annual average. The result of these two situations is the low rate per direct labor hour.

The next step in the analysis is to determine the cause for the high and low expenditure for supplies in the two periods. The question is: are the increase and decrease in the rate due to unusual circumstances or are they expected to prevail in the future? Since the supplies expense

MODEL 24. Supplies Expense Rate per Direct Labor Hour (Weekly Averages by Periods).

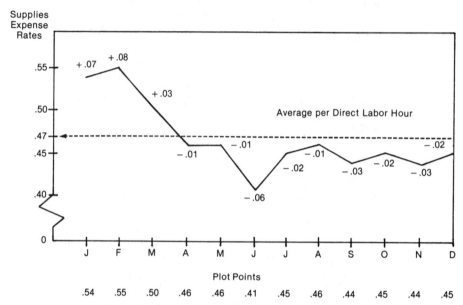

represents the third highest expense in the overhead total, you must give it appropriate attention to make sound budget projections.

Note that the first three months reflected a higher-than-average ($.47/DLH) rate, whereas the succeeding months experienced a lower-than-average rate. The principal cause has to do with the expenses being below average in those periods.

COMPARING FACTORY OVERHEAD ASSESSMENTS

Model 25 reflects a type of analytical report used to assess and measure actual expense results against projected operational budget. This approach highlights the variances by expense account between the prior year's actuals and a proposed budget. The purpose is to determine the cause(s) for an 11.9% increase (32.2 million ÷ $269.8 million) in the 19X4 budget over the 19X3 actuals.

As shown in the model, the two most significant dollar value increases occurred in indirect labor (14.9 million) and in other labor benefits ($6.0 million), representing an 11.9% and 12.0% increase, respectively. There were higher percentage increases in some of the other expense accounts, but the relative comparable dollar values were much smaller. The next step in the analysis is to determine why the 19X4 budget reflected the increases. There may be valid planning criteria for this situation, but you

MODEL 25. Comparing Factory Overhead Budgets: 19X4 Operational Budget Versus 19X3 Actuals.

(*in $000s*)

Expense Classifications	19X4 Management Budget	19X3 Actuals	19X4 Budget Over (Under)	% Increase (Decrease)	Rate per Direct Hour 19X4 Budget	Rate per Direct Hour 19X3 Actuals	Ratio % to DL Dollars 19X4 Budget	Ratio % to DL Dollars 19X3 Actuals
Indirect labor	$139,900	$125,000	$14,900	11.9	$3.32	$3.17	64.68	63.13
Retirement plan	13,900	12,500	1,400	11.2	.33	.32	6.43	6.31
Management incentive	2,500	2,500	—	—	.06	.06	1.16	1.26
Other labor benefits	56,000	50,000	6,000	12.0	1.33	1.27	25.89	25.25
Supplies	21,150	18,500	2,650	14.3	.50	.47	9.78	9.34
Taxes and insurance	16,000	14,200	1,800	12.7	.38	.36	7.40	7.17
Repair and maintenance	14,300	12,500	1,800	14.4	.34	.32	6.61	6.31
Depreciation	14,700	13,200	1,500	11.4	.35	.34	6.80	6.67
Equipment rentals	2,550	2,400	150	6.3	.06	.06	1.18	1.21
Utilities	5,500	4,200	1,300	30.9	.13	.11	2.54	2.12
Telephone and telegraph	4,200	4,000	200	5.0	.10	.10	1.94	2.02
Travel	4,200	3,800	400	10.5	.10	.10	1.94	1.92
Professional and outside services	5,050	4,700	350	7.4	.12	.12	2.33	2.37
Entertainment	800	900	(100)	(11.1)	.02	.02	.37	.46
Dues and donations	800	800	—	—	.02	.02	.37	.40
Miscellaneous	450	600	(150)	(25.0)	.01	.01	.21	.30
Totals	$302,000	$269,800	$32,200	11.9	$7.17	$6.85	139.63	139.24
Summary								
Direct labor hours	42,100	39,400	2,700	6.9				
Expense rate per direct hour	$ 7.17	$ 6.85	$ .32	4.7				
Direct labor dollars	$216,300	$198,000	$18,300	9.2				
Overhead ratio to direct labor dollars	139.6%	136.2%	3.4%	2.5				

should conduct a detailed analysis to confirm the reasoning and budget decisions.

Generally, the budget increases can be explained at least partially by the anticipated increase in direct labor hours of 6.9%. This increase, signifying greater operational activity, would influence a rise in indirect labor and other labor benefit expenses.

Figuring the Overhead Expense Rate per Direct Labor Hour

In total, the overhead expense rate per direct labor hour increased 4.7%. The major increases occurred in indirect labor and in other labor benefits, followed by the supplies account. The rate factor provides preliminary and basic criteria for estimating and budgeting expenses predicated on past experience. In the budgeting process, however, you must anticipate future expense and exercise good judgment when it comes to activity projections.

Analyzing the Expense Ratio to Direct Labor Dollars

The ratio of expense to labor dollars increased by 2.5% from 136.2% to 139.6%. The expense ratio factors, based on direct labor dollars, can be and often are used in the budgeting process. Further, you can use the factors in preparing customer proposal estimates for product/contract pricing, particularly if experience has validated your budgeting in the past.

This type of comparative report provides a comprehensive review of expenses in detail not only for comparing the planned budget with the prior year's actuals, but also for measuring the actual data period by period. With this type of report, you can assess expense data and highlight major variances for further analysis and action.

In the model, note that the three most important ratios (because of their dollar magnitude) are indirect labor, other labor benefits, and supplies. They would be the major areas of concentration for control and planning. Shown at the bottom of Model 25 are the overall expense rates per direct hour and the overhead expense ratios to direct labor dollars.

5

How to Assess and Plan Income Objectives by Means of Profitability Ratio Guidelines

CHAPTER HIGHLIGHTS

Inasmuch as the aim of any business is to make a profit, profitability ratios are perhaps the most important in gauging a firm's success. How each element in a business' financial statements relates to the profitability of its activities is the key question. In this chapter, you will become acquainted with profitability ratios. You will learn how to calculate and interpret them in relation to the organization's overall financial position and operating progress.

First you look at the elements in the income statement. Each item is analyzed by means of a ratio, and the results are compared from one period to another. Where appropriate, possible explanations for variances are offered. You will familiarize yourself with the objectives and assessments of profitability ratios in terms of their composition and relationships to gross profit, income from operations, and net income—the "bottom line," particularly in the context of business cycles.

Much the same is then done with the balance sheet. Each element is converted to a ratio, interpreted, and compared by periods. Explanations for variations are again offered when appropriate. You will be given some points to remember when analyzing the turnover of capital employed.

You will then see how to calculate earnings per common share of stock and use this relationship in assessing financial data.

Finally, how do you evaluate the causes for profit variations? How do they relate to sales, production, expenses, or product mix? Which areas are involved in the variance? These questions are answered in the final section of the chapter.

USE OF PROFITABILITY RATIOS

Profitability ratios are generally the most useful to organizations directly involved in manufacturing and selling a product or in performing a service. For comparative purposes, the individual costs and profit ratios to sales are calculated by periods (monthly, quarterly, and so on). These comparisons provide insight into trends and further as a tool for high-lighting significant variances, which may be the occasion for investigation and possibly corrective action or changes in future planning. These ratios therefore enable you to gauge an organization's financial results and establish future objectives.

The use of profitability ratios for analysis and planning is primarily concerned with, but not necessarily limited to

the rate of return on net income from operations

gross margin

total assets

owners' equity

creditor contribution

price earnings

stock yield rate

The data used in developing the ratios are obtained primarily from both the income statement and the balance sheet.

ANALYZING THE INCOME STATEMENT

Model 26 displays a comparative income statement analysis for the years 19X2–19X4. Each item in the statement is expressed in dollars and as a percentage of net sales. For each data element, the percentage represents the element's relationship to the sales volume. Let's analyze each item on the left-hand side of the table:

- The *cost of sales* percentage decreased from 74.6% in 19X2 to 73.6% in 19X4, giving rise to a relative gross profit percent increase from 25.4% to 26.4%. The improved profit could indicate increased man-ufacturing cost control surveillance, operating performance effi-ciencies, improved equipment output, or learning curve results.
- The *G&A and selling expense* percentage of sales declined between 19X2 and 19X4 in spite of increased sales volume. This is a favorable trend toward increased profitability.

MODEL 26. Comparative Income Statement Analysis.

(in $000,000s)

Description	19X4 Amount	19X4 % Sales	19X3 Amount	19X3 % Sales	19X2 Amount	19X2 % Sales	19X4 versus 19X3 Increase (Decrease) Amount	19X4 versus 19X3 Increase (Decrease) %	19X3 versus 19X2 Increase (Decrease) Amount	19X3 versus 19X2 Increase (Decrease) %
							Determining Changes for Analysis			
Net sales	$240.00	100.0	$190.00	100.0	$130.00	100.0	$50.00	26.3	$60.00	46.2
Cost of sales	176.60	73.6	141.00	74.2	97.00	74.6	35.60	25.2	44.00	45.4
Gross profit	$ 63.40	26.4	$ 49.00	25.8	$ 33.00	25.4	$14.40	29.4	$16.00	48.5
G&A expense	$ 13.90	5.8	$ 11.40	6.0	$ 8.06	6.2	$ 2.50	21.9	$ 3.34	41.4
Selling expense	11.30	4.7	8.90	4.7	6.50	5.0	2.40	27.0	2.40	36.9
Subtotal	$ 25.20	10.5	$ 20.30	10.7	$ 14.56	11.2	$ 4.90	24.1	$ 5.74	39.4
Income from operations	$ 38.20	15.9	$ 28.70	15.1	$ 18.44	14.2	$ 9.50	33.1	$10.26	55.6
Other income	$ .48	.2	$ .19	.1	$ .13	.1	$ .29	152.6	$ .06	46.2
Interest expense	.72	.3	.38	.2	.26	.2	.34	89.5	.12	46.2
Subtotal	$ (.24)	(.1)	$ (.19)	(.1)	$ (.13)	(.1)	$ (.05)	(26.3)	$ (.60)	(46.2)
Pretax Profit	$ 37.96	15.8	$ 28.51	15.0	$ 18.31	14.1	$ 9.45	33.1	$10.20	55.7
Provision for taxes (50%)	18.98	7.9	14.255	7.5	9.155	7.05	4.725	33.1	5.10	55.7
Net Income	$ 18.98	7.9	$ 14.255	7.5	$ 9.155	7.05	$ 4.725	33.1	$ 5.10	55.7
Retained earnings (BB)	$ 17.51	7.3	$ 10.255	5.4	$ 4.50	3.46	$ 7.255	70.7	$ 5.755	127.9
Cash dividends	(8.50)	(3.5)	(7.000)	(3.7)	(3.40)	(2.60)	1.500	21.4	3.600	105.9
Retained Earnings (EB)	$ 27.99	11.7	$ 17.510	9.2	$ 10.255	7.91	$10.480	59.9	$ 7.255	70.7

Note: BB = Beginning Balance; EB = Ending Balance
Retained earnings (EB) = Net income + Retained earnings (BB) − Cash dividends

- Although *interest expense* increased slightly, it is attributed to the additional financing requirements for sales growth. However, the overall impact on profits was partially offset by an increase in other *nonoperating income.*

- The net result of these relevant factors is a 7.9% net income relationship to sales in 19X4, as compared to the 7.05% in 19X2. Although the percent increase appears to be minor, the profit dollar factor was 1.07 times greater in 19X4 over 19X2. This situation resulted from the much larger sales volume and relatively lower manufacturing costs and G&A and selling expenses.

The percentage ratios help you to visualize changes from one period to another, investigate unusual circumstances, and possibly take managerial action. These ratios further focus on the need for management to adjust to varying operational changes, such as an increasing or declining sales volume and their associated cost trends.

Analyzing Comparative Statement Changes

Model 26 also reflects the extent of changes, in terms of percentages, in the various operating line items between 19X2 and 19X3, and between 19X3 and 19X4. This type of reporting forms a basis for horizontal analysis of the income statement.

Note the following from Model 26:

- *Net sales* in 19X3 increased a significant 46.2% over 19X2, compared with only a 26.3% increase in 19X4 over 19X3.

- The *cost of sales percentages* were comparable to the increase in sales volume, and thus the differential effect on gross profit was nominal in both periods compared.

- *Income from operations* showed a gain of 55.6% in 19X3 over 19X2, while the gain in 19X4 over 19X3 was only 33.1%. The increase is attributed primarily to the higher gross profit with a relatively minor offset in increased G&A and selling expenses.

- The 55.7% increase in *net income* in 19X3 over 19X2 was due to the 7.5% return on sales, compared to the 7.05% in 19X2.

SUMMARY

The comparative income statements are analyzed by means of two complementary approaches:

1. *Vertical analysis* provides the *distribution of income from sales* among the functions involved in producing it.

2. *Horizontal assessment* indicates the *rate or ratio of change* in the criteria affecting income.

You should use both methods when analyzing the income statement since changes in the vertical assessment influence the horizontal evaluation.

How to Interpret Changes in Net Income as Percentages of Sales

Model 27 presents another approach to analyzing net income changes between annual periods (19X3 and 19X4 in this instance) and ascertaining the net variation as a percent of sales. In Model 26, the net income as a percent of sales is calculated to be 7.9% in 19X4 versus 7.5% for 19X3. The lower section of the model indicates that the 19X4 income increased by $4.725 million, which is 33.1% greater than in 19X3. Model 27, the alternate analysis, outlines the specific factors causing the increase or decrease between the two annual periods and their *resultant effect* as a percent of sales.

Let's look at Model 27 item by item:

- The calculated differences between the 19X4 and 19X3 income statement items represent increases or decreases to the income variations.

- Initially, net income increased because of a higher gross profit, the difference between a greater 19X4 sales volume of $50 million and a related cost of sales of $35.6 million. The higher gross profit was $14.4 million or a *6% ratio* to sales.

- Compared to gross profit, the *income from operations* was reduced by increased G&A and selling expenses in the amount of $4.9 million or a *2% ratio* to sales. To obtain the ratio of income from operation to sales (4%, as shown in Model 27), deduct the 2% factor from the 6% gross profit to sales increase.

- The *pretax profit ratio* to sales remained the same as income from operations. Although miscellaneous other income increased by $290,000, it was more than offset by the increase in interest expense of $340,000. The resultant difference is negligible in terms of ratio to sales.

- As reflected in the model, the pretax profit increase of $9.45 million led to a tax increase of $4.725 million, which represented a *2% decrease* in the sales ratio. By subtracting the 2% tax increase allowance from the pretax profit increase on sales, you get the "bottom line" increase of 2% in net income as a ratio to sales.

The procedure used in Model 27 complements the one in Model 26. Nontechnical in nature, it can be readily understood by nonaccountants due to its narrative format, which highlights the causes for income var-

MODEL 27. Changes in Net Income as Percentages of Sales.

(in $000,000s)

Description	19X4	19X3	Increase (Decrease) in Dollars	Increase (Decrease) % of Sales
Net Income Increases Due to:				
Gross Profit Increases				
Sales increase	$240.00	$190.00	$50.00	
Cost of sales increase	176.60	141.00	35.60	
Gross profit increase			$14.40	.06
Operating Income Decreases				
G&A increase	$ 13.90	$ 11.40	(2.50)	
Selling expense inc.	11.30	8.90	(2.40)	
Operating income decrease			(4.90)	(.02)
Operating income result			$9.50	.04
Pretax Profit Decreases				
Other income increase	$ .48	$ .19	$ .29	
Interest expense increase	.72	.38	.34	
Profit decrease			(.05)	Negligible
Profit result			$ 9.45	.04
Net Income Decrease				
Increase for taxes	$ 18.98	$ 14.255	(4.725)	(.02)
Net Income Increases			$ 4.725	.02

$4.725 ÷ $240.0 Sales = 2% (19X4 over 19X3)

iation in comparative statement analyses. Further, it presents each of the actual variations between two periods in terms of a ratio to sales volume, a major criterion in profitability assessment.

How to Assess Profitability Ratios

The profitability ratio helps you to measure management's ability to manage and control costs. This ratio assesses whether there is a profitable return on sales activity and other resources invested in the business. The evaluation and planning of profitability involves many facets of the operational and financial results, which are categorically reported in both the income statement and the balance sheet. Since the opinions of accounting professionals vary on this subject, we will take an integrated approach in discussing profitability ratios, their objectives, and their use.

Analyzing gross profit to sales ratio. This basic ratio represents the percentage difference between net sales and the associated cost of sales. The cost of sales represents the direct cost expenditures for producing a product or for performing services: the labor activity, the material usage, and the associated indirect expense support, such as factory overhead (operating supplies, maintenance, repairs, utilities, and the like).

To succeed, business must achieve and maintain a profitable gross margin to sales ratio. Product demand and competitive climate govern the magnitude of the gross margin. As competition increases, pervading the product/service demand, gross profit contracts and narrows. Conversely, as demand increases in proportion to supply, prices and profit margins tend to increase. This phenomenon is natural. The objective of every progressive organization is to sell its products/services at the highest prices consistent with volume and competitive proposals. Gross profits must not only support G&A/selling expenses and operational financing (interest expense) costs, but also yield an adequate net income on sales and return on investment.

Weighing gross profit ratio considerations. As shown in Model 26, the gross profit to sales ratio is the difference between the sales percentage of 100% and the cost of sales. In other words, when calculated as an individual item, it is simply the gross profit value divided by the net sales volume dollars. The gross profit ratio is governed by the variations in the cost of sales relationship to sales. In turn, each of these variables is affected by product demand and price. An assessment of the changes in *sales and cost of sales* includes the following considerations:

1. *Changes in sales values result from:*
   a. The magnitude of product volume, assuming that there is *no change in selling price.* Thus, to obtain the resultant sales volume dollars, multiply the change in volume by the individual product selling price (or by the average product price if more than one product is involved).
   b. If the variation in the sales volume is attributed to a *change in the selling price,* then multiply the product volume by the price differential to obtain the increase or decrease in the sales dollars.
   c. If the variation in sales value *involves both volume and selling price,* then multiply the volume or quantity by the price differential to arrive at the change in sales dollars.
2. *To calculate changes in cost of sales,* follow the same steps.

Influencing factors on gross profit are as follows:

- Business conditions or environment changing market conditions influence product demand, thereby affecting gross profit.
- Material/supplies purchasing. Effective purchasing policies relative to quantity and price procedures govern product cost and therefore affect the magnitude of the gross profit.
- Effectiveness of operational efficiencies and sales results. In terms of manpower utilization and quality/quantity output, operating efficiencies affect labor costs which, in turn, definitely influence product cost and gross profit. Strict surveillance and control of operating expenses are mandatory for competitive product pricing which affects both product demand and gross profit results. (See Chapter 3 for direct product costs and associated ratios.)

Deriving the Income from Operations Ratio to Sales

This ratio is of major significance in the assessment of the income statement. To derive it, reduce gross profit dollars by G&A/selling expenses, by R&D requirements, and by any initial lien on gross profits. The ratio represents the return from operations prior to its adjustment for other income and deductions, plus an allowance for federal income taxes.

Analyzing G&A/selling expense ratio. This ratio to sales indicates the control and surveillance exercised over these expenses relative to sales activities. Even in periods of financial difficulties, these expenses must be paid before bond interest, principal, or stock dividends take their bite out of profits.

The ratio of each of these expenses to sales generally decreases with increased volume. Expenses that increase proportionately with sales generally indicate that management is not exercising proper attention and control, although extenuating circumstances could support increased expenditures.

Analyzing the research and development (R&D) ratio. R&D costs, like G&A/selling expenses, are reductions to gross profit to obtain income from operations. Investment in R&D, as a planned/controlled cost, can be increased or decreased depending on the nature of the "need." Many organizations divert funds and effort either to enhance their current product design or to develop new products for future exploitation. This investment can be substantial, particularly in the highly competitive automotive, aircraft, and defense industries. Although minimal expenditures can lead to improved short-term profits, they can adversely affect profitability in the long run, particularly if their competition's R&D activities are aggressive.

How to Calculate the Pretax Profit Ratio

To obtain the pretax profit value:

1. Add other miscellaneous income (sales discounts, gain on sale of fixed assets, interest income) to the operational income.
2. Then reduce this amount by other deductions, such as interest expense, project abandonments, deferred development, and loss on the sale of fixed assets.
3. Divide the result by net sales to obtain the pretax profit ratio.

Other income and deductions represent nonoperating items in most organizations. The items of other income and deductions vary among organizations depending on their types of business and the accounting procedures.

Calculating the Net Income to Sales Ratio

Every business is managed and controlled to make income, and its success is reflected in terms of its "bottom line"—the net income after taxes in the income statement. The ratio of *net income to sales* measures the sales profitability. Although sales represent a dynamic force in the business enterprise cycle, profitability is a major criterion in assessing operational performance.

Variations in net income. The variations over a period of years in the ratio of net income to sales result from the same type of circumstances that affect the ratio of operating profits: the state of the business environment, competitive influences, management attention and controls, and the cost of borrowed capital. Relative to borrowing funds, a sound and profitable financial structure generally enables an organization to obtain adequate financing at favorable rates.

How business cycles affect net income. To a degree, changes in the business cycle—periods of normality, of high earnings, and of depressed situations—affect every organization. In normal and high earning periods, management must therefore conserve its resources and maintain profitability so that it can cope financially with future adverse situations. To achieve its goals, management must be ever on the alert to take advantage of technological advances, investment opportunities, cost control, and maintain sound financing practices. It must continually assess competition to avoid an unfavorable operating/marketing position. Profitability, stability, survival, and progress all result from constructive financial policies with a continuing appraisal of their objectives and status.

LIMITATIONS OF FINANCIAL STATEMENTS IN RATIO ANALYSIS

There are certain common limitations associated with the use of financial statement data for ratio analyses that should be recognized and understood in the assessment process and the acceptance of results from conclusive findings for decision making. The major limitations and problem situations are highlighted as follows.

- The contents of financial statements are predicated on *generally accepted accounting principles* which have been developed and refined over a period of years by accounting professionals. The relevant exactness of the reported data is nearly impossible to achieve because the statements represent circumstances and conditions that cannot be precisely postulated. There exist differences of opinion in the accounting profession relative to the various complex aspects of accounting procedure. For example, *unrealized profits* should not be included in earnings but *unpaid incurred expenses* should be included in the liabilities.

- Financial statements *use historical costs* and thus, in most instances, ignore the inflation factor. Inventories, for example, can be undervalued; therefore, by using the FIFO costing method, higher income would generally be experienced during periods of inflation.

- The net income reported in the income statement is *not absolute but rather relative* depending on the particular conventional procedures used by the organization in its accounting practices. Income figures can be manipulated, either intentionally or unintentionally, by improper reflection of nonrecurring gain on the sale of land or other resources, declining trend in repairs to existing fixed assets (a possible cost control objective), method of inventory valuation in relation to cost of sales, use of diluted profit rates on contracts to provide for management contingency pools, use of estimated overhead rates that are not representative of actual expenses, and so on.

- The statements reflect the *position of the financial accounting* for an organization but may not show the *true financial condition* of the operational results since there are many factors that are not a part of the financial data reporting. *Informative footnotes* could provide clues to existing or anticipated financial position situations.

- There are *inherent estimations* in the accounting measurement process such as the life of the individual fixed assets and associated depreciation values, which affect operating expense and income, warranty provisions, estimated income tax provisions, projected disallowances (particularly on government contracts), and anticipated project abandonment write-offs.

The statement limitations pose a problem in reliably analyzing an organization's financial position, developing meaningful ratios, and comparing operational results with other organizations even in a similar type industry.

ANALYZING THE COMPARATIVE BALANCE SHEET

Model 28 will help us see how some common practices are employed in analyzing the increases and decreases among assets, liabilities, and equity. It also highlights information that is pertinent to other aspects of profitability and that can be used in conjunction with the income statement operating results.

Examining the Balance Sheet

The balance sheet in Model 28 reports data for the years ending 19X3 and 19X4. Although the various elements and format in the statement are typical of most organizations, the data can be of greater or lesser detail. The item classifications may also vary somewhat among organizations depending on their types of operations and specific reporting requirements. The single balance sheet emphasizes an organization's *financial position*, whereas comparative reporting concentrates on the *changes* between two or more time periods and financial *trends*.

The changes in the balance sheet items are the effects of the period's operational activities, and they reflect the interactions among assets, liability, and capital accounts. Most significantly, the comparisons provide an opportunity to analyze and evaluate the financial position trends of an organization in terms of the specifics reported.

Analyzing Comparative Statements

In the vertical approach to balance sheet analysis, *each of the total asset items is divided by the total asset value.* This computation provides the quantitative positional relationships among the reported items at a particular point in time. *Each liability and equity item is divided by the aggregate total,* which equals the total asset value.

Let's take a look at the comparative values and their percentages:

- Accounts receivable and inventories represented the major elements in the current assets. Although the receivables decreased $4.0 million or 12.2% in 19X4 over 19X3, the decrease was offset primarily by a $3.3 million increase in cash and securities. Relative to inventories, raw materials and finished goods increased by $9.3 million; the increase, however, was mostly offset by a $9.0 million decrease in WIP inventories.

- The total overall current assets for the two reporting periods remained in a static position with only a .6% decrease in 19X4 versus 19X3.

- Net fixed assets increased by $1.2 million or 3.5% in 19X4 over 19X3. Deferred charges decreased by $.8 million or 47.1% in 19X4 as compared to 19X3. In effect, the net fixed asset increase was primarily offset by a $.8 million decrease in deferred charges.

- Accounts payable represented the largest current *liability*, indicating that there was $4.4 million or 26.4% increase in 19X4 as compared to 19X3. This situation is generally considered to be unfavorable unless production/sales requirements increased accordingly (which they did, as shown in Model 26). Further, the increase was more than offset by the $4.6 million decrease in notes payable—a favorable liability reduction trend.

- In the aggregate, total current liabilities increased by $.85 million or 2.8% in 19X4 versus 19X3. Such an increase, in relative terms, is not significant when production costs increased by 25.2%, as shown in Model 26.

- As a result of decreased current assets of $450,000 and increased current liabilities of $.85 million, the net effect on working capital in 19X4 was a decrease of $1.3 million or 2.6%. The *current ratio* (current assets ÷ current liabilities) was a 2.6 factor in 19X4 versus 2.7 in 19X3. These ratios are considered favorable, particularly in manufacturing operations.

- The decrease in *total liabilities* of $1.55 million or 2.5% is primarily attributed to the reduction in long-term debt of $2.1 million or 7.3%. This is a favorable trend in light of the $50,000 increase in total assets and a $1.5 million increase in stockholders' equity, as displayed in Model 28.

- Stockholders' equity in the form of paid-in-capital decreased $7.68 million, and common stock equity decreased $1.3 million. The decreases were offset by a $10.48 million increase in retained earnings (Model 28). The net result was a 2.7% increase in the 19X4 stockholders' equity.

MODEL 28. Comparative Balance Sheet Analysis.

(in $000,000s)

	19X4 Amount	19X4 %	19X3 Amount	19X3 %	19X4 Increase (Decrease) Amount	19X4 Increase (Decrease) %
Current Assets						
Cash	$ 3.50	3.0	$ 2.50	2.1	$ 1.00	40.0
Marketable securities	3.30	2.8	1.00	.9	2.30	230.0
Accounts receivable	28.70	24.5	32.70	27.9	(4.00)	(12.2)
Inventories:						
Raw materials	26.80	22.9	19.20	16.4	7.60	39.6
Work in process	10.70	9.1	19.70	16.8	(9.00)	(45.7)
Finished goods	7.30	6.2	5.60	4.8	1.70	30.4
Subtotal	44.80	38.2	44.50	38.0	.30	.7
Prepaid Expenses	.25	.2	.30	.2	(.05)	(16.7)
Total Current Assets	$ 80.55	68.7	$ 81.00	69.1	(.45)	(0.6)
Property, Plant and Equipment						
Land	2.30	2.0	2.30	2.0	—	—
Buildings/improvement	20.00	17.1	19.70	16.8	.30	1.5
Machinery/equipment	31.40	26.7	29.40	25.0	2.00	6.8
Subtotal	53.70	45.8	51.40	43.8	2.30	4.5
Less: Accumulated depreciation	17.90	15.3	16.80	14.3	1.10	6.5
Net fixed assets	35.80	30.5	34.60	29.5	1.20	3.5
Deferred Charges	.90	.8	1.70	1.4	(.80)	(47.1)
Total assets	$117.25	100.0	$117.30	100.0	.05	
Current Liabilities						
Notes payable	$ 1.40	1.2	$ 6.00	5.1	$(4.60)	(76.6)
Current portion—LT debt	2.50	2.1	2.30	2.0	.20	8.7
Accrued payroll	3.60	3.1	2.90	2.5	.70	24.1
Accounts payable	20.85	17.8	16.50	13.9	4.35	26.4
Income tax payable	2.60	2.2	2.40	2.0	.20	8.3
Total current liabilities	$ 30.95	26.4	$ 30.10	25.5	$ .85	2.8
Deferred Income Taxes	1.90	1.6	2.20	1.9	(.30)	(13.6)
Long Term Debt	26.70	22.8	28.80	24.6	(2.10)	(7.3)
Total liabilities	$ 59.55	50.8	$ 61.10	52.0	$(1.55)	(2.5)
Stockholders' Equity						
Common stock	$ 3.70	3.1	$ 5.00	4.3	$(1.30)	(26.0)
Paid-in capital	26.01	22.2	33.69	28.8	(7.68)	(22.8)
Retained earnings	27.99	23.9	17.51	14.9	10.48	59.9
Total equity capital	$ 57.70	49.2	$ 56.20	48.0	$ 1.50	2.7
Total liabilities/capital	$117.25	100.0	$117.30	100.0	$ .05	
Working Capital	$ 49.60	—	$ 50.90	—	$(1.30)	(2.6)
Current ratio (2.6:1)	2.6	—	2.7	—	(.1)	—
Ratio to sales	—	20.7	—	26.8	—	(6.1)

SUMMARY

Using both the vertical and horizontal approaches to financial statement analysis, you can thoroughly assess operating results. Either type of analysis contributes uniquely to data assessment. Use the calculated percentages as result indicators, which may require additional interpretation and further use in analysis and planning. You must determine whether the various proportions and changes are favorable or unfavorable to the organization's objectives.

Making Comparative Assessments of External Organizations

You can use the same process to compare the financial positions of two or more *external* organizations in related industries at a point in time. If the dollar magnitudes are great, you might prefer to make the comparisons on a percentage basis. Comparisons expressed in dollar values may be misleading due to the relative sizes of the organizations. Converting dollar items to percentages undoubtedly clarifies the relative proportions of the financial elements.

CAUTION

Be careful. The balance sheet data must be compatible and comparable in terms of basic accounting procedures. Follow the guidelines set forth by AICPA as common standards.

APPLICATIONS

Comparative balance sheet analysis provides informative insight into the overall financial position/percentage changes (increases or decreases) between periods. It also reflects the interactions among assets, liabilities, and capital, as well as the respective trends of each.

How to Analyze Changes in Stockholders' Equity

The changes in stockholders' equity schedule highlight and summarize financial variations and reports their effect on the capital position.

Model 29 displays an assessment of capital changes. *Increases in assets* and *decreases in liability accounts* represent the factors causing an *increase in capital.* Conversely, *decreases in assets* and *increases in liabilities* result in *capital reductions.* As shown in Model 29, the change in the 19X4 capital position is the difference between the increases and decreases in the plus amount of $1.5 million or 2.7% over 19X3. In other words, the factors that increase capital represent the source for the increases (cash, securities, and so on), whereas the reductions to the capital account are considered to be capital applications (increased payables and decreased receivables, as examples).

If you require more detail on fixed assets and accumulated depre-

MODEL 29. Assessing Changes to Stockholders' Equity.*

December 31, 19X3–19X4
(in $000,000s)

Summary of Stockholders' Equity		19X4	19X3
Common stock		$ 3.70	$ 5.00
Paid-in capital		26.01	33.69
Retained earnings		27.99	17.51
Subtotal		$57.70	$56.20
Increase in capital		—	1.50
Totals		$57.70	$57.70
1. Factors Increasing Capital			
Increase in Assets			
Cash	$1.00		
Marketable securities	2.30		
Net inventories	.50		
Net fixed assets	1.20	5.00	
Decrease in Liabilities			
Notes payable	4.60		
Deferred income taxes	.30		
Long-term debt	2.10	7.00	12.00
2. Factors Decreasing Capital			
Decreases in Assets			
Accounts receivable	4.00		
Prepaid expenses	.05		
Deferred charges	.80	4.85	
Increases in Liabilities			
Current portion— LT debt	.20		
Accrued payroll	.70		
Accounts payable	4.55		
Income tax payable	.20	5.65	10.50
Increase in Capital			$ 1.50

Capital Ratios	%	%
Capital to sales	24.0	29.6
Net income to capital	32.9	25.4
Retained earnings to capital	48.5	31.2
Capital to total assets	49.2	48.0
Capital to total liabilities	96.9	92.3

*Refer to Models 26 and 28 for operating and balance sheet detail.

ciation than are shown in the model, you would show the individually categorized *gross asset increases* as *increases in assets* and the increases in classified depreciation groupings as *increases* under major item 2—"Factors Decreasing Capital."

How to use stockholders' equity ratios. In Model 29 are examples of equity ratios that can be used in assessing the capital position and changes. In some organizations, these ratios may be relevant and useful, but in others they may be considered inconsequential. By evaluating your own organizations, you can determine which ratios are significant in assessing the capital position.

With respect to the ratios in Model 29, note the following:

THE FORMULA

$$\text{Investors' capital to sales ratio} = \frac{\text{Stockholders' Equity}}{\text{Sales}}$$

As shown in Model 29, the equity capital relationships to sales for 19X4 and 19X3 were 24.0% and 29.6%, respectively. The decrease in the 19X4 ratio is primarily attributed to a 26.3% increase in 19X4 sales over 19X3 with only a 2.7% increase in capital.

APPLICATIONS

Although not commonly used, this ratio may have useful application in certain organizations to indicate the proportion of sales financed by stockholders' equity. A further 25% of sales is financed by creditor liabilities, and the operational activity is supported by the cash flow from operations. Let's analyze this relationship from another perspective: The ratio of sales to capital in 19X4 is 4.16 to 1.00 ($240 million sales ÷ capital equity of $57.7 million). The comparison indicates that the sales volume exceeds the stockholders' equity by four times the investment.

THE FORMULA

$$\text{Net income to capital ratio} = \frac{\text{Net income}}{\text{Capital}}$$

The net income to capital ratio was 32.9% and 25.4% for 19X4 and 19X3, respectively. These ratios indicate the *returns* on stock equity achieved in 19X4 and 19X3. The increase in 19X4 is primarily attributed to a 33.1% increase in net income (Model 26) with a relatively modest increase (2.7%) in equity.

SPECIAL NOTE

When developing ratios involving balance sheet items (assets, liabilities, equity) versus operational data (sales, net income, and the like), generally you obtain more reliable results by using *averaged balance sheet data* and *annualized operational data.*

APPLICATION   This analysis represents the capital or equity *profitability* for the periods ending 19X4 and 19X3. The 19X4 ratio indicates a favorable trend of capital investment return.

THE FORMULA $$\text{Retained earnings ratio to capital} = \frac{\text{Retained earnings}}{\text{Capital}}$$

The retained earnings ratio in Model 29 was 48.5% in 19X4 and 31.2% in 19X3. The large increase in 19X4 resulted from a 59.9% increase in net income, which was only partially offset by a small increase in capital.

APPLICATION   This ratio indicates a favorable situation: The major contributing factor to capital financing is being achieved from operational results and thus reducing the pressure on outside investor contributions and dividend disbursements.

THE FORMULA $$\text{Capital ratio to total liabilities} = \frac{\text{Capital}}{\text{Total liabilities}}$$

This ratio reports the amount of the total liabilities supported by outstanding capital, both the investors' and retained earnings.

As displayed in Model 29, the ratio factor was 96.9% and 92.3%, respectively, for 19X4 and 19X3. The higher ratio in 19X4 is primarily attributed to decreased total liabilities and a modest increase of $1.5 million in capital.

APPLICATION   This ratio presents to creditors an organization's financial stability in terms of contracting and meeting its debt obligations. For example, an analytical assessment of the ratio in the model indicates that every dollar of the total liabilities is supported by $.97 and $.92 in capital for 19X4 and 19X3.

Comparing Equity Capital to Noncurrent Assets

To obtain this ratio, divide the capital value by the noncurrent assets.

Example: The following factors are derived from data in Model 28:

	19X4	19X3		
Net fixed assets*	$35.8	$34.6	19X4	$57.7 ÷ $36.7 = *157%*
Deferred charges	.9	1.7		
			19X3	$56.2 ÷ $36.3 = *155%*
Total	$36.7	$36.3		

*Some organizations may use gross fixed asset costs depending on their situations. The calculated ratios are 157% and 155%, respectively, for 19X4 and 19X3.

APPLICATION The significance of this ratio is that the stockholders' equity supports the noncurrent assets and that the surplus is available for current asset operating requirements. Generally, the greater the ratio is over 100%, the more favorable is the organization's financial position from the standpoint of meeting creditor commitments and debts.

How to Gauge Turnover of Total Capital Employed

The ratio of sales to average total assets represents the turnover of the total capital employed in operations. The turnover formula is as follows:

THE FORMULA
$$\text{Total assets employed ratio} = \frac{\text{Net sales}}{\text{Average total assets}}$$

Included in the total assets are the typical balance sheet items as shown in Model 28, such as cash, receivables, inventories, net fixed assets, and so on. Marketable securities and other forms of investment are excluded because they do not contribute directly to operational requirements and are separate producers of nonoperating income. Note that the asset distribution represents all of the sources of capital both borrowed (short- and long-term), as well as the stockholders' investment plus retained earnings.

Example: The following calculations are made from Model 28 data:

(in $000,000s)

	19X4	19X3		Asset Turnover
Total capital	$117.25	$117.10	19X4	$\frac{\$240.00^*}{\$113.95} = 2.11$
Less: Securities	3.30	1.00		
Adjusted capital	$113.95	$116.10	19X3	$\frac{\$190.00^*}{\$116.00} = 1.64$

*Net sales data from Model 26.

The annual sales and year-end asset figures are used instead of the average in order to compare the two years. If only 19X4 sales were compared with the two years' asset average, the resultant ratio would be 2.08. If monthly or quarterly comparative data were used, you would use annualized sales and asset averages.

The increase in the capital employed turnover rate in 19X4 over 19X3 indicates that assets are being utilized more effectively in 19X4 (2.11 versus 1.64). In other words, the assets supported more sales per dollar in 19X4 as compared to 19X3.

Calculating the rate of return on total capital employed. In addition to analyzing the asset turnover status, you have to determine and evaluate asset profitability. To make this assessment, combine the asset turnover with the profit rate on sales. Depending on organizational practices and requirements, you can calculate two rates of return for analyzing operational results: (1) income from operations and (2) net income. The calculating formulas are as follow:

1. *Approach A:* Rate of return   Rate on income   Asset
   on total assets = from operations × turnover
              or Net income

   a. Income from operations $\dfrac{38.2}{240.0}$ = 15.9% return on operating income
      19X4 Sales

      Asset turnover   2.11 × 15.9% = <u>33.5%</u> Operating return
                                             on adjusted total
                                             assets

   b. Net income $\dfrac{18.98}{240.00}$ = 7.9% Return on
      19X4 Sales   net income

      Asset turnover   2.11 × 7.9% = <u>16.7%</u> Net income return
                                             on adjusted total
                                             assets

2. *Approach B:* $\dfrac{\text{Operating income}}{\text{Total assets}} = \dfrac{\text{Income}}{\text{Sales}} \times \dfrac{\text{Sales}}{\text{Total assets}}$

   a. Income from operations $\dfrac{38.20}{113.95} = \dfrac{38.2}{240.0} \times \dfrac{240.00}{113.95}$
      19X4 Total assets

                               33.5% = 15.9% × 2.11

                               33.5% = <u>33.5%</u> Operating return
                                             on total assets

   b. Net income $\dfrac{18.98}{113.95} = \dfrac{18.98}{240.00} \times \dfrac{240.00}{113.95}$
      19X4 Total assets

                               16.7% = 7.9% × 2.11

                               16.7% = <u>16.7%</u> Net income return
                                             on total assets

Points to remember about return on total capital employed. Here are some things to remember about this relationship:

- An improved asset turnover generally means an increase in the rate of return on total assets employed.

Example: Using the 19X4 and 19X3 results already developed, the following comparison is made:

	19X4	19X3	
Adjusted capital employed	$113.95	$116.00	
Net sales	240.00	190.00	
Turnover ratio	2.11	1.64	
Profit rate on operating income	15.9%	15.1%	
Return on capital employed	33.5%	24.8%	(8.7% increase in 19X4)
	(2.11 × 15.9%)	(1.64 × 15.1%)	

- The *increased sales* in 19X4 of 26.3% over 19X3 and a decrease of 1.9% in total capital employed resulted in an 8.7% increase in the asset return.

- Generally, an organization selling higher-priced items (automobiles or machinery, for example) has a *lower turnover rate* than one selling lower-priced units. The *lower-priced units have a higher-profit margin* in order to achieve a favorable return on the capital assets employed.

- A *high rate of turnover* in capital employed usually indicates efficiency in the utilization of capital.

- *Use of average total assets and appropriate annualized sales* provides a realistic assessment of profit return on total capital employed despite unusual fluctuations among time periods.

CALCULATING EARNINGS PER COMMON SHARE

Investors in common stocks are generally more interested in and concerned with the earnings per share (influencing factor on market price) of their stock than with the dividend return. (The exceptions might be stockholders who depend on their dividends for their livelihoods.) The stockholders assume the ultimate risk in the business enterprise if it should fail since all creditor claims must be satisfied before any investment reimbursement is made to the owners. The investors' stock ownership represents tangible evidence of their claim against the net assets of the organization.

To derive earnings per share, divide the net income by the number of common stock shares outstanding in the possession of the stockholders.

Example: Let's assume that the main and only concern is common stock since no preferred or other type equivalent stock is involved in this situation:

Earnings per Share
(in $000,000s)

	19X4	19X3
Net income	$18.98	$14.255
Average shares outstanding	3.43 = $5.53*	3.36 = $4.24*

*Earnings per share

Rate of Return on Stockholders' Equity
(in $000,000s)

	19X4	19X3
Net income	$18.98	$14.255
Stockholders' equity	57.70 = 32.9%	56.20 = 24.4%

The increase in earnings per share in 19X4 is attributed to a 33.1% higher income with only a 2.1% increase in shares outstanding 3.43 − 3.36 million shares = .07 ÷ 3.36).

The common stock equity is generally the total stockholders' equity less the par value of the preferred stock. So, if there were dividend requirements for *preferred stock,* deduct the amount from the net income before calculating the earnings per share of common stock.

Calculating the Price-Earnings Ratio per Share

This ratio represents the relationship between earnings per share and the market price. To obtain it, divide the market price per share by the comparable earnings per share.

Example: The market prices per share of stock are $16 and $14, respectively, for 19X4 and 19X3.

	19X4	19X3
Market price per share	$16 = 2.89 times	$14 = 3.3 times
Earnings per share*	$5.53 earnings	$4.24 earnings

*Calculated in previous example.

The price-earnings ratio is calculated to be 2.9 and 3.3 times earnings.

ASSESSING THE CAUSE FOR PROFIT VARIATION

By using cost variation analyses, you not only determine the reasons for the variance in planned profit goals, but also ascertain whether some type of corrective action is required or whether income anticipations were too optimistic. Essentially, you try to answer such questions as these: Can the cost assessment provide the necessary insight as to where and how cost deviations occurred? Can the deviations be reduced and profits increased?

Most progressive and successful organizations plan their profit objectives in advance rather than accept whatever results materialize at the end of a reporting period. With a "planning" philosophy, you must initiate cost control standards for cost of sales and G&A/selling expenses. You must also carefully plan and then assess sales volume anticipations and product profit margins.

The Basic Causes for Variations

At the end of the reporting period, compare the planned profits to the actuals and then calculate the difference in terms of increases or decreases. Next, determine the cause or causes. Some of the common reasons for profit variations are changes in

> sales volume
> direct production costs
> G&A/selling expenses
> product sales prices
> product line mix sales

Let's look at each of these causes more closely:

Sales volume. The planned sales objective may be either not achieved or exceeded, with generally a resultant increase or decrease in profits. An analysis would help you to pinpoint the problem: an "unaccepted" product line, a schedule slippage or acceleration, a "blown" contract or sales order, a "tough" sales territory, and so on.

Direct production costs (cost of sales). Variations in these costs can be attributed to a number of factors, such as machine downtime, poor learning curve results, wage increases, fluctuations in the price of raw materials and operating costs, excessive rework, schedule slippage, and so on. The detailed work order and cost sheets can generally provide the reasons for these variations.

G&A/selling expenses. These expenses may have exceeded estimates due to increased advertising, acceleration and expansion of sales activity, higher than anticipated administrative costs, increased corporate office expense allocations, and so on.

Product sales prices. Product prices can be lower than expected due to many factors, such as price concessions to favored customers because of competitive pressures, large-quantity sales at discount prices, poor estimates of product cost and gross margin markup, exploitation of new market outlets, and so on. The marketing organization is undoubtedly aware of the details.

Product line mix sales. In an organization with varying product lines and different gross margins, the estimated sales for the individual product lines may or may not materialize. In other words, low-priced items, with their low-profit margins, may have represented most of the projected sales. A detailed analysis of the sales by product line would reveal "what happened" to dilute profit.

Analyzing Gross Profit Variance

Model 30 displays the formulas used to derive the gross profit variances and to determine their specific causes. As shown in the model, the overall gross profit variance is the difference between the actual and standard gross profits. To ascertain the causes for the difference, use the following formulas:

Cost of sales	= Standard cost of sales − Actual cost of sales
Sales price list at dis-count	= Actual net sales − Price list sales at standard discount
Standard gross profit variation by product line	= Standard gross profit on cost of sales − Standard gross profit on actual price list sales by product line
Standard gross profit variation on sales volume	= Standard gross profit on actual price list sales by product line − Standard gross profit

The sum of the increases and decreases derived from these calculations represents the causes for the net profit variation, as shown in Model 30. Note that the G&A/selling expenses are not displayed since they do not generally influence gross profit; they are rather subsequent deductions to derive income from operations.

Segregating Gross Profit Variations
by Causes

Model 31 demonstrates the calculations for Product Lines A and B and their totals. Segregation of the variance analyses is by *cause*. The sum total of the gross profit variations resulted in a decrease of $670,000 for

MODEL 30. Analyzing Gross Profit (GP) Variance.

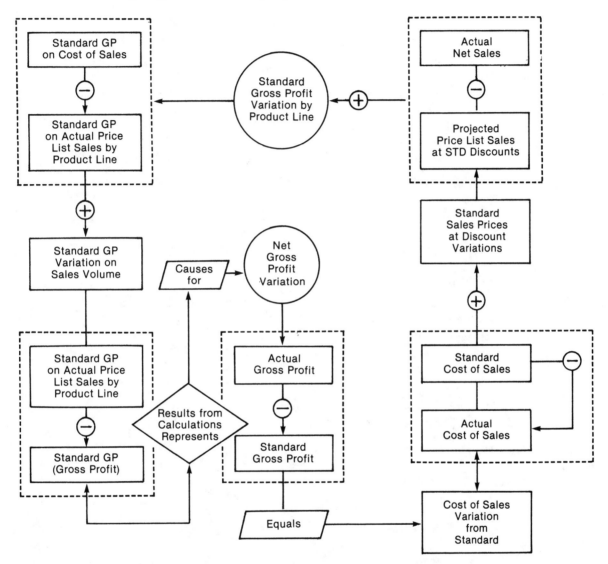

Product Line A and an increase of $1.34 million for Product Line B, with a net total increase of $670,000 for the combined product lines.

The bottom of the model displays a summary of the gross profit variations by causes for each product line. This type of analysis and reporting provides management with a rapid overview of the causes for gross profit variations and permits positive action, if required, to correct unfavorable situations.

The variations indicate that Product Line B had favorable variations in gross profit with the exception of sales volume dollar results, which indicate that discounted price actuals were $1.0 million less than the projected standard.

MODEL 31. Calculating Gross Profit Variations by Causes.

(in $000,000s)

	Product Line A	Product Line B	Combined Total
Gross Profit (GP) Variation			
Actual	$ 2.23	$ 9.04	$11.27
Standard or estimated	2.90	7.70	10.60
Increase (decrease)	$ (.67)	$ 1.34	$ .67
Analysis of GP Increases (Decreases)			
Cost of Sales			
Standard	$ 3.20	$12.40	$15.60
Actual	3.32	11.96	15.28
Increase (decrease)	$ (.12)	$ .44	$ .32
Sales at Price List or Discounted			
Actual net sales	$ 5.55	$21.00	$26.55
Price list sales at discount	5.80	20.70	26.50
Increase (decrease)	$ (.25)	$ .30	$ .05
Standard GP Variation by Product Line			
Cost of sales	$ 2.60	$ 8.30	$10.90
Actual price list sales discounted	2.50	6.70	9.20
Increase (decrease)	$ .10	$ 1.60	$ 1.70
Standard GP Variation on Sales Volume			
Actual price list sales discounted	$ 2.50	$ 6.70	$ 9.20
Standard gross profit	2.90	7.70	10.60
Increase (decrease)	$ (.40)	$(1.00)	$(1.40)
Summary of Variation Analysis			
Actual gross profit	$13.85	$48.40	$62.25
Standard gross profit	14.52	47.06	61.58
Increase (decrease)	$ (.67)	$ 1.34	$ .67

Variation Analysis by Causes

	Product Line A	Product Line B	Combined Total	Percentage Increase (Decrease)
Cost of sales	$(.12)	$ .44	$ .32	.478
Sales price or discounted	(.25)	.30	.05	.075
Standard GP variation by product line	.10	1.60	1.70	2.537
Standard GP variation on sales volume	(.40)	(1.00)	(1.40)	(2.090)
Net increase (decrease)	$(.67)	$ 1.34	$ .67	1.000

6

How to Use Ratio Analysis for Industry Comparisons

CHAPTER HIGHLIGHTS

Financial analysts, as well as managers, may utilize comparison ratios to assess and interpret data for planning and controlling operations. Industry comparisons can be extremely helpful, but their use has its pitfalls. As the analyst, you must be familiar with the role of ratio guidelines in making comparisons, as well as with the possible deficiencies in data reliability.

Some ratios are used to uncover problems relative to receivables, inventory, income, sales, financing, and fixed assets.

Other ratios assess the implications of solvency relative to fixed assets to net worth, working capital to sales, and inventories to working capital.

These ratios also play an important role in trend analysis. The procedure for their use is explained, as is the significance of similar industry comparisons.

COPING WITH THE DILEMMA IN THE INITIAL USE OF RATIO ANALYSIS

Ratio analysis was initially used to assess an organization's financial position and performance in the early 1900s by financial and banking institutions. The purpose was to determine an organization's financial stability, particularly its ability to meet debt obligations on schedule. This assessment provided a basis for an organization's decision to extend credit to a borrower. Originally, the lender's concern was with the organization's *current ratio*—the relationship of current assets to current liabilities. The borrower's ratio was analyzed individually and with respect to the related industry.

Subsequently, both investors and financial analysts realized that their prevailing ratio approach was, by itself, not an adequate assessment of an organization's financial stability, progress, and performance. They then scrutinized other ratios for their use in data analysis to supplement and validate the financial status indicated by the *current ratio*.

A series of applicable ratios was developed. Although many users were captivated by the newly found possibilities of these ratios, analysts were unfamiliar with their significance and limitations. As a result, these ratios were often misapplied and misinterpreted. Users found that the application and use of the broad ratio approach to evaluate an organization's performance and financial progress were not the panacea originally envisioned. Care and judgment had to be exercised in using and interpreting ratios.

RECOGNIZING THE INHERENT WEAKNESSES IN RATIO ANALYSIS

A number of factors can influence the reliability and validity of ratio performance indicators, thus placing limits on their unqualified utilization for management's financial and operating decisions. Here are some of the major limitations and possible drawbacks. If you are to use ratio analysis on a firm basis and accept the results with confidence and finality, you should bear the following in mind:

- In business problem solving and planning, quantitative data analyses are not the sole criterion. Management's judgment and its operating effectiveness play vital roles in decision making and assessing performance results.

- To interpret the implications of changes in ratios reliably, you must analyze the variations in the two or more variables representing the relationship. For example, given unusual fluctuations in the current ratio, you must investigate the individual current assets and liabilities to determine whether the trend of change is temporary or permanent.

- Inherent exceptions can be involved in any ratio interpretation since the standard of content and calculation is not absolute. If data compatibility is not assured, comparisons with industry averages may be misleading and invalid.

- Persons involved in the reporting and analysis processes may overlook or "gloss over" significant information. Consequently, ratios do not necessarily provide a *thorough and accurate overview* of the financial statement content, relationships, and results.

- Profit is a key area of analysis. Yet the ratio assessment of income return on equity and total assets can be distorted. The reported income figures might include profits before or after deducting depreciation and interest expenses, or federal income taxes might not have been given consideration. For a generally sound criterion in judging the profit generated, you might use pretax profit from operations.

- Ratios are sometimes accepted as the "final say" in result analysis. However, do not overlook other relevant and influencing criteria, such as (1) the effects of inflation, (2) changes in product mix and its effect on the operating/sales environment, (3) receivable/inventory turnover factor, (4) adverse cash flow, (5) changes in credit policy, (6) prevailing sales/backlog status and trends, and (7) excessive investment in capital facilities.

- Although you may use ratios for planning, do not ignore the fact that they represent historical experience and past relationships. Although past performance is and should be of considerable interest, the emphasis is on correcting deficiencies and improving future results. The prevailing ratios aid in reconciling and developing projections for the future. Nevertheless, the key requirements for success and profit are judgmental decisions, marketing intelligence, anticipated operating environment, planned goals, and effective management control.

- Ratios of similar types of organizations can be so misleading that they hamper a realistic comparative analysis of data results and meaning. You should consider (1) the relative sizes of the organizations, (2) their uniformity in accounting procedures, (3) lengths of accounting periods being reported, and (4) type of customers. Each of these factors can influence the interindustry comparison of performance results by means of ratios.

HOW TO USE PERIODIC TRENDS TO MEASURE PERFORMANCE

By using ratio analyses as representatives of past experience, you can effectively plan financial objectives and gauge future operating environments. In so doing, your concern must be directed toward the underlying direction and intensity of changes in operating results. The situation may be static and quiescent, requiring only minor changes in future operating decisions. Major trend changes would call for a thorough review of the operating plan and perhaps significant changes to meet new challenges.

TYPE OF MEASUREMENTS

The common measurements in financial data analysis fall into two primary groupings:

1. The first type of assessment is concerned with the *item element relationships* in current performance reporting.
2. The second is directed toward the *item changes* in a series of time-reported statements.

Current or single report analysis measures results only at a point in time. Assessing a series of time reports is a dynamic approach in performance evaluation because you can determine patterns of progress and trends for establishing future planning goals. Further, you can redirect operational trends that are inconsistent with management's prerogatives and objectives.

The use of trend measurement, in conjunction with ratio comparisons and data evaluation, provides a supplemental and logical basis for sound planning. Trend measurement and projections are affected by estimates or approximations and their computation. The latter method involves the principles of semi- or moving-averages and the least squares procedure approach.

The progressive organization depends on successful operating performance results, their appropriate assessment and interpretation, sound financial planning, and adequate controls. When an organization lacks financial success or fails, it generally has not paid enough attention to data result analyses, and possibly the financial accountants and analysts who prepare the reports for management review might have erred. Sound, factual, and relevant communication between management and staff is often the key to successful operational activities.

UNDERSTANDING THE ROLE OF RATIO GUIDELINES

PRESENTING YOUR ANALYSIS TO MANAGEMENT

As the financial analyst, your assessment of operating results may indicate that receivable and/or inventory balances are too high, that fixed assets are excessive when compared to sales and net worth, that bank loans are disproportionate to asset requirements, and so on. Although your presentation may be perfectly valid, your viewpoint could be overruled by management. However, if you point to prevailing situations and results in other similar organizations, you make your point more convincingly. At least, you obtain supportive interest and attention from management, who might further explore and analyze the causes for the data results and differences. To show management, therefore, that certain components of the financial structure are out of balance or represent problem situations, compare the organization's data with that of similar organizations and/or similar industry averages.

Yet data comparisons even among similar industry organizations can be difficult to support due to the following important factors:

- uniformity of accounting systems, procedures, and time periods
- dissimilarity in size and organizational structures
- different types of customers with their particular effects on credit terms and extension and receivable collections
- age, cost, composition, and utilization of fixed assets
- capitalization requirements and availability
- somewhat different products which affect various elements in the financial structure
- failure of past results to indicate the future and its trends
- management effectiveness
- varying external standards and goals among organizations, rendering comparisons invalid and incompatible in assessing internal results and planning future objectives

Comparing the dollar value results among organizations is very often unsatisfactory and meaningless. Generally, more effective and reliable comparisons can be effected through the *use of ratios.* Ratios may not be the panacea, but they serve a useful purpose. The major drawback occurs when an individual organization's ratios are compared with averages.

A *ratio* is a computation that expresses the relationship of two or more sets of data in terms of a *percentage* or a *multiple,* as in the case of the common *current ratio.* Ratios are usually classified as

- *static*—balance sheet items, point in time
- *operating*—costs versus sales
- *velocity*—relationship of certain income and expense items to balance sheet items

WHERE TO OBTAIN COMPARATIVE RATIOS

LIST OF SOURCES

The major sources of ratio information are as follows:

> Dun & Bradstreet, Inc.
> Standard & Poor's Corporation
> Moody's Manual of Investments
> Robert Morris Associates
> Value Line
> Various trade associations for their members

In addition, organizations whose stock is traded on the security exchanges file annual reports with the Securities & Exchange Commission (SEC). These reports are generally more useful for comparisons than the stock-holders' annual reports because the SEC prescribes a uniform format and terminology, and they contain more detailed information than that provided to stockholders.

Prime Ratios Published

- current ratio (current assets to current liabilities)
- net income return on tangible net sales
- net income as a percentage of net working capital
- net income as a percentage of tangible net worth
- net sales as a percentage of net working capital
- receivable collection period (length of)
- net sales to inventory
- fixed assets to tangible net worth
- current debt to tangible net worth
- total debt to tangible net worth (equity ratio)
- inventory to net working capital
- current liabilities to inventory
- funded debt to net working capital

These ratios are published for retail, wholesale, and manufacturing lines in the Dun & Bradstreet publication. Robert Morris Associates publishes balance sheet items as percentages of total assets, and costs as percentages of sales. They further report the ratios of sales/receivables, cost of sales/ inventory, day sales in inventory, sales/inventory, and sales/total assets. These ratios are all discussed and illustrated in this book.

REPORTING REQUIREMENTS FOR SECURITY EXCHANGE COMMISSION

All organizations who have securities registered under the Securities and Exchange Act of 1934 are required to file an annual report containing certified balance sheets as of the close of the last two fiscal years, plus statements on profit and loss and on the application of funds. The annual report on Form 10–K is to be filed within 90 days after the fiscal close and the report contents are illustrated in Model 32, part A. Form 10–K is prepared in accordance with the Commission's regulation S–X, which prescribes the form and content of financial statements. Item 1 of the

MODEL 32. Securities and Exchange Commission Form 10–K.

A. *Summarized Financial Information*

Company or group of companies for which report is filed: _____

Profit and loss information for the _____ months ended _____

	Current Year	Preceding Year
1. Gross sales, less discounts, returns, and allowances	$_____	$_____
2. Operating revenues	_____	_____
3. Total captions 1 and 2	$_____	$_____
4. Costs and expenses:		
(a) Cost of goods sold	$_____	$_____
(b) Operating expenses	_____	_____
(c) Selling and G&A expenses	_____	_____
(d) Interest expense	_____	_____
(e) Other deductions, net	_____	_____
Total costs and expenses	$_____	$_____
5. Income (loss) before taxes and extraordinary items	$_____	$_____
6. Provision for taxes on income	_____	_____
7. Income or loss before extraordinary items	_____	_____
8. (a) Extraordinary items, less applicable income tax	_____	_____
(b) Minority interest	_____	_____
9. Net income (or loss)	$_____	$_____
10. Earnings per share data:		
(a) Per share of common stock and common stock equivalent:		
(1) Income before extraordinary items	$_____	$_____
(2) Extraordinary items, net of tax	_____	_____
(3) Net income	$_____	$_____
(b) Per share of common stock, assuming dilution:		
(1) Income before extraordinary items	$_____	$_____
(2) Extraordinary items, net of tax	_____	_____
(3) Net income	$_____	$_____
11. Dividend declared per share	$_____	$_____

form requires the *summary of earnings* for the last five fiscal years to be updated to preclude the file information from being misleading. Supplemental data are required for Item 2, which includes an analysis of sales and revenues and net income or loss by product lines of the business enterprise.

MODEL 32. Securities and Exchange Commission Form 10–K (cont.)

B. Capitalization and Stockholders' Equity

Date:_____(Latest fiscal quarter)

Debt	Amount
Short-term loans, notes, etc.	$_____
Long-term debt including parenthetically portion due within one year (list separately convertible debt)	_____
Total debt	$_____
Deferred credits	$_____

Stockholders' equity	Shares Outstanding	Amount
Preferred stock (list separately convertible and non-convertible preferred stock)	_____	$_____
Common stock	_____	_____
Capital in excess of par value		_____
Earned surplus		_____
Balance at beginning of current fiscal year		_____
Prior period adjustments; if any (show credits and charges separately)		_____
Net income (income statement, Item 9)		_____
Dividends		(_____)
Other credits (charges)—explain nature and amounts		_____
Balance at end of interim period		_____
Treasury stock (identify class of security, number of shares and basis at which stated)	_____	_____
Total stockholders' equity		$_____

Notes to Income Statement

SEC further requires additional information in the form of notes to the statement. This information deals with

  installment or deferred sales

  intercompany profit/losses

  depreciation, depletion, obsolescence, and amortization

  accounting treatment of maintenance, repairs, renewals and betterments, and adjustment of accumulated reserves

In consolidated statements, statements are required as to the principle of consolidation and the reconciliation of the parent's investment in the subsidiaries with the equity of the parent in the net assets of the subsidiaries. This information is an integral part of the statement and a helpful supplement to the data contained therein.

The Form 10–K instructions also require disclosure of any information that is necessary to correct potential misleading report data. Such a statement might explain, for example, that the results for the interim period are not necessarily indicative of the results to be expected for the year due to seasonal or other specified factors, or it might offer an explanation of an unusual increase or decrease in *net sales or income.*

Importance of summarized financial data reported to SEC (part A of Model 32). The SEC report and the pertinent comments provide a basis for making detailed ratio comparisons, particularly in similar industries. In the standard format, the reported information is specifically outlined and in more detail—such as earnings per share before and after dilution of extraordinary items. More varied data are included than is generally reported in the basic income statement. Declared dividends per share are also reported for the current and prior year.

Capitalization and Stockholders' Equity

In addition to the income statement, a capitalization schedule must be provided. The statement's format is displayed in Model 32, part B. The form and content of the schedule conform generally to that in the balance sheet and the notes appearing in the annual report filed with the Commission. Minority interests are stated separately. The number of shares of each class of security reserved for conversion, warrants, options, and other rights is disclosed separately.

Importance of capitalization and stockholders' equity data reported to SEC. The considerable detail provided in Model 32, part B can be used in organizational comparisons. This information provides a thorough assessment among organizations in similar industries. Ratios developed for debt, equity, and income analysis are more meaningful and explicit. If unusual gains and losses on securities or fixed assets are included in the financial statements, data comparability among organizations between time periods is destroyed. The problem with using financial statement data is that the information is limited to what is recorded in the books of account. Other reported data supplement the information contained in the traditional financial statements.

Notes to Balance Sheet Data

SEC requires additional information in the form of notes appended to the statement and filed with it. As applicable, the following information must be included:

- assets subject to lien
- intercompany profits and losses affecting balance sheet items
- preferred shares, if callable and if so, when; arrears in cumulative dividends; preference on involuntary liquidation
- pension and retirement plans
- restrictions that limit the availability of surplus for dividend purposes
- contingent liabilities

Other special forms with instructions are used for specific purposes:

- S–1: sale of common stock used by major utility organizations
- S–8: employee savings plan
- S–9: sale of debt

The largest number of registrations and annual reports are filed on Forms S–1 and 10–K.

HOW TO USE RATIO ANALYSIS TO DETERMINE PROBLEM SITUATIONS

UNCOVERING PROBLEMS

You can use various ratios to assess and highlight current and potential operational problem situations. To gauge the significance of a ratio, you must test the ratios to determine their applicability, relevancy, and use in the organization's operations.

Some areas that require constant surveillance and have a decided influence on financial stability are

- accounts receivable
- inventory
- net income
- sales activity
- financing
- fixed assets

APPLICATIONS

Accounts receivable ratio. This aspect of an organization's operations is important because funds are rendered unavailable until collected. The ratio that reveals the most about the status and acceptability of the receivable position is the *average collection period,* an informative guide in comparing an organization's collections with the industry as a whole. This average is used in evaluating the effectiveness of its credit and collection functions. If there is a collection problem, review the credit policies and/ or take corrective actions to accelerate customer reimbursements.

Inventory ratios. One of the prime causes of business failures and involuntary liquidations is an either excessive or unbalanced inventory. Only with constant and aggressive surveillance can you avoid this type of situation. Except for possible speculation, management would seldom intentionally plan to build an excessive inventory. Ratios do not reveal an unbalanced inventory. They can, however, be used as a guide in determining if the inventory totals are in line with those of other organizations in the industry or with goals set by management in projecting financial requirements.

The most recognized and used ratios in inventory assessment and control include the following:

Cost of sales to inventory, which indicates inventory turnover.

Sales to inventory, which is a prime indicator of too much or insufficient inventory to meet the sales volume demands and objectives.

Days of sales in inventory, which reveals inventory turnover and is also an indicator of too much or too little stock.

Inventory to working capital, which shows how the least liquid portion of current assets compares to the total position.

The *disadvantages of excessive inventory* are:

1. Too much *working capital* is being utilized. As a result, the organization may not be able to meet current obligations, which are primarily supported by the cash and accounts receivable assets.

2. *Obsolescence* may be a problem. When the inventory does not turn over within a reasonable time, it can deteriorate or a new product may require different type inventory.

3. The *price* of raw materials may decline. In this case, the inventory has to be written down to reflect the true value. This situation may cause larger losses than if the inventory was at a nominal level.

4. Excessive inventory creates *additional costs,* such as interest on investment, storage, insurance, and taxes. Further, excessive inventory may necessitate plant expansion. These factors lead to increased costs without adding value to the product.

The *problems with insufficient inventories* are:

1. With *excessive out-of-stock conditions,* small procurement orders have to be placed, thus increasing paper work and receiving costs. Even-

tually, these conditions lead to higher production costs, resulting from additional setups, short runs, and the like.

2. *Delays in customer deliveries* and possibly cancellation of orders may result.

3. Work activity and machine usage may *slow down or even stop* since there is inadequate inventory to be processed in the manufacturing environment.

Net income ratios. These ratios, used to assess profitability results, are under constant surveillance by most organizations. Net income represents the bottom-line of operational achievement. Useful ratios for comparing the profitability of an organization with others in the industry include net income to sales, to net worth or equity, and to total assets.

- The *net income to sales ratio* is used to answer two questions: (1) Are the profit margins compatible with those of other comparable organizations? (2) Do they meet organizational goals? If the information is available, a more detailed and realistic comparison is *gross profit to sales.*

- The *net income to net worth (equity)* ratio indicates whether management has the ability to earn a reasonable return on the owners' investment. As an assessment guideline, compare the income return results to the prevailing interest rates on accepted *secure investments,* such as government bonds, money market certificates, bond savings, and the like. The earnings on those investment instruments should be considered as the break-even point of acceptability. You should have profit above this figure to attract investor capital since investment in any organization poses a greater risk than that of the so-called "safe and secure" investments.

- *Net income to total assets* ratio tests whether management can achieve a favorable rate of return on all assets employed in the business enterprise.

Here are some considerations in profit ratio comparisons and analyses:

1. Know whether the profit figures are before or after income taxes. The comparative results make quite a difference in profit assessment.

2. Another problem in making profit comparisons relates to the owner-manager salaries in closely held corporations. Owners may be drawing more or less than the prevailing salaries for comparable managers. The owner should determine what he or she would pay a professional manager to perform the job. This figure is then substituted for the actual owner's salary and reflected in the pretax and

after-tax income figures for making comparisons. A true salary figure must be reflected in the data used for comparisons.

APPLICATIONS   *Sales activity ratios.* These ratios are used to determine whether an organization is over- or undertrading (selling). The primary ratios used are:

- The *sales to working capital* ratio is used to indicate the amount of working capital required to support varying sales volumes.
- The *sales to equity ratio* is used to determine if the owners are investing too much or too little for the sales volume involved. Further, it is a valid check on whether the owners' equity is being employed effectively.

The *sales to total assets* ratio actually supplements the sales to equity ratio. It is an indicator as to whether the organization is using an excessive amount of creditor capital.

Major financial ratios. Financing for an organization is divided into two major categories:

- *Acquisition of funds* from owners/investors, long-term financing, and short-term creditor sources.
- *Appropriate allocation and proper balance* of available funds among cash, receivables, inventory, and fixed assets.

Certain ratios are used in evaluating the relative balance in the *source of funds,* as follows:

- Current ratio.
- Current debt to owners' equity, which indicates whether the suppliers may be providing too much capital.
- Total debt to owners' equity, which supplements the current debt to equity ratio and highlights whether an organization is undercapitalized.
- Funded debt to working capital, which is a reasonable test to determine if an organization could liquidate its long-term debt from the prevailing working capital. A ratio that exceeds 100% is a criterion that an organization has invested too much in fixed assets.

Fixed asset ratios. As a generally recognized management principle, only a certain amount of equity can be invested in fixed assets. Two common and basic ratio guidelines are used to highlight the soundness of an organization's financial structure and investment policy relative to fixed assets.

The *fixed asset to capital equity* ratio indicates the proportion of total equity that is invested in property, plant, and equipment. Comparison to other organizations in a similar industry can provide a basic guideline as to whether an organization is overly invested or "in-line" with the average practices.

Sales to fixed asset ratio may disclose that an organization has too large or too small a facility for the prevailing or anticipated sales volume. In making comparisons of sales to fixed assets, give consideration to another possible problem. Normally, fixed assets are carried at the original value less depreciation. If the assets were purchased in years when the value of the dollar was higher and thereafter was heavily depreciated, this would result in a very high ratio.

Conversely, a low ratio reflects an excessive valuation of fixed assets. So if an organization's ratios are out of line with the industry ratios, you must apply considerable judgment before drawing specific conclusions or initiating actions based on the comparisons.

USING RATIOS FOR ASSESSING SOLVENCY

Generally, these ratios are considered to be the tests for and the *keys* to solvency. With them, you can ascertain the ability of an organization to withstand such adverse situations as a recession, strikes, declining sales market, and/or other major setbacks. The pertinent ratios are:

- fixed assets to net worth or equity
- working capital to sales
- inventories to working capital

Net Fixed Assets to Net Worth

Net fixed assets include the book value of land, building, machinery, and furniture/fixtures less the accumulated depreciation (not on land). *Net worth* is the invested owners' equity and excludes all intangibles such as patents, trademarks, and goodwill. An organization's investment should be in proper relationship to the owners' equity.

What is the "right" relationship? There is no specific guideline. It generally depends on the type of operational requirements and/or industry. A major consideration, however, is that a buildup in fixed assets results in higher costs such as taxes, insurance, maintenance, depreciation, and storage. Further, increased costs raise the *break-even point* which, in turn, may create profit problems for the organization if the sales decrease substantially.

Some organizations may reason that they are successful if they maintain an expanded facility and the most advanced equipment. The general assumption is that, if demand increases for their product(s), they can readily capitalize on this demand and increase profits. What may be overlooked in this thinking is that, when a great proportion of equity is invested in fixed assets, then less funds are available for working capital requirements such as receivables, inventories, and cash. On the optimistic side, the organization may be in a position to meet increased product demands, but they may not have sufficient working capital to support the greater sales volume. Naturally, the adverse situation is a higher break-even point and possibly the need for *reducing sales volume* due to insufficient capital to support their receivable and inventory requirements.

Net Working Capital to Sales

The ratio of working capital to sales should be in proper proportion. Yet there is no specific guideline as to the "proper" proportion. The relative size of an organization and its operational requirements generally govern the magnitude of the working capital needs. To determine relative averages and to guard against "overselling," you can compare similar types of organizations in the same industry. The assumption is that, the more an organization sells, the more profits it reaps. In some cases this may be true, but additional sales may tie up more capital in receivables and inventory.

If the organization does not provide the additional capital, it must then borrow the capital fund requirements either by making short-term loans or by delaying creditor payments. Borrowing can create serious problems for the organization, particularly if the sales volume declines significantly and the organization cannot meet its outstanding obligations. An accepted adage is that business failures can occur just as quickly by *selling too much,* as well as by *selling too little.*

Inventories to Working Capital

The inventory investment should be compatible within the structure of the organization's net working capital. When inventories exceed net working capital, the current liabilities may exceed cash, marketable securities, and receivables. Under these circumstances, the organization is forced to liquidate some of its inventory to meet its current obligations, particularly if the organization is faced with adverse operating results.

THE IMPORTANCE OF RATIOS IN TREND ANALYSES

Generally, comparing a single ratio for an organization against published information may not reveal a significant trend. Because preparing, compiling, and publishing industry financial statements take considerable time, the data may be unavailable for months. Usually, industry averages do not vary substantially from year to year unless the general economic conditions change considerably as a result of recession, inflation, relevant government regulations, and so on. To assess trends, therefore, plot ratios for a number of years on graph paper. Enter each ratio on an individual sheet of graph paper, on which comparable industry ratios are also plotted. You can then make a realistic comparison with other organizations in a similar industry based on years of experience. Model 33 shows the Dun and Bradstreet ratio figures plotted for the upper, median, and lower quartiles. This type of visual comparison provides an immediate view of an organization's ratio and trends relative to similar industry results as a whole.

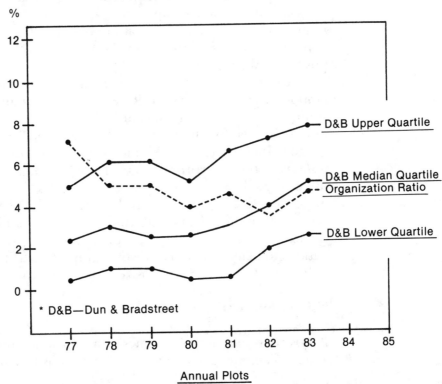

MODEL 33. Net Income to Net Sales Ratio: Organization Versus Dun and Bradstreet (D&B) Quartiles.

ADVANTAGES OF PLOTTING Plotting these ratios enables you to highlight the trend so that management can review and assess it. Whereas a one-year comparison with industry averages might indicate a healthy situation, the trend may actually be in the wrong direction. Plotting presents an immediate overview of the situation and the annual trend direction.

Inevitably, the question is, How do you know if the ratio is out of line? For the answer, you have to determine the specific reasons for deviations when the organization's ratio is outside the upper or lower quartile range. Generally, the organization's ratios are assumed to be in line with the average results when they are between the upper and lower quartiles. In Model 33, the organization's ratio trend is above the median quartile, dips in 19X2, but continues to climb in 19X3. Why did the trend decline in the annual periods shown? Only a detailed assessment will reveal the cause for the variations.

THE SIGNIFICANCE OF SIMILAR INDUSTRY COMPARISONS

Ratio comparisons with organizations in the same industry may be valid, but you must exercise analytical assessment before accepting this assumption completely. Some of the ratio figures may be approximately the same in many manufacturing lines, but peculiar industry characteristics can invalidate a comparison with a composite of all industry. Since some ratios can have wide variations based on the nature of the industry, make your comparisons within the industry rather than with any composite overall average.

A well-balanced financial structure is a *must* for the successful operation of any organization. Rarely is capital unlimited, so the available funds must be allocated judiciously. Naturally, when too much is invested in one segment of the business, then another function/operation is neglected. Inefficient use of capital can result from too much *overall investment* in the enterprise. Relatively few formulas indicate the optimum use of capital.

Yet valuable guidance can be obtained by comparing organization ratios with industry and determining the causes for unusual variances. An excellent presentation tool for highlighting varied and unusual situations to management is a display graph of pertinent organization and industry ratios, which emphasizes both trends and variances.

Using Comparative Ratios

Ratios represent only guidelines in assessing financial data and in operational planning. There may be valid reasons for an organization's ratios to vary significantly from those in a similar industry. Most important, be aware that differences do exist and that you must determine the reasons for them.

Ratios should not be used as absolutes. For example, it may be totally justifiable to build inventory if a material shortage is threatened. Even if the fixed asset to equity ratio varies from industry averages, *plant expansion* may still be logical and desirable, and the investment may be based on the anticipated growth in sales volume. If properly interpreted and used, ratios can serve as revealing and valuable guides for analyzing financial results, planning operations, and making management decisions.

Ultimately, the usefulness of ratios depends on a thorough understanding of ratio logic, data compatibility, operational objectives, and analytical investigation as to their appropriateness.

SUMMARY OF LIMITATIONS INVOLVING RATIO ANALYSIS

- A ratio is only as reliable as the quality of its component makeup. The question arises as to the validity of the data being used. For example, a high current ratio may be reflecting poor quality receivables, inventories, and securities. There could be intentional delays in inventory replenishment, which could affect payables and funding. Incurred current liabilities reporting may have been cut off prior to the actual closing date, and so on.

- *Varying accounting procedures* among external industry organizations can complicate and distort valid industry comparisons. Treatment and use of various period-end adjustments would invalidate reliable comparisons. There is always the problem of *categorizing similar industries* due to differences in diversified products, objectives, and procedures. Through historical experience and checkout over a period of time, selective organizations may be identified that reflect and have compatible accounting and reporting similarities that make them acceptable for valid comparisons.

- *Ratios involve quantitative data* which are not always indicative or sole criteria in assessing performance results and/or providing planning factors. Management expertise, judgment, and experience are the basic fundamentals in evaluating performance results and decision making.

- In making organization comparisons, it is very important that the analyst know what is the *ratio composition.* In using net income figures, for example, it must be ascertained whether the income is before or after giving effect to interest expense and depreciation.

In the case of cash flow, some organizations may consider net income and depreciation expense as cash inflow, whereas it is really net working capital resulting from their operational activity.

- It is advisable to use a number of *different ratios* in making comparisons in order to gain a more realistic insight or perspective on actual performance analysis and results.

- *Caution and judgment* must be exercised in using ratios for *projecting* an organization's financial position and trends. Ratio development is predicated on historical performance and, as such, may not be a valid indicator of the future. A thorough ongoing review of past results based on prevailing operational circumstances plus future operating plan anticipations must be considered in establishing financial goals and performance objectives. Under reliable circumstances, *ratios may provide valuable guidelines* in future planning.

- *Inflation influences* (*changes in purchasing power of the dollar*) have a decided effect on ratio analysis. This factor is difficult to incorporate in the ratio assessment of performance results. A possible approach in overcoming this problem is to include price level data effects as supplementary information to the ratio analysis. The inflation impact can distort performance trends and relevant individual ratios. Similar problems arise when there are significant changes in sales revenues—either in growth or a declining trend.

7

Evaluating an Organization's Financial Position

CHAPTER HIGHLIGHTS

What are the objectives of financial position reporting? How do both internal and external users employ such reports? This chapter deals with these questions. It offers an insight into the key ratios used in evaluating an organization's financial position. Model 34, an overview of one organization's financial status, provides the illustrative data for developing and analyzing relevant ratios. This chapter discusses:

- the usefulness and importance of structural ratios
- ratios relative to an organization's liquidity, such as current ratio, acid test, cash, and cash turnover
- the relationships of working capital to current assets, sales, current liabilities, and inventory balances
- common fixed asset ratios, which are calculated relative to total assets, turnover, owners' equity, funded debt, and sales
- various debt ratios, such as owners' equity to total liabilities, aspects of the capital structure, equity to total capital employed, funded debt, and so on

Not all the ratios described are relevant to all organizations. Historical experience can suggest which ratios are relevant and helpful to an organization's performance assessment and operational planning.

The financial status of an organization at a particular point in time consists of the assets owned by an organization and the claims against the assets in the form of liabilities and the owners' or stockholders' equity. Specifically, the data are reported and identified in a balance sheet (or statement of financial position). Explanatory notes to this statement augment the monetary values in the formal report.

USERS OF FINANCIAL POSITION REPORTING

USERS INSIDE AND OUTSIDE THE BUSINESS

At any time, a number of concerned parties have an active interest in the financial position of an organization. Internally, various *management levels* use the information to review and evaluate the organization's current position and progress, to initiate corrective action decisions as required, and to determine the course of their future planning. *Owners and investors* analyze the financial position data to determine the solvency of the operations, as well as the degree of risk in making or continuing an investment. *Creditors* (such as vendors or banks) and credit agencies have a marked interest in ascertaining an organization's debt-paying capability and its financial outlook. *Stockbrokers* may use the information to advise and influence the investments of their clients. Certain *government agencies* may take an interest in the reported information for regulatory enforcement, awarding contracts based on adequate financing for contract performance, and possible taxation aspects. *Similar industry organizations* use the information to compare results, thereby assessing their performance and progress relative to their competitors. These are the major users of financial position reports outside the organization.

Within an organization, and in addition to management, many other parties use and analyze balance sheet data: management accountants, financial planners, and certain operational personnel concerned with inventory status and fixed asset acquisition and control. Executive operational management has a particular interest in the financial progress of an organization that results from operational activities.

SETTING OBJECTIVES FOR BALANCE SHEET STATEMENTS

Balance sheet reporting serves the following basic objectives:

1. *Identification* of the various types of *financial resources* (cash, receivables, inventories) that are available within an organization to meet operational goals.

2. The *means* (sources) by which the resources were obtained (investment by owners, borrowings, creditors, and so on).

3. *Valuation* of specific types of resources, such as

   - receivables less the reserve for doubtful accounts
   - gross fixed assets reduced by the reserve for depreciation/amortization

- marketable securities at cost or current market value
- inventories at lower of cost or market price

4. *Supplemental information* that is not reflected in the formal statement, such as contingencies and explanatory data, and that may be important to the report users in assessing the financial position for the decision-making actions.

The balance sheet—the statement of financial position—reflects a static situation. It presents the data at a point in time, which changes immediately after the reporting date since new transactions are constantly occurring (cash receipts and disbursement, purchases, sales, and the like). The balance sheet reflects the results of all the activities, actions, and decisions since the organization's inception. As a record of the results from past performances, it can serve as an index to future events. Other reports, such as an income statement and cash flow schedule, are required to provide the answers as to "how" the organization arrived at its current financial position.

VIEWING THE BALANCE SHEET
AS AN OVERVIEW OF FINANCIAL STATUS

Model 34 presents an overview format of an organization's financial position by quarterly periods. As reflected in the model, the financial structure of a business enterprise involves three primary elements: assets, liabilities, and owners' equity (capital stock and retained earnings). The relationship of the three elements is represented by the equation:

$$\text{Assets} = \text{Liabilities} + \text{Owners' equity}$$

This equation can also be represented as follows:

$$\text{Liabilities} = \text{Total assets} - \text{Total equity capital}$$
$$\text{Equity capital} = \text{Total assets} - \text{Total liabilities}$$
$$\text{Total assets} = \text{Total equities (owners' and creditors')}$$

Understanding Structural Ratios

Reasonable relationships generally exist among the various items in the financial structure. In Model 34, ratios are developed among the reported items at year-end for 19X3 and 19X4. On the asset side, each individual asset is divided by the total asset value. Also, each liability and owners' equity is divided by the total liabilities and equity. This type of analysis provides not only a structural relationship among the various items for the two year-end periods being reported but also the *trend* between the time periods.

AN ILLUSTRATION

A review of the data indicates that the current assets as a percentage of total assets decreased from 84.98% in December 19X3 to 83.39% in 19X4. The principal cause is the 19X4 increase in cash, which was more than offset by the decrease in receivables. Total assets decreased by 1.6% in December 19X4 as compared to 19X3, due to a 3.5% decrease in current assets ($419.6 to $405.1 million). Although fixed assets increased by 13.8% in 19X4, much of the increase was diluted by a 20% increase in accumulated depreciation.

As shown in the model, current liabilities decreased by 5.5% in 19X4 as compared to 19X3 ($300.2 to $283.8 million). This situation is attributed to decreases in payables, taxes, and customer advances, which were partially offset by an increase in notes payable. The long-term debt remained a relatively stable percentage, but the net overall debt result was a 4.8% decrease in the 19X4 total liabilities.

Total equity increased by 5.6% in December 19X4 over 19X3, which was attributed to an 8.4% increase in retained earnings, while the capital stock remained consistent at $50.5 million. The overall liabilities and equity total (as in the case of total assets) was 1.6% lower in 19X4 for reasons already discussed. Working capital increased by 1.6% (119.4 million to $121.3), indicating a favorable trend.

APPLICATIONS

Structural and trend *ratios* can be very useful in assessing the basic characteristics of capital structure relationships, particularly if calculated by monthly and quarterly periods. Further, the trend indicators provide a basis for planning, at least on a preliminary basis. By analyzing the developed ratio data, you can determine unusual highlights and deviations, which can lead to management actions and decisions.

Balance Sheet Limitations in Ratio Analysis

In assessing balance sheet reported data and calculating ratios, consideration should be given to the following information limitations that would be reflected in that type of reporting. The effect of the limitations could jeopardize the reliability of ratio development and utilization.

- The balance sheet may not reflect the *true market value of the assets*. Inventories may not be truly presented at the market value or cost, whichever is lower (data value conservatism). Receivables may not

MODEL 34. Structure of the Statement of Financial Position.

(in $000,000s)

Assets:	19X3 December	% of Total Assets	March	June	September	December	% of Total Assets
				19X4			
Cash	$ 22.9	4.64	$ 38.0	$ 32.9	$ 36.6	$ 35.5	7.31
Marketable securities	8.0	1.62	7.5	8.5	8.0	6.0	1.24
Accounts receivable	125.0	25.31	110.4	111.5	102.3	105.1	21.63
Inventories	247.8	50.18	260.0	268.5	256.9	243.4	50.10
Advances to subcontractors	5.9	1.20	5.1	4.2	3.7	3.4	.70
Prepaid expenses	10.0	2.03	9.5	8.6	15.7	11.7	2.41
Total current assets	$419.6	84.98	$ 430.5	$ 434.2	$ 423.2	$ 405.1	83.39
Fixed assets, gross	128.8	26.08	133.5	138.1	142.1	146.6	30.18
Accumulated depreciation	-65.4	-13.24	-68.6	-71.8	-75.1	-78.4	-16.14
Net fixed assets	63.4	12.84	64.9	66.3	67.0	68.2	14.04
Investment in subsidiaries	5.5	1.11	5.5	5.5	5.5	5.5	1.13
Deferred charges	5.3	1.07	6.2	6.0	6.9	7.0	1.44
Total assets	$493.8	100.00	$ 507.1	$ 512.0	$ 502.6	$ 485.8	100.00

MODEL 34. Structure of the Statement of Financial Position (cont.).

		% of Total L/Eq.						% of Total L/Eq.
Liabilities:								
Notes payable	$ 70.0	14.18	$ 95.0	$ 100.0	$ 95.0	$ 85.0		17.50
Accounts payable	91.5	18.53	84.4	83.1	76.9	76.7		15.79
Accrued salaries & wages	18.6	3.77	21.4	21.8	19.0	19.3		3.97
Estimated federal income taxes	15.8	3.20	12.8	10.7	10.8	9.3		1.92
Customer advances	75.0	15.19	66.8	68.8	65.0	64.0		13.17
Miscellaneous liabilities	29.3	5.93	30.4	28.8	34.9	29.5		6.07
Total current liabilities	$300.2	60.80	$ 310.8	$ 313.2	$ 301.6	$ 283.8		58.42
Long-term funded debt	42.6	8.62	42.6	42.6	42.6	42.6		8.77
Total liabilities	$342.8	69.42	$353.4	$355.8	$ 344.2	$ 326.4		67.19
Stockholders' Equity:								
Capital stock	$ 50.5	10.23	$ 50.5	$ 50.5	$ 50.5	$ 50.5		10.39
Retained earnings	100.5	20.35	103.2	105.7	107.9	108.9		22.42
Total equity	$151.0	30.58	$ 153.7	$ 156.2	$ 158.4	$ 159.4		32.81
Total liabilities/equity	$493.8	100.00	$ 507.1	$ 512.0	$ 502.6	$ 485.8		100.00
Other Relevant Data:								
Working capital	$119.4	—	$ 119.7	$ 120.0	$ 121.6	$ 121.3		—
Sales volume	—	—	252.8	274.9	276.2	273.1		—
Net income	—	—	4.9	5.7	4.7	3.0		—
Annualized sales	—	—	1011.0	1100.0	1105.0	1092.0		—

be adjusted for doubtful accounts. Prepaid expenses may not reflect period write-offs. Short-term investments may be over- or under-valued. Direct material costs may be over- or understated depending on the method of valuation.

- It is common management procedure to review the various data line-items of the balance sheet at period-end and *take appropriate actions* that would enhance the organization's financial position and achievement (window-dressing) results in the opinion of current stockholders, potential stock investors, credit agencies, and funding institutions. An important approach is to reduce or eliminate out-standing debt obligations. Therefore, in calculating debt and equity ratios, a weighted-average debt value would be used rather than a year-end balance. This action would generally reflect a more positive debt position. Further, year-end data comparisons to other orga-nizations could be distorted and misleading. On the other hand, analysts might even adjust financial statements in order to compare favorably within the reported values of industry.

     A device used to create a high current ratio would be to delay the replenishment of inventories in the period preceding the closing of the books. Another approach would be to hold cash receipts open after the closing date to reflect a favorable cash position.

- *Liabilities could be undervalued* due to a pending or anticipated lawsuit for which information would not be reflected in the balance sheet. Debt ratios would be distorted and comparative data with other organizations would be misleading and inappropriate for an ade-quate operational assessment.

- Certain *assets could be overvalued;* particularly, in the case of obsolete or deteriorated inventory. Changes in product mix may have created certain material to be surplus due to changed product requirements. Material prices may have declined substantially whereas the inven-tory value is being carried on the books at the original higher prices. This situation would distort such relevant ratios as: current, inven-tory to working capital, turnover, and average age. Industry inven-tory comparisons would undoubtedly be questionable as to reliability.

- Another limitation of balance sheet reports could involve the exist-ence of *undervalued assets* such as marketable securities if they were reported at cost value but the market prices were greater. This situation would affect both the current and acid ratios. Net working capital would be understated. Other ratios such as current and total assets to sales and equity would be affected.

- *Ratios are static* and do not necessarily reflect future conditions and expectations. Careful past experience evaluation, anticipated events to occur in the future (from market intelligence and trends, management objectives, identification of potential problem areas) and judgment must prevail in their usefulness in the planning process.

To correct for the limitations discussed above for the balance sheet assessment and ratio development, the financial analyst could *footnote any relevant data* pertinent to items listed above or others that the analyst may be aware of in order to clarify the reality of the data presented. This would alert management as to the true significance and inherent limitations that were being reported. In making comparisons to industry organizations, their internal data manipulations would not be known from their reporting but comparative result findings and any actions would be tempered by the knowledge that *inconsistencies do exist* among organizations in their reporting process.

HOW TO USE THE LIQUIDITY RATIOS

The *liquidity* of a business organization is its potential to meet current debt obligations. A reasonably sound liquidity position permits an organization to obtain financial resources to take advantage of investment opportunities and adequately respond to operational emergencies.

The degree of liquidity is generally linked to the size of the working capital position at a given point in time. The *ratio* of current assets to current liabilities—rather than the monetary difference between them— is the measure of liquidity. (The difference between current assets and current liabilities represents the *net working capital,* whereas the single identification of current assets indicates the *aggregate working capital.*) Working capital represents the portion of current assets that is not supplied by current creditors. If no funded debt exists, then the working capital is the owners' equity in the current assets, as differentiated from the owners' equity in the fixed assets.

Using the Current (Working Capital) Ratio

THE CALCULATION

$$\text{Current ratio} = \frac{\text{Current assets}}{\text{Current liabilities}}$$

This traditional ratio is commonly used in the business environment as a guideline to the financial margin of safety or solvency. It indicates the *number of times* current assets will pay off the current liabilities. Historically a two-to-one ratio has been considered the ideal minimum. Yet there may be exceptions. Some organizations with a "two-to-one" ratio may have more varied and difficult problems than those with a lower ratio factor.

Example: From the information provided in Model 34 the following *current ratios* are developed:

	19X3			19X4	
	December	March	June	September	December
	1.40:1	1.39:1	1.39:1	1.40:1	1.43:1

This indicates a fairly consistent pattern for the periods reported. Any unusual deviations among periods are cause enough to investigate the differences to determine whether a trend (up or down) will prevail in the future or will result from unusual circumstances. The 1.43 factor in December 19X4 represents a favorable liquidity trend position.

Using the Acid Test Ratio

This ratio determines an organization's *immediate* capability to pay its current obligations. Quick assets generally include cash, marketable securities, and accounts receivable. Inventories are excluded because they must first be sold and customer billings collected before they represent assets usable in paying current debts. Advances to subcontractors are also not available until contract performance has been achieved and settlement made. Prepaid expenses are not included in quick assets because they will be used and therefore provide no resources for paying current debts. The equation for calculating the acid test ratio is as follows:

THE CALCULATION

$$\text{Acid test ratio} = \frac{\text{Cash} + \text{Marketable securities} + \text{Accounts receivable}}{\text{Current liabilities}}$$

Example: From the information provided in Model 34, the following acid test ratios are derived:

	19X3			19X4	
	December	March	June	September	December
	.519 ($155.9 ÷ 300.2)	.502	.488	.487	.517

The size of the ratio (approximately 50% of current liabilities) highlights the fact that the inventory values represent the major current asset item. Conversely, the current liabilities could be excessively high in comparison to the quick assets.

The low ratio of 48.7% in September resulted from a relatively low quick asset period value of $146.9 million, compared to prior periods, which was not offset by a low current liabilities amount. The higher ratio in December 19X3 is attributed to the greater quick asset value versus the lower current liabilities. The same comment applies to the December 19X4 period.

You must exercise caution in the use and interpretation of the acid test ratio. Although the ratio implies that only three current assets will be available to pay current liabilities, such may not always be the case. Some of the inventory may very well be converted into cash before all of the current obligations mature for vendor/creditor payment. Further, notes and accounts payable payments could be deferred to coincide with the quick asset position. Payment of miscellaneous and other liabilities may be delayed with possibly no major consequences. The material purchase schedule may be extended. So before making any decisions based on the application of the acid test ratio, be sure you have thoroughly assessed its applicability to your organization.

Using Cash Ratios

THE CALCULATION

Some organizations may use another liquidity test ratio. In this instance, the formula is as follows:

$$\text{Cash ratio} = \frac{\text{Cash + Marketable securities}}{\text{Current liabilities}}$$

Example: Using the data in Model 34, the following ratio data are prepared by quarterly periods:

19X3	19X4			
December	*March*	*June*	*September*	*December*
10.3% ($30.9 million ÷ $300.2)	14.6%	13.2%	14.8%	14.6%

These cash ratios indicate that, using this method (which is far more conservative than the acid test ratio), there is enough liquidity in the cash and marketable securities to pay only 10.3% to 14.8% of the current obligations. In some cash–sales-oriented organizations that maintain minimum receivables, the usefulness of this ratio is justified. Yet its universal acceptance as a criterion of assessing an organization's position to meet current debts on a scheduled basis is doubtful.

MAKING USE OF THE CASH TURNOVER RATIO

With this ratio, you can analyze and assess the effectiveness of an organization's use of its cash position. The equation is as follows:

$$\text{Cash turnover} = \frac{\text{Sales volume}}{\text{Cash balance}}$$

Example: Using the 19X4 *quarterly* data in Model 34, the following ratios are obtained for comparative purposes. (The more precise method is to use annualized sales.)

		19X4		
March	*June*	*September*	*December*	
6.65:1 ($252.8 million	8.36:1	7.55:1	7.69:1	
÷ $38.0)				

The highest ratio, in June 19X4, is attributed to a below-average quarterly cash position versus a high sales volume of $276.2 million. The low turnover rate in March 19X4 resulted from a low sales volume of $252.8 million, whereas the quarterly cash position was above average.

The increase in the turnover rate in December 19X4 over March indicates an increased effectiveness in the use of cash in supporting the sales volume. The turnover rate is useful in determining preliminary cash balance forecasts based on sales projections. In March, for example, the $252.8 million sales, divided by the 6.65 factor, results in a $38 million cash balance.

The annual cash turnover ratio is calculated to be approximately 30:1. This value is obtained by dividing the annual sale of $1,077 million by an average cash balance of $35.75 million.

EMPLOYING THE TOTAL ASSET TURNOVER RATIO

This ratio assesses how effectively an organization is utilizing its total assets. It gauges management's efficiency in controlling the use of assets based on sales volume activity. The equation is as follows:

$$\text{Asset turnover} = \frac{\text{Sales (usually annualized)}}{\text{Average total assets}}$$

Example: For purposes of illustration, the quarterly balances for total assets are the averages for the period. The following quarterly ratios are developed from the basic data in Model 34.

		19X4		
March	*June*	*September*	*December*	
49.9% ($252.8	53.7%	55.0%	56.2%	
÷ $507.1)				

These ratios indicate that the asset turnover is improving—56.2% in December versus 49.9% in March. The high ratio in December is attributed to a declining total assets, whereas sales volume remained relatively constant. The decrease in total assets resulted primarily from a reduced inventory position.

The average turnover for the year is 2.15, a rate derived by dividing the annual sales of $1,077 million by the annual average asset of $501.8 million. The annual ratio is more indicative and informative of the actual total asset turnover position because the annual sales volume was used versus the annual average assets. Note that if the four quarterly ratios are totaled (214.8%—note 2.15 above) and divided by four, the average quarterly ratio is 53.7%.

Using the Total Asset Relationship to Sales

With this ratio, you can determine the total asset requirements based on sales volume. This approach is the converse of that of the asset turnover ratio. To obtain this ratio, simply divide total assets by sales volume.

Example: The following quarterly ratios were developed from data in Model 34:

	19X4			
March	*June*	*September*	*December*
2.01:1 ($507.1 million ÷ $252.8)	1.86:1	1.82:1	1.78:1

Given an annual quarterly average of total assets of $501.8 million and total annual sales of $1,077 million, the ratio is 2.15:1. Totaling the ratios (7.47) and dividing this value by four results in a ratio of 1.87:1. The difference is due to the use of the annual average of total assets versus total sales volume, as opposed to quarterly period calculations.

The low average ratio of 1.78:1 in December indicates a favorable trend in that reduced assets are used in supporting the sales volume.

As a preliminary planning guide (if historically consistent and adjusted for trends) the estimated asset requirements based on sales would be projected by multiplying sales volume by the ratio factor; for example, as shown above $252.8 million sales times 2.01 would approximate total assets of $508.1 million.

MAKING USE OF WORKING CAPITAL RELATIONSHIPS

INFLUENCES ON WORKING CAPITAL

The working capital ratio, one of the most widely used in business, reveals the proportion of capital provided by the enterprise and the contribution share from creditors, hence its importance to creditors and short-term loaning institutions. The working capital position is affected by a number of operating/financial factors, such as the turnover velocity of receivables and inventory, the size of the credit obtained from vendors, and the amount of capital provided by the investment owners.

Receivables and inventory turnover is of prime importance in the adequacy of the working capital position. Receivable turnover is affected by business conditions in general, by credit terms, and by the organization's collection policy, control, and enforcement. Inventory turnover is primarily influenced by product price, by the extent of inventory obsolescence, by production demands, and by the size of the inventory in relation to sales. To achieve a desirable turnover ratio management must keep a constant watch on the organization's receivable/inventory status.

Comparing Working Capital to Current Assets

To derive this relationship, divide average working capital by average current assets.

Example: The following quarterly ratios are calculated, using data in Model 34.

19X3	19X4			
December	*March*	*June*	*September*	*December*
28.5% ($119.4 million ÷ $419.6)	27.8%	27.6%	28.7%	29.9%

These ratios indicate that working capital represented an annual average in 19X4 of 28.5% (annual average working capital divided by annual average current assets) of the current assets. The high ratio of 29.9% in December 19X4 is primarily due to the relatively lower current asset value of $405.1 million, whereas the working capital remained fairly constant when compared to prior period results.

This type of ratio, if proven historically to be reasonable and valid, can be used to assess current versus past performance in terms of the working capital/current asset relationship. Further, you can use it as a planning guide to future anticipations in the development of the annual operating plan. In other words, having projected current assets, you apply the average working capital position. By subtracting this value from planned current assets, you obtain the anticipated current liability values.

Using the Current Assets to Working Capital Ratio

The ratio of the current assets to working capital is simply the converse of working capital to total current assets. To obtain this ratio, divide average current assets by the average working capital.

Example: The following results are obtained using data in Model 34.

	19X3		19X4		
	December	*March*	*June*	*September*	*December*
	3.51:1 ($419.6 million ÷ $119.4)	3.60:1	3.62:1	3.48:1	3.34:1

The decreased ratio in December 19X4 resulted from a relatively low current asset value in comparison to the rather consistent working capital position of prior periods. The principal contributing factor is the reduction in inventories (a high of $268.4 million in June 19X4 to $243.4 million in December).

On the current liability status, there was a favorable decrease in the December 19X4 notes payable when compared to the quarterly periods in 19X4. Accounts payable was reduced to $76.7 million in December 19X4 as compared to the high of $91.5 million in December 19X3.

APPLICATIONS These ratios can be used in planning and/or in assessing data projections developed by more detailed conventional methods. Here is a method for forecasting current liabilities. If working capital values were initially projected (although this is generally not the planning sequence), you can estimate current assets by multiplying the working capital value by one of the preceding ratios to obtain the anticipated current asset values. Then subtract the projected working capital from the developed current asset values to obtain the projected current liabilities.

Comparing Working Capital to Current Liabilities

In analyzing the current position of a business enterprise, you must determine the adequacy of working capital. One such approach is to determine the ratio of working capital to current liabilities. This relationship enables you to compare the resources supplied by the current creditors versus the proportion provided by the owners, long-term creditors, or both. You should interpret this ratio in the context of the turnover rate of current assets versus that of current liabilities.

As a general rule, a rapid turnover of current assets with a slower turnover of current liabilities requires a lower working capital ratio. The opposite is true with a rapid turnover of current liabilities and a slow turnover of current assets; you need a higher working capital ratio.

To determine the ratio between working capital and current liabilities, divide average working capital by average current liabilities.

Example: The following ratios are calculated using data in Model 34.

19X3			19X4	
December	*March*	*June*	*September*	*December*
39.8% ($119.4 million ÷ $300.2)	38.5%	38.3%	40.3%	42.7%

The high ratio in December 19X4 is attributed to a relatively low current liability position compared to prior periods, whereas the working capital remained at one level.

Another approach is to determine the relationship of *current liabilities to working capital.* To calculate this ratio, divide the average current liabilities by average working capital.

Example: The developed relationships are as follows:

19X3			19X4	
December	*March*	*June*	*September*	*December*
2.51:1 ($300.2 million ÷ $119.4)	2.60:1	2.61:1	2.48:1	2.34:1

These ratios indicate that the current liabilities are at an average of 2.51 times the working capital. Note that the current asset ratio to working capital averaged about 3.5 times working capital—a more favorable relationship than if the current liabilities ratio were higher.

APPLICATION   This type of ratio can be used to assess financial performance and to evaluate the validity or reasonableness of data developed by more detailed methods.

Comparing Inventory to Working Capital

This ratio is an indicator of the inventory position at a point in time. It reflects the portion of working capital invested in inventories. In other words, it shows how the least liquid part of current assets relates to its total. Inventories that are greater than net working capital signify that current liabilities exceed the liquid current assets represented by cash, marketable securities, and accounts receivable. In this type of situation, the organization might have to consider decreasing, at least in relative proportion, a part of its inventory.

From another viewpoint, this relationship represents the ratio of the inventory to the owners' equity in the current assets, providing there are no fixed liabilities to consider. Establishing a universal standard ratio is difficult because it depends on the type of business and its requirements, asset turnover, and the sales demands. Further, this ratio is an indirect statistical situation, compared to the acid test which is both understandable and direct in concept and use.

To develop this ratio, divide average inventory by average working capital.

Example: The following ratios are developed using the data in Model 34:

19X3			*19X4*		
December		*March*	*June*	*September*	*December*
2.08:1 ($247.8 million ÷ $119.4)		2.17:1	2.24:1	2.11:1	2.01:1

The average is 2.12:1, with the highest ratio of 2.24 occurring in June 19X4. The principal reason is the increased June inventory in comparison to the other quarterly periods, while the working capital position remained relatively constant.

APPLICATION As always, exercise evaluation and judgment in using this ratio for any practicable benefit. It may be suitable in some organizations as a preliminary planning factor and/or as a means of comparing performance results among periods. While the ratio represents a possible analytical guideline, segregating working capital into its individual component parts is difficult, if not plain unrealistic.

Relating Sales to Working Capital

The sales volume of an organization bears a definite relationship to the amount of its working capital in support of sales. Generally, a substantial sales volume requires large working capital. With increased sales volumes, receivables, and cash, the organization has to invest more in maintaining adequate inventories. The increases in current assets, however, are somewhat offset by increased current liabilities, such as purchase requirements (material and supplies). This results in greater accounts payable balances, as well as higher accrued salaries wages, due to increased labor activity and possibly short-term loans to support the higher volume. The owners' investment would also have to be greater to finance increased sales activity.

Establishing a standard for sales/working capital relationship in industries as a whole is difficult due to various influencing factors, such as the prevailing velocity of current assets and current liabilities among organizations. These and other factors must be given due consideration before you can establish ratio validity and accept it as a reasonable criterion for data assessment and planning.

To determine the relevancy and usefulness of this ratio to an organization's performance assessment and planning, you should explore two versions of the relationship. The equations used in calculating the ratios are as follows:

$$\text{Working capital to sales} = \frac{\text{Average working capital}}{\text{Sales (usually annualized)}}$$

$$\text{Working capital turnover} = \frac{\text{Sales (usually annualized)}}{\text{Average working capital}}$$

Working capital to sales. Using this ratio, you can estimate working capital needs based on sales volume (sales multiplied by the ratio factor). The usefulness of this ratio is contingent on its being proven consistent and valid by experience.

Example: The quarterly working capital ratio to sales are calculated using data in Model 34:

19X4			
March	*June*	*September*	*December*
47.3% ($119.7 million ÷ $252.8)	43.7%	44.0%	44.4%

The high ratio of 47.3% in March 19x4 is attributed to the lower sales volume of $252.8 million as compared to the other periods. At the same time, the working capital position remained relatively constant with the other periods.

Working capital turnover. This version measures the number of times working capital is employed or turned over during a given period. The use of working capital becomes more efficient as the turnover rate increases. A low ratio generally signifies poor performance in the use of working capital, whereas a high ratio usually indicates efficient capital employment.

Example: Model 34 provides the quarterly data for calculating the working capital turnover rates, as follows:

19X3			
March	*June*	*September*	*December*
2.11:1 ($252.8 million ÷ $119.7)	2.29:1	2.27:1	2.25:1

On a *period annualized sales basis,* the capital turnover ratios are calculated as follows (also represent four times the quarterly ratios):

	19X4			
March		*June*	*September*	*December*
Annualized sales	$1,011.2 (millions)	$1099.6	$1104.8	$1092.4
Ratios	8.44:1	9.16:1	9.08:1	9.00:1

The low ratio in March 19X4 is attributed to a lower sales base in comparison to the subsequent periods, while the working capital remained practically constant.

This ratio may be useful in some organizations, if verified to be relatively consistent, in determining or planning approximate working capital requirements based on sales volume. To use it in this way, divide the quarterly annualized sales by the appropriate ratio factor. The use of sales and working capital trend ratios over an extended period may be the most effective means of establishing or verifying their relevance.

HOW TO ANALYZE FIXED ASSET RELATIONSHIPS

Net Fixed Assets to Total Asset Ratio

This ratio enables you to determine the relationship of net fixed assets to total assets based on past experience. To calculate the ratio, divide average net fixed assets by average total assets.

Example: The following quarterly ratios are calculated using data in Model 34:

19X3			*19X4*	
December	*March*	*June*	*September*	*December*
12.8% ($63.4 million ÷ $493.8)	12.8%	12.9%	13.3%	14.0%

The increasing trend in the ratio is due to increased investment in fixed assets, while total asset value was declining, particularly in the September and December 19x4 quarterly periods (partially offset by increasing depreciation reserve). The main cause for the decrease in total assets is a low current asset position. The significance of this situation is that fixed assets represent a greater share of the total assets and that the current working assets, which directly support operational activity, are declining. This can be an unfavorable trend unless additional fixed assets are required for expansion, more efficient or new equipment, or modernization of existing facilities.

APPLICATIONS   You may use these ratios in a couple of ways: (1) as guidelines in estimating fixed asset expenditures based on projected total assets, (2) as a tool for measuring fixed asset growth or decline in relation to fluctuations in the total asset position.

Computing the Fixed Asset Turnover

The objective of this ratio is to analyze the use of fixed assets based on sales volume activity. It generally indicates how effectively an organization is employing its fixed asset investment in relation to sales volume and objectives. The equation is as follows:

$$\text{Fixed asset turnover} = \frac{\text{Sales (usually annualized)}}{\text{Average net fixed assets}}$$

Example: The following quarterly turnover ratios are developed based on the data in Model 34:

	19X4		
March	*June*	*September*	*December*
3.90:1 ($252.8 million ÷ $64.9)	4.15:1	4.12:1	4.00:1

The high turnover ratio of 4.15 in June is attributed to increased sales ($274.9 million) versus a minor increase in fixed assets to $66.3 million. The decrease in the turnover ratio in December resulted from a decrease in quarterly sales with an increase in net fixed assets. The increase and decrease amounts are conservative but sufficient to reduce the turnover ratio.

This type of ratio may be somewhat misleading if used to compare it with other organizations in the same industry, particularly if an organization, for example, leases buildings rather than owning them. The effect is a more favorable ratio. In another instance, the gross fixed assets might greatly depreciate over a period of time (such as in long established organizations), and thus the net fixed asset values are lower with a resultant higher turnover rate. The opposite is true—the net value (aspect of depreciation) is larger—with a heavy investment in new facilities.

APPLICATIONS   You must exercise judgment when using this ratio. These ratios may be used to assess performance among periods, as long as they prove to be consistent and realistic. The ratios may not only indicate valid trends, but they may also act as planning guidelines in projecting the need for fixed asset acquisitions. They can reveal too much capacity—or too small a plant with insufficient machinery and equipment to support a given sales volume.

Figuring the Net Fixed Assets to Owners' Equity

With this ratio, you can analyze and assess the proportion of an organization's fixed assets financed from the owners' equity capital. Large fixed asset investments result in greater fixed costs (depreciation, taxes, maintenance, and the like), with its predictably increased break-even point. If the sales volume is reduced substantially, other related problems, such as the attendant effect on profits, may result.

Generally, as the proportion of fixed asset investment increases from owners' equity, less funds are available for working capital requirements, such as accounts receivable, inventory, and cash. Although the investing organizations enhance their capacity to meet increased product demand, they may not have sufficient working capital to support the larger sales volume. Thus, an organization may actually have to decrease its sales volume due to a lack of funds to support their operations. Too much investment in a business, if not properly justified, usually indicates an inefficient use of capital.

To calculate this relationship, divide average net fixed assets by average tangible owners' equity.

Example: The following ratios are developed using data in Model 34.

19X3		19X4			
December	*March*	*June*	*September*	*December*	
42.0% ($63.4 million ÷ $151.0)	42.2%	42.4%	42.3%	42.8%	

These ratios indicate a consistent net fixed asset investment trend. Fixed assets increased from $63.4 million in December 19X3 to $68.2 million in December 19X4. The owners' equity increased from $151.0 million in 19x3 to $159.4 million in December 19X4.

VERIFYING THE RATIO

To evaluate the reasonableness of the fixed asset investment ratio, compare it to those of other organizations of comparable size in the same line of business. Management must exercise judgment, however, in such comparisons. There may be extenuating circumstances for major differences, such as current large investments in plant modernization or unusual expansion expenditures to meet projected new product demands. Excessive fixed asset investments can lead to insufficient working capital to meet adequately operational needs, the accumulation of expensive long-term indebtedness, and possibly financial instability. The prime value of fixed assets to a business depends on their earning power.

Ratio of Net Fixed Assets to Funded Debt

This comparison is a reasonable indicator, to a lending organization, of the integrity of its investment. To determine this ratio, divide the average net fixed assets by the average funded debt.

Example: The following quarterly ratios are calculated using data in Model 34.

19X3			19X4	
December	*March*	*June*	*September*	*December*
1.49:1 ($63.4 million ÷ $42.6)	1.52:1	1.56:1	1.57:1	1.60:1

> For every $1.00 of funded debt, there is $1.60 (December 19X4) net book value of property, plant, and equipment. The increase in the ratio trend is attributed to an increase in fixed asset acquisitions, whereas the funded debt remained constant.

To determine the reliability and usefulness of this relationship, make comparative analyses and management judgments relative to other organizations in the same industry.

Relating Sales to Net Fixed Assets

Use this ratio to measure the size of the fixed asset investment relative to the sales volume activity. This ratio may give you an insight as to whether an organization has too much capacity and associated machinery/equipment or too small a plant for a given sales volume. In making this comparison with other organizations in the same industry, give consideration to the age of the assets, price levels when they were purchased, and the depreciation policies with their effect on fixed asset valuation. If the assets were acquired in years when the value of the dollar was high and thereafter heavily depreciated, the result is a higher ratio. This situation is due to the lower net fixed asset value. Conversely, a low ratio indicates an excessive valuation of the fixed assets without a comparable increase in sales. If the organization's ratios are out of line with the industry as a whole, then you must make a judgment as to the differences and causes before drawing specific conclusions.

Fixed assets in themselves do not produce sales, but generally without them only limited sales can be made in a product-oriented organization. Sales results from many factors, such as product demand, favorable markets, effectiveness and efficiency of sales promotion, and so on. To calculate this ratio, divide annualized sales by the average net fixed assets.

Example: The following quarterly ratios are developed using data in Model 34:

	19X4		
March	*June*	*September*	*December*
3.90:1 ($252.8 million ÷ $64.9)	4.15:1	4.12:1	4.00:1

The low ratio of 3.90 in March is attributed to the relatively low sales volume, whereas net fixed assets had a conservative increase over December 19X3. The high ratio of 4.15 in June resulted from an 8.7% increase in sales over March, but the fixed assets were only 2.2% greater.

These developed ratios indicate that the sales volume is approximately four times greater than the net fixed asset position. In other words, fixed assets averaged 25% of sales dollars.

Depending on whether they prove valid, these ratios can be used in assessing period performance, in planning asset requirements, and in making comparisons with other organizations in the same industry.

HOW TO EVALUATE KEY DEBT RATIOS

ASSESSING RISK When a business is financed by creditors, a considerable degree of risk is involved. For example, if there is a significant decrease in sales activity or in receivable turnover, the business may be unable to meet its obligations. Substantial interest on loans (borrowed capital) may even exceed earnings, hence, a *loss* situation.

The overall industry debt overload in 1982 is attributed to excessive borrowing during the 1970s, low stock market prices, and high inflation rates. Many organizations assumed that they could repay borrowed capital with cheaper dollars if inflation continued at double-digit rates. The reasonableness of many an organization's debt capacity was underemphasized. As a result, a number of organizations had to seek Chapter 11 protection, restructure their debts, seek relief from creditors in the form of extending debt payment schedules, and further negotiate with vendors/creditors for reduced interest rates. In 1982, bankruptcies were at their highest levels since the 1930s. Some major firms encountering financial problems included Lockheed Aircraft, Chrysler, Braniff Airlines, Martin Marietta, DuPont, and other large corporations.

Relating Owners' Equity to Total Liabilities

This ratio relates the amount of investment resources provided by the owners to that provided by creditors. Creditors are investors in an organization because in essence, money is borrowed and/or other debts created presumably to achieve a higher rate of return from operational activities.

To calculate this ratio, divide the average owners' equity by average total liabilities.

Example: The following quarterly ratios are developed using the data in Model 34:

19X3			19X4	
December	March	June	September	December
44.0% ($151 million ÷ $342.8)	43.5%	43.9%	46.0%	48.8%

The owners' investment equity is 48.8% in December 19X4. The primary cause for the favorable trend is decreasing liabilities with an increasing owners' equity (greater retained earnings). The increased owners' equity, in comparison to the creditors', is one indicator of a stronger financial position trend.

Computing the Capital Structure Ratio

This ratio indicates the proportion of long-term debt to the owners' equity plus long-term debt. To calculate this ratio, use the following equation:

$$\text{Capital structure ratio} = \frac{\text{Average long-term debt}}{\text{Owners' equity} + \text{Long-term debt}}$$

Example: Using data in Model 34, the following quarterly ratios resulted:

19X3			19X4	
December	March	June	September	December
8.6% ($42.6 million ÷ $493.8)	8.4%	8.3%	8.5%	8.8%

The variations in the ratios among periods are due to the fluctuations in the total liabilities plus owners' equity.

Relating Owners' Equity to Total Capital Employed

This ratio indicates the relative proportions of invested and borrowed capital to the total capital employed in the business enterprise. *Owners' equity* includes the owners' investment (primarily capital stock) plus retained earnings. *Borrowed capital* includes both current liabilities and long-term debt commitments (debentures, for example).

APPLICATION This ratio acts as a guideline in evaluating the adequacy of invested capital and the security of borrowed capital. Generally, the greater proportion of owners' equity that an organization possesses in terms of resources, the more assurance the creditor has that debt obligations will be met. An accepted baseline is that invested capital should exceed borrowed capital, but this criterion may not be true in some organizations depending on their type of operations. Borrowed capital in excess of invested capital indicates that there is a sharing of propriety risk with the creditor and that the security of debt repayments may result in financial jeopardy.

To calculate this ratio, divide the average owners' equity by the average total capital employed.

Example: The following quarterly ratios are developed using data in Model 34:

19X3		19X4		
December	*March*	*June*	*September*	*December*
30.6% ($151 million ÷ $493.8)	30.3%	30.5%	31.5%	32.8%

The ratio of owners' equity to total capital employed over a period of time usually reflects an organization's financial policy and objectives—and gives an insight as to management's fiscal responsibility. Operating with excess creditor investment, however, may be fully justified and acceptable under certain circumstances.

Relating Working Capital to Funded Debt

Use this ratio to evaluate and determine if an organization could liquidate its long-term debt obligations from working capital. Although an organization may have a more than adequate earnings' position, it still may not have maintained enough liquid capital to meet long-term debt obligations. To calculate this ratio, divide the average working capital by average funded debt.

Example: The following quarterly ratios are calculated using data in Model 34:

19X3		19X4		
December	*March*	*June*	*September*	*December*
2.80:1 ($119.4 million ÷ $42.6)	2.81:1	2.82:1	2.85:1	2.85:1

The ratio of 280% for December 19X3 indicates there is $2.80 of working capital for each $1.00 of funded debt. The ratio trend increased to 285% in September and December of 19X4, which is more conservatively favorable to meet debt obligations.

Analyzing Funded Debt Disposition

Here is another approach to working capital versus funded debt evaluation.

Example: The data are extracted from Model 34:

	Millions		*Millions*
Current assets	$405.1	Current liabilities	$283.8
Noncurrent assets	80.7	Funded debt	42.6
		Capital	159.4
Totals	$485.8		$485.8

December 19X4

Current assets of $405.1 million, less current liabilities of $283.8 million, provides a working capital of $121.3 million. Since the funded debt is $42.6 million, the total amount of the funded debt is represented by current assets—$121.3 million versus $42.6 million. None of the long-term debt has to be supported by the noncurrent assets. This financial position is favorable both for the concerned organization and for its long-term creditors because of the liquidity potential.

Relating Current Debt to Owners' Equity

Use this ratio to determine whether the short-term creditors are providing too much capital resources to support the operational environment relative to material, supplies, and services. To calculate this ratio, divide the average current liabilities by the owners' equity.

Example: The following quarterly ratios are calculated using data in Model 34:

19X3		*19X4*		
December	*March*	*June*	*September*	*December*
1.99:1 ($300.2 million ÷ $151.0)	2.02:1	2.01:1	1.90:1	1.78:1

The 19X3 ratio signifies that vendors were providing $1.99 (December) of credit support for each $1.00 of owners' equity. A more favorable trend was experienced in December 19X4, which resulted from decreasing current liabilities as compared to an increasing owners' equity (higher retained earnings).

Determining a reasonable ratio is difficult because it depends on several factors, such as the velocity of receivable and inventory turnovers, characteristics of the operational environment, working capital position, and the comparative ratio averages being experienced by other organizations in a similar industry. Continual periodic analyses and historical experience results may help you to make a judgmental decision as to acceptable ratio guidelines.

Comparing Total Debt to Total Assets

With this ratio, you can evaluate an organization's debt position in relation to its total asset position, both current and noncurrent. It is one indicator of how much debt an organization can incur and still cope without financial difficulty. To develop this ratio, divide the average total debt by average total assets.

Example: The following quarterly ratios are calculated using data in Model 34.

19X3		19X4			
December		*March*	*June*	*September*	*December*
69.4% ($342.8 million ÷ $493.8)		69.7%	69.5%	68.5%	67.2%

These ratios indicate that total liabilities represented 67.2%–69.7% of the total assets. In other words, approximately 70% of the total assets are being financed by external vendors and creditors.

On the surface, this situation implies possible difficulties in meeting scheduled debt obligations, but this may not be the case in reality. Current assets may turn over quickly, thereby permitting timely debt payments. Certain current liabilities, such as payables, may be extended in due date payments. Long-term debts can be restructured for delayed payments. Increased earnings may be anticipated based on improved business outlook, and so on. As discussed in a prior example, the organization's working capital was considered to be adequate based on industry-wide comparisons. Current assets were in a 1.4:1 ratio to current liabilities (common to this industry).

Figuring the Total Debt to Owners' Equity Ratio

This ratio is another approach in evaluating whether an organization has enough capital to support its operations and debts. The merits of this measurement, however, can be misleading. To calculate this ratio, divide the average total debt by average owners' equity.

Example: The following quarterly ratios are derived from data provided in Model 34.

19X3			19X4	
December	*March*	*June*	*September*	*December*
2.27:1 ($342.8 million ÷ $151)	3.00:1	2.28:1	2.17:1	2.05:1

The developed ratio for December 19X4 indicates that the total debt is twice (2.05) the amount of the owners' equity. The trend is declining, as current liabilities decrease and owners' equity increases. In view of the reasonably strong position, financial difficulties are unanticipated. Current assets are adequate to support the total debt, with undercapitalization of minor importance in this particular organization.

Pros and Cons of Debt Ratios and Financing

Trading on equity—or on what is known as "leverage" in some organizations—refers to the use of borrowed capital to achieve a higher rate of return on the owners' equity than could otherwise be accomplished without the use of the creditors' capital. For example, if funds can be borrowed at a rate that is lower than can be earned with the capital, then borrowing is considered to be both practical and profitable. Conversely, if the organization's earning power is lower than the interest cost on the borrowed capital, then the owners will earn less than if part of the capital had not been borrowed.

Trading on equity involves the risk of some losses, but it can also be rewarding. This ratio represents the relationship between the amount of borrowed capital and the owners' equity. Creditors' capital must be repaid, and so must interest expense, whether earned or not. When liquidation is a possibility, creditors have first claims against the assets over those of the owners. Thus the inappropriate use of creditors' capital presents risks both to the creditors and to the owners. The point is that operating capital is not affected by the maturity dates of owners' equity but rather by the due dates of the creditors' capital.

The prime objective of debt ratios is to focus management's attention on potential problems associated with the use, size, and repayment of creditors' capital. You must also give consideration, however, to other influencing ratios, such as earnings, cash flow, working capital, capital structure, and so on. This is the only way to review properly financial objectives and operational planning in terms of creditors' impact on an organization's financial stability.

8

Understanding Data Relationships for Effective Cash Flow Planning

CHAPTER HIGHLIGHTS

Cash flow might be described as the blood flow of an organization. Cash flow can be decelerated, when required, or accelerated. The opening section of the chapter explains how you can do either.

You are then acquainted with a computerized cash collections and ratio analysis process, including cost-incurred contracts, sales deliveries, and progress payments. The development of progress payments, determining available funding, and anticipations of liquidation are very important with respect to fixed price contract collections, particularly on government contracts.

The step-by-step outline of an automated cash flow and reporting process is presented, although the procedures may vary somewhat among organizations.

Using an illustrative model, you will familiarize yourself with a numerical cash schedule, with ratios among the cash receipts, disbursements, and balances. By means of the two other models, you will come to understand the relationships among sales, receipts, and receivables. A similar approach is used for payable costs, disbursements, and payable balances. Finally, accrued salaries/wages and payable costs, disbursements, and balances are outlined and highlighted.

The cash flow statement and its associated data reveal the in- and outflow of cash, its availability, the need to borrow funds to support operational activities, and problem areas.

Cash flows into the organization as the result of product sales and/ or performance of services. Typical input for cash flow systems arises from such systems and processes as sales deliveries, accounts receivable, costs incurred, and progress or partial payments. Receipts are also provided by customer advances, borrowings, and issuance of capital stock.

Cash flows out of the organization in the form of major cash disbursements for salaries/wages, accounts payable, capital asset expenditures, interest expenses, taxes, loan repayments, dividends, and so on.

The amount of cash available at any point in time can be calculated. First obtain the prior period's cash balance from the cash actuals report. Combine that total with the current period's receipts. From this total, deduct the cash disbursements. The result is an ending cash balance for the period.

The next question is whether cash is indeed available, or if borrowing is in order. To answer this question compare the cash balance to the organization's pre-established cash requirements.

UNDERSTANDING THE DYNAMICS OF CASH FLOW

In recent years, many organizations, both large and small, have experienced inadequate cash flow, with its characteristic problems—one of which is their inability to meet their debt obligations. A few notable examples of the early eighties are Chrysler, Lockheed, DeLorean, Braniff, United Airlines and Caterpillar Tractor. Many others are forced to plead bankruptcy under Chapter 11 guidelines. These problems can be attributed to overextension of credit, selling to poor credit risks, delays in collecting receivables, large interest commitments on borrowings, overexpansion, acquisitions, economic reversals, cost-profit competition, and possible reductions in sales volume.

This chapter is concerned with the various aspects and details of billings, collections, and cash situations. The ratios and other guidelines in the following sections can aid your organization in achieving and maintaining financial stability, as well as in cash planning.

How to Decelerate Cash Outflow

If you determine that a cash shortage is imminent, then, outside of borrowing, certain actions are feasible. One you should consider is *decelerating cash outflow* (at least temporarily). Cash outflow can be decelerated as follows:

STEPS FOR DECELERATION

Defer, where possible, the payment of specific accounts payable commitments to a later period through vendor negotiations.

Delay normal vendor payments to the last possible billing day or as long as you can without jeopardizing purchase discounts.

Restructure long-term debts to delay scheduled due date payments.

Reschedule capital expenditure projects until funds become available. (In some instances, this is not feasible because of immediate operating needs.)

Postpone dividend payouts and interest payable if cash flow becomes an acute problem.

Try to negotiate with vendors to establish payment dates during peak receipt periods.

How to Accelerate Cash Receipts

Certain situations lend themselves to accelerating *cash inflow:*

STEPS FOR ACCELERATION

Emphasize the collection of receivables, particularly if they are past due and/or delinquent. A more stringent credit policy may be necessary.

Initiate prompt customer billings, such as invoicing the customer on the following working day after product shipment has been made or service performed.

Make a concerted effort to reduce receivable and inventory balances to conservative levels. This may mean a change in the customer credit policy and a delay in making major purchases.

Provide payment incentive discounts to selected customers.

Reduce advances to subcontractors and subsidiaries.

Use lock-box procedures to accelerate the availability of customer remittances to meet the more immediate vendor payments.

IMPLICATIONS OF CASH FLOW FROM OPERATIONS

Cash flow from operations represents *cash receipts from sales* (product/services) less the costs and expenses associated with producing a product or performing services. This would include supervisory, administrative/selling expenses. The financial reporting information provided would include an income statement, balance sheet and undoubtedly changes in financial position in terms of source and application of funds. The objective in this process is to determine the net increase or decrease in working capital resulting from sales revenues versus expenses.

The general procedure followed in the calculations is to adjust net working capital to reflect the changes that occurred in the current asset and liability accounts as a result of operational sales revenues. In essence, increases in current liabilities are combined with asset decreases and from this resultant value is deducted the combination of liability decreases and asset increases.

A simplified illustration of this procedure is noted as follows:

Dollar Values in Millions			
Net working capital from operations		*Cash flow from operations*	
Net income	$10.0	Increase in accounts receivable	$ 5.0
Depreciation/amortization	1.5	Decrease in inventories	(3.0)
Other (deferred debts)	.1	Decrease in prepaid expense	(.5)
		Increase in payables	2.5
		Increase in accrued expenses	1.0%
Net working capital	$11.6	Net total	$ 5.0

The $11.6 million less $5.0 million equals $6.6 million net cash flow from operations. It should be noted that the cash balance (to meet operational requirements) and fixed asset accounts (replacement/expansion) are generally also affected by fluctuations in sales revenues but these items are not usually reflected in the accepted format of changes in financial position.

It is pointed out that interest and fixed charge ratios should not only be based on profit but also the cash from operations as illustrated above since favorable cash flow is what pays the expenses. Financial position ratios and cash flow planning are further discussed in Chapters 7 and 8, respectively. Future cash flows are the determinate factor in assessing an organization's projected capability in meeting its debt obligations.

MAPPING THE COMPUTERIZED CASH COLLECTION PROCESS

Model 35 shows how customer billings and collections can be processed. The system includes:

1. cost-type contract collections
2. sales deliveries
3. progress or partial payments

Cost-Type Contract Billings

Costs plus fixed fee are generally collected in 15 days; put another way, they are lagged by a factor of 50%. Thus 50% of the costs billed in one period fall into the following period for collection. To derive the total contract billing collections for the current period, combine the *prior period's* lagged amount balance with the *current period's* collectible amount. The lagged amount, based on historical experience, may vary from one organization to another.

MODEL 35. Computerized Billings and Collection Process.

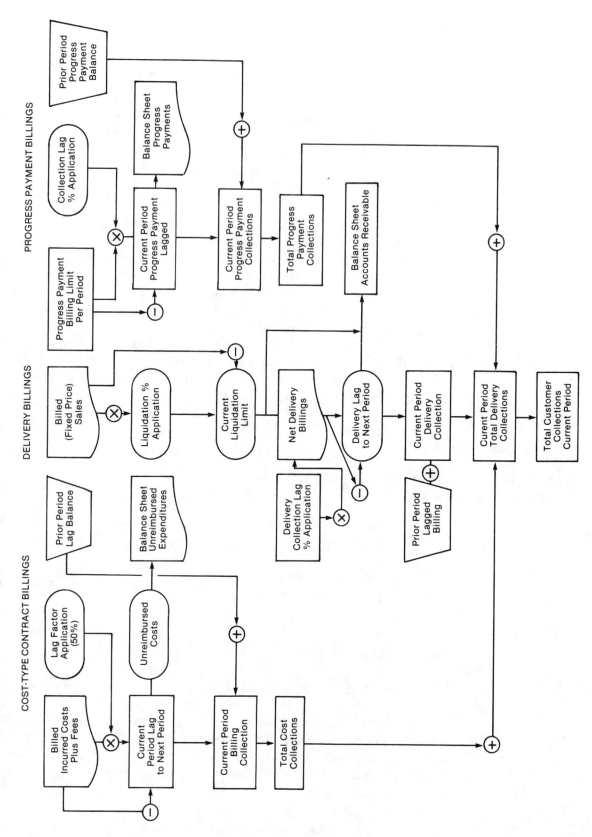

196

Delivery Billings/Collections

First negotiate a liquidation factor with the customer. Then apply the factor to the billed sales. The result represents the *current period's liquidation* value. Deduct that amount from the billed sales to derive the net delivery billing amount. To this value, apply the delivery collection lag percentage to obtain the delivery amount to be lagged to the subsequent period.

To derive the value that is *collectible* in the current period, subtract the developed delivery lagged value from the delivery billing amount. This amount is combined with the prior period's lagged billing to obtain the current period's *total delivery collections*. Note that the value lagged into a subsequent period represents an *accounts receivable* in the balance sheet.

Progress Payment Billings

As shown in Model 35, the collection lag percentage is applied to the progress payment billing limit to obtain the value of the progress payment to be lagged to the next period for collection. Deduct the lagged amount from the billing limit to obtain the current period's collectible value based on the lag application.

Combine the prior period's progress payment balance with the current period's collectible amount to obtain the total progress payment collections in the current period.

Total Customer Collections

To derive the total customer collections (bottom center in Model 35), add cost-type contract collections to the sales delivery and progress payment collections. The *lagged values* represent a collectible current asset in the subsequent period.

COLLECTION STEPS

Basically, the process involves four steps:

1. Determine the amount of the billing that, based on experience factors, will be delayed in the collection until the following period.

2. Subtract the lagged amounts from the current period's billings to derive the collectible values in the current period.

3. Combine the prior period's lagged amounts with the current period to obtain the current period collections in the billing categories, displayed in Model 35.

4. Combine the three categories of collections to arrive at the total customer anticipated cash receipts in the current period.

Using Ratios in Connection with Automated Billings/Collections

Model 36 reflects the flow-charted data system in Model 35. It provides the data value assumptions for the three types of billings: cost incurred, deliveries, and progress payments. The dollar values may be used for the development of ratios, which in turn serve as a basis for comparative analyses in subsequent periods. The proviso, as always, is that the ratios must prove to be *consistent and valid* over a period of time under similar operational circumstances.

Calculating Ratios to Cost-Incurred Billings

As illustrated in Model 36, the process is simple. As costs are incurred and billed, you apply a collection lag percentage (or substitute a dollar value). The lagged amount—$50,000 or 50% of costs in this example—falls into the following period for collection. The lagged portion represents *unreimbursed expenditures*.

AN ILLUSTRATION

Deduct the lagged amount from the incurred costs ($100,000) to determine the amount to be collected in the current period ($50,000). To this value add the prior period's lagged amount ($45,000) to obtain the total collections for the period ($95,000).

The following ratios can be developed for analysis and planning:

- The relation of *current period collection to incurred costs* is 50% (a 15-day lag in billing collection, generally based on historical experience and/or customer negotiations). The calculation process is illustrated in Model 36.

- The *prior period billings to total collections* is calculated to be 47.4%, which indicates a consistent pattern in the collection process based on the data provided.

- *Lagged prior period billings to current period cost ratio* is determined to be 45%. This ratio may not be valid or significant. Only experience can gauge or verify its usefulness.

- Total *current and prior billings to current costs,* as represented by a 95% factor in the model, may provide a valid statistic for future planning and/or assessing collection realities and trends.

- *Current unreimbursed expenditures ratio to incurred costs* is a reciprocal of current period collections to cost. This ratio, if proven valid over several periods, may be useful in projecting unreimbursed expenditure balances for a forecasted balance sheet, either in total or by specific contracts.

MODEL 36. Ratio Aspects of the Billings/Collection Process.

Cost Incurred Billings: Assumptions (in $000s)		Ratio Development	%	$
Total incurred costs	$100.0	Current collections to costs	50.0	(50 ÷ 100)
Billing collection lag	50.0	Prior billings to collections	47.4	(45 ÷ 95)
Prior lagged billings	45.0	Prior lagged billings to costs	45.0	(45 ÷ 100)
Total cost collections	$ 95.0	Current and prior billings to costs	95.0	(95 ÷ 100)
		Unreimbursed expenditures to costs	50.0	(50 ÷ 100)

Delivery Billings: Assumptions (in $000s)			%	$
Billed sales	$ 60.0	Liquidation limit to sales	60.0	(36 ÷ 60)
Liquidation limit	36.0	Current liquidation lag to sales	40.0	(24 ÷ 60)
Current liquidation lag	$ 24.0	Delivery collection lag/liquidation		
Delivery collection lag	9.0	limit	25.0	(9 ÷ 36)
Current delivery collections	27.0	Delivery collections to sales	45.0	(27 ÷ 60)
Prior billings	12.0	Prior billings to total collections	30.8	(12 ÷ 39)
Total delivery collections	$ 39.0	Current collections to total	69.2	(27 ÷ 39)

Progress Payment (PP) Billings: Assumptions (in $000s)			%	$
PP billing limit	$ 40.0	Collection lag to billing limit	50.0	(20 ÷ 40)
Current collection lag	20.0	Prior billings to total collections	47.4	(18 ÷ 38)
Prior billing lag	18.0	Current collections to total	52.6	(20 ÷ 38)
		Total collections to billing limit	95.0	(38 ÷ 40)
Total PP collections	$ 38.0			

Customer Collection Summary (in $000s)

	Current Period	%	Prior Billings	%	Total Collections	%
Incurred costs	$50.0	51.6	$45.0	60.0	$ 95.0	55.2
Billed deliveries	27.0	27.8	12.0	16.0	39.0	22.7
Progress payments	20.0	20.6	18.0	24.0	38.0	22.1
Totals	$97.0	100.0	$75.0	100.0	$172.0	100.0

Computing Ratios to Delivery Billings

Model 36 displays the basic assumption values used in developing the total delivery collections and associated ratio factors.

To obtain the *current liquidation value* ($36,000), apply the liquidation application percentage (liquidation limit) to the billed sales. Subtract this value from the billed sales to derive the balance of the uncollectible ($24,000), which represents a receivable for the next period.

AN ILLUSTRATION

The current liquidation limit of $36,000 represents net delivery billings. Apply delivery collection lag of 25% to the billings ($36,000) to obtain the uncollectible delivery portion of $9,000. The liquidation limit of $36,000, less the $9,000, represents the *current period's delivery collection.*

Combine the *prior period's lagged balance* of $12,000 with the current period's delivery collection to obtain the *total delivery collections.*

The pertinent ratios are as follows:

- The *liquidation limit to billed sales* is 60% ($36,000 ÷ $60,000). The liquidation limit percentage establishes the amount that can be liquidated in the current period. The limit is based on past experience and/or customer negotiations. This ratio can be used as a planning factor in establishing liquidation limits based on projected billed sales.

- The *current liquidation lag value to sales* is calculated to be 40%, which is the reciprocal of the 60% liquidation limit noted above. (You can use either factor application to obtain the other.)

- The *delivery collection lag to the liquidation limit* is calculated to be 25%, as shown in the model. The dollar lag value may be a direct input, and it represents a receivable in the following period.

- The *current delivery collections to sales* ratio is 45%. This ratio may be useful in projecting current delivery collections based on forecasted billed sales activity.

- The *prior period billings relation to total sales* is calculated to be 30.8%. The reciprocal percentage represents the current period collections (69.2%). Either factor may be useful in planning current collections and prior period billings based on anticipated total collections.

Figuring Ratios for Progress Payment Billings

AN ILLUSTRATION

Model 36 displays the dollar value assumptions used in developing the total progress payment collections and related ratios. The progress payment *billing limit* is developed as illustrated in Model 36. Or you can apply an applicable percentage to the cumulative *progress payment potential* to derive a period billing limit. To obtain the value of the *uncollectible* progress payments to be lagged into the following period, apply a *collection lag percentage* to the billing limit. The value of $20,000 (based on a 50% collection lag) is deducted from the period progress payment limit of $40,000 to obtain the progress payments to be collected in the current period. Then combine the prior period's lagged amount of $18,000 with the current period's collectible to derive the total payments of $38,000 for the period.

Useful ratios can be developed from these data:

- The *current collection lag relative to a billing limit ratio* is calculated to be 50%, as shown in Model 36. The ratio can vary among contracts depending on the terms of negotiation. This is a useful planning factor in projecting the current period's progress payment collections based on the billing limit.

- As shown in the model, the *prior period's billing to total collections* is calculated to be 47.4%. The ratio of the current period's collections to the total collections is 52.6%, which is a reciprocal value of the prior period's lagged collections. *Either factor* can be used in planning the anticipated component values of the total collections in a given period, provided they have been proven to be valid over a period of time.

- Comparing the *total collections to the billing limit* results in a 95% ratio. Use this ratio in planning with caution due to possible changes in the operational environment and in customer negotiated guidelines.

Summarizing Customer Collection

The customer collection summary at the bottom of the model is based on the data detailed in the upper part of the exhibit. This summary indicates the relative proportions of incurred costs, deliveries, and progress payments as they apply to collections for the current and prior periods. The summary's objective is to determine the primary source of collections, which in this case were incurred costs with an overall 55.2%. Current period billings accounted for 56.4% ($97,000 ÷ $172,000) of the total collections.

You can apply these factors, given similar operating circumstance, to total projected collections to obtain, at least preliminarily, the segregated sources of the collections, reflected in the balance sheet as unreimbursed expenditures, accounts receivable, and uncollected progress payments. Further, if the ratio proves to be historically valid, approximately 56.4% of the total collections may be assumed to represent current period billings.

DEVELOPING PROGRESS PAYMENTS AND LIQUIDATIONS

Model 37 displays the computerized process for developing progress payments and liquidations. You can use this process for each contract, project, or combination of the two, providing you give consideration to the realistic averaging of the percentage involved (progress payments, funding, and liquidations).

On a contract or project basis, the developed information can be readily consolidated through automated processes. Thus the detailed information can be reported for analysis and assessment, as well as for future planning.

When you use the consolidated contract approach, you lose the detail. When changes, additions, and deletions are required by contract, the percentages must be recalculated and re-inputted unless a computer program routine is developed to accomplish this task.

Let's look more closely at Model 37.

Processing Progress Payments

In this process, you combine work in process costs with the changes in material and supply (M&S) costs, to obtain the total period's incurred costs. Apply a negotiated or planned progress payment percentage to the incurred costs to obtain the progress payment on period cost value. Combine period advances to vendor changes with the progress payments on costs to derive the progress payment potential. The period values are accumulated to obtain the cumulative progress payment potential. Collections depend on the constraints of negotiated available funding.

Calculating Funding Availability

Certain contracts—particularly government-negotiated contracts—have provisions specifying the funding percentage available to meet progress payment requirements. Model 37 displays the general process involved. A brief description of the procedure follows:

- Accumulate the period's incremental funding by contract to obtain the cumulative funding available to date.

- Apply the funding limit percentage or ratio to the cumulative funding value to ascertain the cumulative funding available in a specific period.

- At this point, compare the cumulative progress payment potential to the available cumulative funding. The *lesser value* represents the cumulative progress payment limit for collection. The resultant value

MODEL 37. Development of Progress Payments and Liquidations: A Computerized Process.

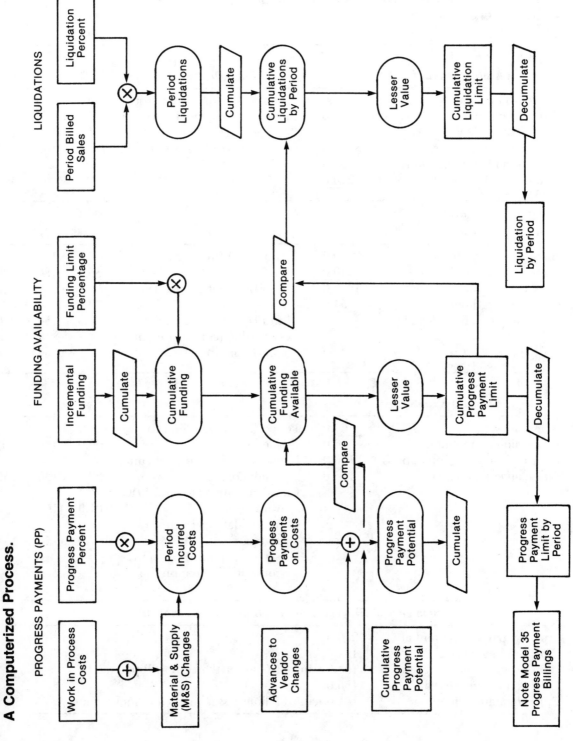

203

MODEL 38. Ratios for Progress Payments and Liquidations: A Computerized Approach.

Progress Payments (PP)

Assumptions (in $000s)		Ratio Development	%	$
Current period costs	$100.0	PP on costs to incurred cost	50.0	(50 ÷ 100)
Progress payments on costs	50.0	Current PP potential to cum PP	28.6	(60 ÷ 210)
Advances to Vendors	10.0	Prior period's PP to cum PP	71.4	(150 ÷ 210)
Progress payment potential	$ 60.0	Period incurred costs to cum PP	47.6	(100 ÷ 210)
Prior period accumulation (PP)	150.0			
Cumulative PP potential	$210.0			

Funding Availability (FDG)

Assumptions (in $000s)			%	$
Incremental funding	$ 80.0	Incremental funding to cum		
Prior period cum funding	140.0	FDG	36.4	(80 ÷ 220)
Cumulative funding to date	$220.0	Cum FDG limit to total cum		
Cum funding limit—70%	154.0	FDG	70.0	(154 ÷ 220)
Remaining funding lagged	$ 66.0	Cum FDG to cum PP limit	73.3	(154 ÷ 210)
		Lesser value (cum represents cum PP limit)		154

Liquidations

Assumptions (in $000s)			%	$
Billed sales	$ 60.0	Period liquidation limit to		
Period liquidation limit	36.0	billed sales	60.0	(36 ÷ 60)
Prior accumulated liquidations	120.0	Liquidation limit to total cum		
Cumulative liquidations	$156.0	liquidations	23.1	(36 ÷ 156)
		Cum liquidations to cum FDG available	101.0	(156 ÷ 154)
		Cum liquidations to cum PP limit	101.0	(156 ÷ 154)
		Lesser value (cum FDG represents cum liquidation limit)		154

Summary of Progress Payments/Liquidations (note above)	
Progress payment potential	$210.0
Cum funding available	154.0
Cum progress payment limit	154.0 (cum FDG lesser than cum PP potential)
Cum liquidations to date	156.0
Cum liquidation limit	154.0 (cum PP limit lesser than cum liquidations)

is *decumulated* to obtain the progress payment limit for a given period. As shown in the model, this is the maximum value for collection as reflected at the top of Model 35 under the caption of "Progress Payment Billing Limit."

Step-by-Step Billing Liquidation Procedure

The progress payment liquidation process is displayed at the extreme right of Model 37, as follows.

- Apply the *liquidation percent to the period billed sales.* In so doing, you determine the amount that may be liquidated in a given period provided that the cumulative value at a point in time does not exceed the cumulative progress payment limit.

- Accumulate the period liquidations, as shown in the model, and compare the amounts to the cumulative progress payments. The *smaller value* of the two represents the cumulative liquidation limit. In other words, this value is the maximum that can be liquidated within the period.

- Decumulate the cumulative liquidation limit to obtain the potential liquidation by period. The period liquidation amount cannot exceed the established progress payment limit by period.

ASSESSING THE RATIO ASPECTS OF PROGRESS PAYMENTS AND LIQUIDATIONS

Model 38 illustrates the data used in developing progress payments, funding, and liquidation ratios. The computation procedure reflects the processing steps shown in the flowchart in Model 37.

How to Determine Progress Payment Ratios

AN ILLUSTRATION

Apply the assumed progress payment of 50% to the current period's total incurred costs of $100,000 to obtain the value lagged for collection in the following period. The difference between the $100,000 and the lagged payments of $50,000, plus the *advances to vendors,* represents the current period's progress payment *collection potential.* Consolidate the potential amount with the prior period's progress payment total of $150,000 to obtain the cumulative progress payment potential of $210,000.

The following comments pertain to the ratio development.

1. The *progress payments on costs to period incurred costs* is calculated to be 50%, as shown in Model 38 ($50,000 ÷ $100,000). Use this ratio to determine the progress payment value to be lagged to the next period. The difference from incurred costs represents the potential collectible portion in the current period. A valid ratio can be useful in projecting future progress payment collections.

2. The *current progress payment potential to the cumulative progress payments* is calculated to be 28.6%. Make use of this ratio in estimating current progress payments based on the cumulative total. Conversely, to estimate the current progress payments, if the factor proves to be consistent, multiply the cumulative progress payments ($210,000) by 28.6%.

3. The *prior period's progress payment to cumulative progress payments* is represented by a ratio of 71.4% ($150,000 ÷ $210,000). This statistic may be useful in estimating the prior period's progress payment accumulation. Subtracting this value from the cumulative payments to date results in the current period's payment potential. This calculation assumes, of course, that the ratio factors prove to be reliable over historical time periods and that the operating circumstances remain relatively consistent.

4. Comparing *period incurred costs to cumulative progress payments* results in a 47.6% ratio. This factor can be used to project preliminary period incurred costs if the cumulative progress payments have been initially estimated. This can be useful in several ways in planning, but an organization must experiment with past data results to determine which approach most effectively meets its purposes.

Determining Funding Availability Relationships

AN ILLUSTRATION   The period's *incremental funding* is $80,000, as shown in Model 38. The prior period's accumulated funding is $140,000, which is combined with the current period's funding to obtain the *cumulative funding to date* of $220,000. To derive the cumulative funding limit of $154,000, apply a funding limit percentage of 70% to the cumulative funding. This value represents the maximum funding available within a period. The difference between cumulative funding and the maximum available in the current period is $66,000, which is lagged to subsequent period(s).

The following comments pertain to the development of these ratios:

1. The ratio of the *period's incremental funding to the total cumulative funding to date* is 36.4%, as shown in Model 38. If the incremental funding is very sporadic and its amounts vary, this factor may not be reliable

for future planning. Exercise care in its use for planning—but it does represent a possibility.

2. The *period's cumulative funding available (or limit) to total cumulative funding* is generally a customer-negotiated situation—in this instance, 70%. A maximum of 70% of the cumulative funding is available for collection. The funding available limit factor can vary among projects and contracts depending on customer negotiations. This ratio is very important in planning the availability of future funding, which is vital to realistic cash flow projections.

3. Comparing *the cumulative funding available to cumulative progress payment potential limit* yields a ratio of 73.3%, as shown in Model 38. This factor indicates that the progress payment potential ($210,000) is greater than the available funding of $154,000. This means that the funding limit prevails as the basis for progress payment collections. This comparison enables you to plan the extent that progress payments can be collected. The cumulative funding available (the lesser value) therefore represents the cumulative progress payment limit.

Calculating and Using Liquidation Ratios

To determine the amount of liquidations, apply a liquidation limit percentage to the billed sales. Based on the data in Model 38, the liquidation amount for the period is $36,000. The difference between this value and the billed sales of $60,000 is deferred to the next period. To obtain the cumulative total to date, which is $156,000, combine the liquidation limit with the prior accumulated liquidations. Compare this value to the established cumulative payment limit to determine the cumulative liquidation limit of $154,000. This amount is the lesser of the cumulative payment limit or the cumulative liquidations (note the flowchart in Model 37).

The following comments pertain to these ratios:

1. The *current period liquidation limit to total cumulative liquidations* is calculated to be 23.1%, as shown in Model 38. This factor is probably not valid for projection since it represents only a point in time. Its prime importance is in comparing and assessing period-to-period trends in the liquidation limit based on cumulative totals. This assessment indicates whether the limit is growing or decreasing. Either direction has an impact on customer collections, which are of vital concern in the cash flow process.

2. To determine the ratio of the *period liquidation limit to billed sales,* divide the liquidation limit by the billed sales value. The percentage is calculated to be 60%, which is usually a negotiated limit.

3. The ratio of *cumulative liquidations to cumulative funding available* is calculated to be 101%. Since the liquidations exceed the available funding, the funding limit of $154,000 prevails in establishing the cumulative liquidation limit. The ratio can be used to verify the relative size of liquidations versus funding availability. Determining its utilization is difficult depending on the reliability of historical experience and future anticipations.

4. The ratio of *cumulative liquidations to cumulative progress payment limit* is the same as liquidations to funding (101%). The funding is the lesser amount ($154,000) of progress payment potential ($210,000), and thus represents the maximum that can be collected within this time period.

At the bottom of Model 38 is a summary of the data included in the schedule. It presents the prime information used in developing the various ratios.

AUTOMATED CASH FLOW PROCESS AND REPORTING

Model 39 presents an overview of cash flow processing in the computerized environment.

Setting Input and Processing Guidelines

- Product sales and service performance are the basis for *customer billings, receivables, and cash collection scheduling.* The billings represent operating receipts.

- *Nonoperating receipts* result from other cash flow items, such as cash from the sale of capital stock, disposal of fixed assets, bank borrowings, interest income, and so on, as shown in Model 39.

- Operating and nonoperating receipts are combined to obtain *total receipts.*

- The various types of classifications of cash disbursements are shown in the model, and their summary represents the *total cash disbursements.* The lag interval on disbursements will vary among the various items depending on the due dates of scheduled payments.

- The total receipts less the disbursements equals the *net cash increase (decrease)* for the period. To this value, the period beginning cash balance is added to obtain the *end of period balance.*

- Compare pre-established period cash requirements to the period end balance, and calculate the difference as shown in Model 39. If

MODEL 39. Automated Cash Flow and Reporting Process.

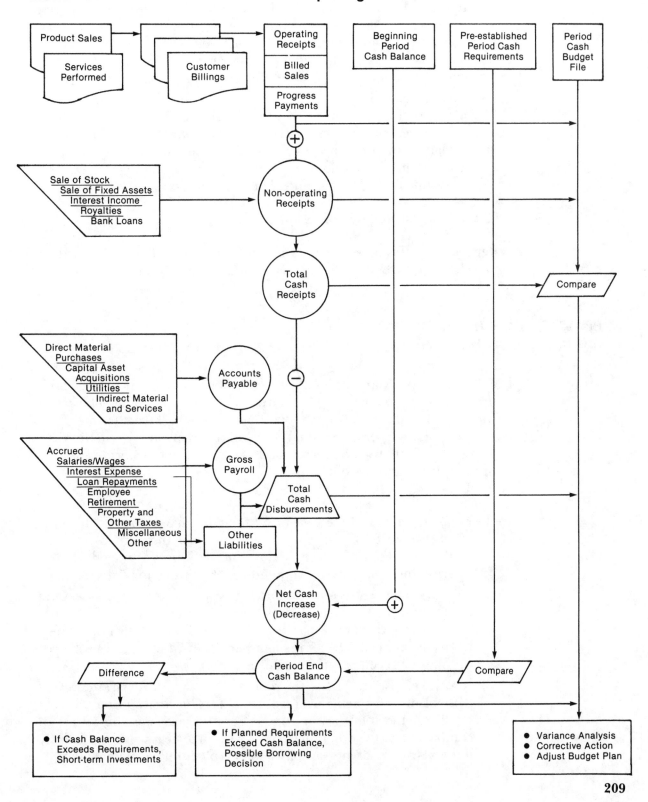

209

the actual cash balance exceeds the cash balance requirements, you might emphasize short-term investment opportunities, loan repayments, and upgrading facilities. If planned requirements exceed the actual cash balance, consider short-term bank borrowings, delaying certain disbursements, accelerating receivable collections, and so on.

- Receipts and disbursement items, as well as the ending cash balance, are compared automatically to the period budget to *determine variances* for possible corrective action and/or adjustments to future cash budget planning. This system is fairly common to most organizations. Item classifications may vary depending on the organization's operations, procedures, and chart of accounts.

Setting Output Requirements

Reports from this system include a period and year-to-date cash schedule, as well as a budget comparison report indicating line item variances.

PREPARING A CASH RECEIPT AND DISBURSEMENT SCHEDULE

Model 40 displays a typical internal cash flow schedule including ratios for assessment, performance measurement, and/or planning. The objective of meaningful ratios is to provide a basis for performance measurement, highlighting problem situations, and future planning—in this case, cash flow projections. The format and processing steps coincide basically with the flowchart in Model 39.

Let's analyze this schedule:

1. Major receipts represent *billed sales and progress payments*, which averaged about 88% of the total collections for the year as reflected by their ratio to total receipts. Customer advances averaged 7% and interest and bank loans accounted for the remaining 5%.

2. The first quarter receipts had the lowest quarterly collection ratio (21.5%) during the year. This is attributed to the low receipts from billed sales and progress payments (ratio of 77.3%). The low receipts were partially offset by a bank loan receipt of $20,000 or 14.6% ratio of the total receipts for the quarter.

3. Relative to disbursements, the ratio of *accounts payable and gross payroll* of total disbursements averaged 91.7%. The first quarter ratio of 22.8% to the total disbursements for the year was the lowest in comparison to the other quarters. The primary cause is the relatively low dollar value of the payables and payroll disbursed in that quarter.

MODEL 40. Cash Flow Schedule:
Cash Receipts, Disbursements and Balances.   *(in $000s)*

Cash Receipts:	*March*	*%*	*June*	*%*	*September*	*%*	*December*	*%*	*Total*	*%*
Billed sales	$ 58.5	42.7	$ 90.0	54.6	$ 86.0	52.7	$ 84.0	49.0	$318.5	50.1
Progress payments	47.3	34.6	54.8	33.3	63.0	38.6	75.4	43.9	240.5	37.8
Customer advances	9.1	6.6	13.0	7.9	12.2	7.5	10.3	6.0	44.6	7.0
Interest income	2.0	1.5	2.0	1.2	1.9	1.2	1.9	1.1	7.8	1.2
Bank loans	20.0	14.6	5.0	3.0	—	—	—	—	25.0	3.9
Total cash receipts	$136.9	100.0	$164.8	100.0	$163.1	100.0	$171.6	100.0	$636.4	100.0
Quarterly receipt ratios to total annual collections		21.5		25.9		25.6		27.0		100.0
Cash Disbursements:										
Accounts payable	$ 85.1	59.0	$ 87.9	56.1	$ 97.1	60.5	$ 97.5	56.8	$367.6	58.0
Payrolls, gross	51.1	35.5	53.9	34.4	54.4	33.9	53.7	31.3	213.1	33.7
Federal income taxes	2.2	1.5	2.2	1.4	1.0	.6	1.0	.6	6.4	1.0
Property and other taxes	1.2	.8	2.7	1.7	2.1	1.3	4.7	2.7	10.7	1.7
Retirement fund	3.5	2.4	—	—	—	—	3.0	1.7	6.5	1.0
Loan repayment	—	—	8.0	5.1	5.0	3.1	10.0	5.8	23.0	3.6
Interest paid	1.1	.8	2.0	1.3	1.0	.6	1.92	1.1	6.02	1.0
Total cash disbursements	$144.2	100.0	$156.7	100.0	$160.6	100.0	$171.82	100.0	$633.32	100.0
Quarterly disbursement ratio to total annual payouts		22.8		24.7		25.4		27.1		100.0
Net cash increase (decrease)	(7.3)		8.1		2.5		(.22)		3.08	
Beginning balance	8.9		1.6		9.7		12.20		8.90	
Ending balance	$ 1.6		$ 9.7		$ 12.2		$ 11.98		$ 11.98	
Ending balance ratio to average annual balance	($8.87)	109.0			138.0		135.0			

$$\frac{18.0}{1.6 \div 8.87} = 18$$

211

4. The various percentage ratios in Model 40 provide a rapid means to compare period results to the annual averages. With them, you can readily highlight deviations for further analyses and possibly corrective action.

5. As a result of the greater disbursements and lower receipts in the first quarter, there was a $7,300 decrease in cash, which resulted in an ending balance of only $1,600. This balance was 18% below the average quarterly balance for the year. The situation was corrected in the second quarter due to an $8,100 increase in receipts over disbursements. The third and fourth quarters also reflected modest increases over the average in the ending cash balances.

Comparing Quarterly Receipt Ratios to Annual Collections

As displayed in Model 40, the quarterly collection ratios to the year's total ranged from 21.5% in the first quarter to 27.0% in the fourth quarter. This range indicates that an assessment of these major differences is in order. A review of the data reveals that the variances are attributed to the following:

1. The fourth quarter *billed sales collections* are 6.3% (49.0% versus 42.7%) greater than those of the first quarter. The annual average is 50.1%. The differences require detailed analysis but the explanatory data are not available in Model 40.

2. The fourth quarter progress payment collections exceed the first quarter receipts by 9.3% (34.6% versus 43.9%). The annual average is 37.8%.

3. The lower sales and progress payment receipts in the first quarter are primarily offset by a 14.6% borrowing receipt (versus zero in the fourth quarter).

Comparing Quarterly Disbursement to Annual Payout Ratios

The *quarterly disbursement ratios to the year's total* ranged from 22.8% in the first quarter to 27.1% in the last quarter. Here are the following contributing causes:

The fourth quarter's combined accounts payable and gross payroll percentages are lower than the first quarter (88.1% versus 94.5%). The difference, however, is partially offset by the higher percentages in the fourth quarter for property and other taxes (2.7%) *plus* loan repayments (5.8%).

Comparing the Quarterly Ending Balance to Annual Average

The quarterly ending balance average is calculated to be $8,870. The ratio of the ending balance to the average balance is 18%, 109%, 138%, and 135%, respectively for the four quarters. The first quarter ratio was significantly below the other quarter ratios, which were all above 100%. The problem in the first quarter requires detailed investigation as to specific causes.

To gauge a need to borrow funds to meet anticipated debt obligations with automated cash flow planning, compare the pre-established cash balance requirement to the resultant cash balance projection. In the actual environment reflected in Model 40, note that $20,000 was borrowed to finance the cash flow deficiency.

ANALYZING RELATIONSHIPS AMONG THE SALES, CASH RECEIPTS, AND RECEIVABLES

Model 41 displays the development of various ratios concerned with the relationships among sales, cash receipts, and receivables. One or more ratios may be valid for use in some organizations but possibly not in others. Their validity and usefulness are predicated on an assessment of historical experience.

Developing the Ratios

Cash receipts to sales deliveries/progress payments. The annual ratio averaged 99.7% ($558.2 ÷ $560.0) as reflected in Model 41. The quarterly ratios range from 98% to 103%. These statistics indicate a reasonable consistency throughout the year. If future experience follows the same pattern, either the period ratio factors or the annual average can provide an acceptable means of projecting cash receipts based on sales/cost anticipations.

The reciprocal of this ratio indicates the relationship of *billed sales/ incurred costs to cash receipts.* Although this information is provided in the model, generally the procedure is to project cash receipts based on the sales/incurred cost forecast, which is the initial planning data in the organization's operating plan.

Ending receivable balance to billed sales deliveries/progress payments. The ratios range from 21.5% to 28.9%, with the largest percentage of 28.9% occurring in the first quarter. The principal cause for the high ratio is the below-average quarterly sales deliveries/cost incurred. Note that *in-*

MODEL 41. Sales, Receipts, and Receivable Balances.

(in $000s)

Accounts Receivable	March	June	September	December	Summary/ Average
Beginning balance	$ 32.6	$ 29.8	$ 32.8	$ 33.8	$ 32.6
Sales deliveries/cost incurred	103.0	147.0	150.0	160.0	560.0
Subtotal	$135.6	$176.8	$182.8	$193.8	$592.6
Cash receipts	105.8	144.0	149.0	159.4	558.2
Ending balance	$ 29.8	$ 32.8	$ 33.8	$ 34.4	$ 34.4
Ratio (%) Development and Analysis					
Receipts to sales/incurred costs	103.0	98.0	99.0	100.0	100.0*
Sales/incurred costs to receipts	97.0	102.0	101.0	100.0	100.0*
Ending balance to sales/incurred costs	28.9	22.3	22.5	21.5	23.8*
Ending balance to sales/incurred costs + beginning balance	22.0	18.6	18.5	17.8	19.2*
Ending balance to receipts	28.2	22.8	22.7	21.6	23.8*
Receipts to ending balance	355.0	439.0	441.0	463.0	424.0*

*Quarterly ratio average was derived by adding the ratios for the four quarters and dividing by four.

curred cost values are generally reflected in the cash receipt *progress payments.*

The *average ratio for the year* is calculated to be 23.8%, as shown in the model. This percentage is based on an average quarterly sales-progress payment of $140,000 and an average ending receivable balance of $32,700.

Ending receivable balance to sales deliveries/progress payments plus the beginning balance. The developed ratios range from 17.8% in the fourth quarter to 22.0% in the first quarter, as shown in Model 41. The average quarterly ratio for the year is calculated to be 19.2%. The annual average is 5.8% ($34.4 ÷ $592.6). To develop the ratio, divide the ending receivable balance by the combined billed sales/progress payments plus the beginning receivable balance. To obtain the quarterly average, divide the sum of the quarters by four in this instance.

The high ratio in the first quarter is attributed primarily to the relatively lower sales deliveries/progress payments as compared to the other periods.

APPLICATIONS   You can use this ratio as a planning factor to estimate the ending receivable balance based on projected billed sales/progress payments plus the beginning balance. Deducting the estimated ending balance from the combined billings plus the beginning balance an *estimated cash collection* value can be obtained. The formula for the first quarter data is:

$$\$135,600 \times 22.0\% \quad = \$29,832 \text{ (ending balance)}$$

$$\$135,600 - \$29,832 = \$105,768 \text{ (cash receipts)}$$

As shown in the model, the ending receivable balance in one quarter becomes the beginning balance in the following quarter or pertinent time period.

Ending receivable balance to cash receipts. The quarterly ratios are comparable to the sales/progress payment ratios because their values are practically on a one-to-one basis with cash receipts ($560,000 versus $558,200 of cash receipts). The figures in the model are annual totals. The quarterly ratios range from 21.6% to 28.2%, with an average of 23.8% per quarter. The high ratio in the first quarter is attributed to the relatively lower cash collection results as compared to subsequent quarters.

APPLICATIONS   This type of ratio can be useful not only for analyzing differences among periods but also as a planning guideline and factor in projecting the ending receivable balance based on cash collection forecasts. Further, if proven to be relatively consistent, the ratio can be utilized to verify or confirm the validity or reasonableness of projected receivable balances that are developed by more detailed and conventional planning procedures.

Cash receipts to ending receivable balance. The quarterly ratios range from a low 355% in the first quarter to a high 463% in the fourth quarter, as shown in Model 41. The ratios are calculated by dividing the cash receipt values by the ending receivable balances. Note that, although *ending balances* are used in the discussion, the more precise method for quarterly periods is to use the *average* for the three-month periods within a quarter. A calculating formula for the first quarter numerically is:

$$\frac{\$105,800 \text{ (receipts)}}{\$29,800 \text{ (receivables)}} = 355\% \text{ ratio}$$

The high ratio of 463% in the fourth quarter is primarily due to the higher-than-average collections, as compared to the other quarterly periods. The receivable balance increased by only 15%, as compared to the first quarter. On the other hand, cash receipts increased 50.7% in the fourth quarter versus the first quarter. Note that the summary total of the quarterly ratios would provide the annual ratio factor.

If the developed ratios prove to be realistic over time and the organization's operations remain reasonably consistent in nature, you may use the factors to estimate cash receipts based on receivable ending balance projections or to check estimated receipts forecasted by other means.

Further, the ratios may be utilized in the "what if" gaming process wherein cash receipts are manipulated by changes in ending receivable balances.

CAUTION IN RATIO USAGE

As useful as ratios are for analysis and planning, you must be aware of their possible shortcomings. As always, be sure that you are using comparable data when comparing one organization's results with those of another. You must also consistently analyze and assess historical experience to establish reliable and meaningful ratio factors.

ANALYZING COSTS, DISBURSEMENTS, AND PAYABLE RATIOS

Model 42 displays various ratios concerned with payable costs, cash disbursements, and accounts payable balances. The ratios are predicated on the data provided in the upper part of the model. The reliability of the ratios depends on the consistency of the operational activity and a thorough assessment of historical experience.

Developing the Ratios

Payable disbursements to payable costs. The quarterly ratios in Model 42 range from a high of 104% in the first quarter to a low of 96.2% in the fourth quarter. To develop the ratios, divide the quarterly disbursements by the quarterly costs. In the first quarter, for example, $85,100 was divided by $82,200 (costs) to obtain the 104% factor.

You can use the ratios for performance assessment of period actuals' activity and for comparisons among periods to determine variations and their causes. Further, the ratios *may be valid* for use in projecting payable disbursements based on payable costs forecasts.

The principal cause for the relatively high ratio in the first quarter is that disbursements exceeded costs whereas the opposite occurred in the fourth quarter with a 96.2% factor.

Payable costs to disbursement ratios. The factors ranged from a low of 96.6% in the first quarter to a 104% in the fourth quarter. This type of ratio may not be much help since disbursements are generally predicated on costs incurred, rather than vice versa. The ratio is therefore presented only as a possible guide when planned disbursements are available and you're estimating a "ballpark" cost figure.

Ending payable balances to costs. The quarterly ratios range from a low of 21.6% in the third quarter to a high of 24.8% in the first quarter, with an annual quarterly average of 23.8%. The primary reason for the low ratio in the third quarter is the high costs incurred, whereas the ending payable balance remained fairly static compared to the first quarter.

MODEL 42. Payable Costs, Disbursements, and Balances.

(in $000s)

Accounts Payable	March	June	September	December	Summary/ Average
Beginning balance	$ 23.3	$ 20.4	$ 21.9	$ 20.7	$ 23.3
Incurred costs	82.2	89.4	95.9	101.4	368.9
Subtotal	$105.5	$109.8	$117.8	$122.1	$392.2
Cash disbursements	85.1	87.9	97.1	97.5	367.6
Ending balance	$ 20.4	$ 21.9	$ 20.7	$ 24.6	$ 24.6
Ratio (%) Development and Analysis					
Ending balance to disbursements	24.0	24.9	21.3	25.2	23.8*
Disbursements to ending balance	417.0	401.0	469.0	396.0	421.0*
Disbursements to costs	104.0	98.3	101.3	96.2	99.9*
Costs to disbursements	96.6	102.0	98.8	104.0	100.3*
Disbursements to BB + costs	80.7	80.1	82.4	79.9	80.8*
Ending balance to costs	24.8	24.5	21.6	24.3	23.8*
Costs to ending balance	403.0	408.0	463.0	412.0	421.0*

Quarterly ratio average was derived by adding the ratios for the four quarters and dividing by four.

The reason for the high ratio of 24.3% in the fourth quarter is an 18.8% ($20,700 to $24,600) increase in the payable balance, as compared to the third quarter. There was only a 5.7% increase in costs ($95,900 to $101,400) for the comparative periods.

Ending payable balance to cost ratios can be used to compare actual results among periods and to provide a projection factor for estimating and planning payable balances based on cost budgets and forecasts. Further, if historical experience is reliable, you can use the ratio to verify projected payable balances that are developed in detail by more conventional planning procedures.

Payable costs to payable ending balance. The ratios are developed in reverse of the order for ending payable balances to cost ratios: divide the costs by the payable balances. As shown in Model 42, the ratios range from 403% in the first quarter to 463% in the third quarter, with an annual quarterly average of 421%. The major cause for the low ratio in the first quarter is the below-average costs. The high ratio of 463% in the third quarter resulted from a comparable ending payable balance to the first quarter but the costs were 16.7% greater ($82.2 to $95.9).

The value of the ratios as planning factors may be questionable, since payable balances are more logically based on cost actuals and projections than this reverse process.

Cash disbursements to ending payable balance. The quarterly ratios range from a low of 396% to a high of 496% in the third quarter, as shown in Model 42. The primary cause for the low ratio in the fourth quarter is the high payable balance, whereas the disbursements are consistent with the third quarter value with its low ending balance.

Using this type of ratio in some organizations may be questionable. The ending payable balance depends more on the disbursement activity than vice versa. In most organizations, cash disbursements are projected first and the ending payable balance results from cost and disbursement calculations. The ratio factors, however, may be helpful as a guide in obtaining "ballpark" disbursement values, but the information must be tempered with caution.

Ending payable balance to disbursement. The quarterly ratios range from a low of 21.3% in the third quarter to a high of 25.2% in the fourth quarter. To develop the ratios, divide the ending payable balance by the disbursement values.

The low ratio of 21.3% in the third quarter can be attributed to the low ending payable balance of $20,700 and the higher-than-average disbursement activity. Conversely, the high ratio of 25.2% in the fourth quarter resulted from the high payable balance of $24,600 versus a disbursement value that was similar to the third quarter with its lower balance.

The ratio factors developed in Model 42 can be used to

- analyze the activity among time periods and assess major variations
- estimate preliminarily ending payable balances based on disbursement values

You have to review historical experience to determine the validity of these factors for use in your organization. Although the ratios demonstrate the relationship among the data, each organization must determine their value, their usefulness for analysis and planning, and possible reservations about their employment.

Payable disbursements to beginning payable balance plus costs. The quarterly ratios vary from 79.9% in the fourth quarter to a high of 82.4% in the third quarter. The low ratio in the fourth quarter is due to high costs, while the disbursements remained relatively the same as in the third quarter. The high ratio of 82.4% in the third quarter resulted from a combined increase of 7.3% in the beginning payable balance and costs over the second period, whereas disbursements increased 10.5%.

APPLICATION   The annual ratio average of 80.8% appears to be fairly representative of the four quarters' financial activity. If the factor proves to be valid, you can project the payable disbursements based on an estimated beginning payable balance plus costs.

If you obtain a consistent disbursement application factor and calculate reliable estimated disbursements, then you can approximate the projected ending payable balances. As shown in Model 42, the beginning balance of $23,300 for the first quarter, plus the payable costs of $82,200 and less the disbursements of $85,100, results in an ending balance of $20,400. This amount becomes the beginning balance in the subsequent period, and so on thereafter for monthly and quarterly periods.

CAUTION   The ratio factors in Model 42 may serve as performance assessment and planning guidelines. As always, their usefulness in an organization depends on the reliability of historical experience and the assumption that future operational anticipations will remain relatively consistent.

ASSESSING ACCRUED SALARIES/WAGES, COSTS, AND BALANCES

In addition to payable costs, assessing gross payroll costs is generally one of the significant costs in operating a business enterprise.

Developing the Salaries/Wages (S/W) Ending Balances

CALCULATION
PROCESS

	Accrued (S/W) beginning balance (prior period)
(+)	Current period accrued payroll costs
(=)	Subtotal (outstanding payroll costs)
(−)	Period cash disbursements
(=)	Accrued (S/W) ending balance (current period)

The following relationships can be employed for assessing financial performance based on historical analysis and planning guidelines.

1. Period cash *disbursements* versus current *period accrued* payroll costs.
2. Period *accrued payroll costs* as a percentage of payroll *disbursements*.
3. Accrued payroll *ending balance* as a percentage of *current period payroll* costs.
4. Period *payroll cost relationship* to accrued payroll *ending balance*.
5. Period payroll *disbursement relationship* to accrued payroll *ending balance*.
6. Period *ended payroll balance* as a percentage of payroll *disbursements*.

7. Period payroll *disbursements* as a percentage of *accrued salaries/wages beginning balance* plus current *period accrued gross payroll costs.*

To calculate all these ratios, divide the first data element indicated by the following data identifier. For example, in the first entry, divide the *disbursements* by the *accrued payroll costs.*

As in the case of payables, you must exercise discretion in the use of these ratios. To determine their reliability and validity in assessing performance and their usefulness as planning guidelines, a thorough analysis must be made of the ratio results.

9

Employing Statistical Techniques for Effective Planning and Operations

CHAPTER HIGHLIGHTS

How do ratios make operations and planning effective? This chapter demonstrates how statistical and graphic display techniques can help you to analyze and interpret financial data with an eye toward fixing operating policies and establishing realistic planning objectives. As always, however, remember that statistical tools provide only basic data assessment. You must supply the judgmental analysis and interpretation before reliably employing the methods for planning or assessment.

The *cost-volume-profit* relationships are concerned with profit optimization, specifically with product sales price, production costs, and volume sold. Break-even analysis is illustrated with graphic display charts. The effects of plant expansion costs, production costs, sales increases, operating income, and plant capacity are all relevant to the break-even point. The advantages and disadvantages of each are explained.

The *profitgraph technique* is explained and its objectives described. You will familiarize yourself with the relevance of break-even analysis and the impact on profit goals. You will see the relationships of cost and operating income analysis, as well as investment assessment criteria and applications, to product line, performance measurement, pricing decisions, and facility expansion.

The *capitalgraph model* is illustrated by means of case data—how it is constructed and used. A practical example demonstrates how the operating capital position results from the status of current assets and liabilities and net fixed assets versus the impact of fluctuating sales volumes.

Although illustrated throughout the chapter, the *least squares correlation* procedure is the focus of the last section of the chapter.

Various statistical techniques can be used not only in analyzing results from operating events, but they can also provide a realistic basis for establishing and achieving financial goals and objectives. To use these techniques, however, you must thoroughly understand the procedures, their significance, and their applicability. You must also assess and interpret your organization's operational results, because some of the techniques in this chapter may not apply to *all* organizations. Yet a thorough screening through practical application will undoubtedly reveal the limitations of these techniques or their potential as a useful and effective tool for an organization's consideration.

The procedures described in this chapter are concerned with

- cost-volume-profit relationships
- operating leverage ratios
- break-even point usage and illustrations
- profitgraph techniques
- capitalgraph assessment
- the principles of least squares correlation

MAKING USE OF COST-VOLUME-PROFIT RELATIONSHIPS

INFLUENCES ON PROFITABILITY   Of basic and sensitive concern in a business enterprise is *profit optimization* and how to accomplish it successfully. The three major influences on an organization's profitability are:

- product sales price
- cost of producing and delivering the product
- product demand and/or volume sold

The product or service sales price is equal to the cost of production or of performing the service plus a reasonable profit. The sales price is generally a governing factor in the volume sold. In turn, the production volume influences the cost; hence, the interaction among price, volume, and cost. An organization must be able not only to measure and understand the impact of these factors, but also how to keep them in proper proportion.

Analyzing the Break-even Point

The fundamental accounting concept is that sales income less costs equals profits. Assessing the break-even point is a common tool used in measuring the relationship among costs (variable and fixed), volume (sales revenue), and net income. The vertical axis (*y*) on a break-even chart represents dollar costs and sales. The horizontal axis indicates volume, which can be expressed in terms of product units, machine hours, pounds, gallons, and so on.

To calculate the break-even analysis, use the following equation:

$$\text{Break-even sales} = \frac{\text{Fixed expenses}}{1 - \dfrac{\text{Variable expenses}}{\text{Sales}}}$$

Example: Let us estimate sales to produce a zero income from operations:

Sales	$300,000
Variable expenses	(234,000)
Fixed expenses	(36,000)
Income from operations	$30,000

Calculation:

$$\text{Break-even sales} = \frac{36,000}{1 - \dfrac{234,000}{300,000}}$$

$$= \frac{36,000}{1 - .78 \text{ or } .22}$$

$$= 163,636$$

The break-even sales are calculated to be $163,636. Let's go one step further and assume that the objective is to estimate sales on a zero pretax profit in which there was an additional expense for interest. In that case, add the interest to the fixed expenses, and recompute the equation to reflect the difference in the break-even point.

Variable expenses (utilities, repairs, supplies) fluctuate with production volume, whereas fixed expenses do not because of their usual constant nature (depreciation, leases, insurance). Some expenses can be semivariable, that is, they may fluctuate to a degree but not in direct proportion to volume changes. At times, segregating semivariable costs from the variable or fixed expenses is difficult, and very often the distinction is one of judgmental categorization.

HOW TO CALCULATE THE OPERATING LEVERAGE RATIO

Fluctuations in sales dollars can have a decided effect on operating profits, particularly when fixed expenses are high. To measure the operating leverage, use the following equation.

THE FORMULA

$$\text{Operating leverage} = \frac{\text{Sales} - \text{Variable expenses}}{\text{Sales} - \text{Total expenses}}$$

Examples: Let's use the data from the previous example.

(1) $\dfrac{\$300,000 - \$234,000}{\$300,000 - \$270,000} = \dfrac{\$66,000}{\$30,000} = 2.2$ times

If the sales increase or decrease by 15% the leverage results change as follow:

(2) $\$300,000 \times +15\% = \$45,000 + \$300,000$ or $\$345,000$

$\dfrac{\$345,000 - \$234,000}{\$345,000 - \$270,000} = \dfrac{\$111,000}{\$75,000} = +1.48$ times

(3) $\$300,000 \times -15\% = -\$45,000; \$300,000 - \$45,000 = \$255,000$

$\dfrac{\$255,000 - \$234,000}{\$255,000 - \$270,000} = \dfrac{\$21,000}{\$-15,000} = -1.4$ times

Example (1) indicates that the operating leverage is 2.2 times sales of $300,000, with variable expenses of $234,000 and total expenses of $270,000. Under the leverage concept, income from operations change 2.2 times the percentage change in sales from the original base. For instance, if there is a 15% change in sales, then the estimated operating income would be approximately 33% (15% × 2.2). In this example, the operating income would change by $9,900 ($30,000 × 33%).

Examples (2) and (3) show how the leverage changes when the sales base increases and decreases by 15%—assuming there are no changes in the fixed and variable expenses (rarely possible). The results are a +1.48 and a −1.4 times the percentage change in the revised sales base.

Making Use of the Leverage Factor

The operating leverage enables you to assess the income risk resulting from a change in sales volume. In Example (3), a 15% decline in sales resulted in an *estimated negative factor* of 1.4 times the income from operations. The *operating risk* results from the level of fixed operating expenses. The *financial risk* in an organization, on the other hand, arises from the use of debt support by creditors—both short and long term. In the evaluation of financial leverage ratios, you can gain an informative insight as to the total operating risk resulting from sales volume fluctuations and increased creditor debt. Fixed expenses have an important impact on an organization's total risk.

HOW TO ILLUSTRATE THE BREAK-EVEN POINT

Typically, break-even charts display graphically the two types of expenses that influence operating profits based on a given sales level. Break-even analyses involve the segregation of costs into fixed and variable. The break-even chart is based on (1) estimated price levels and (2) fixed and variable cost trends. The *break-even point* is the volume at which sales and total costs are equal. Contribution margin represents the difference between sales and variable costs, which is used to absorb fixed costs, taxes, and profits. In essence, this type of analysis is concerned with volume, sales mix, and management operating efficiency in controlling costs and the use of investment resources.

Model 43 demonstrates different versions of break-even analysis.

Sales and Variable Expenses Only

In Figure 1 of Model 43, all expenses are assumed to be variable (not a typical situation), and the operating income of $66,000 represents a 22% ratio to sales. With no fixed expenses, the diagonal line is drawn from the "0" locations to a point on the total variable expense (the vertical axis) representing $234,000. The difference between the sales dollars and expenses represents the operating income. The income at varying sales unit volumes is reflected by the vertical distance between the lines representing sales and variable expenses.

The sales line rising at a 45-degree angle represents the increases in sales (on the vertical axis) and results from increases in unit volume (on the horizontal axis). The principal assumption in this instance is that the product mix and sales price remain constant.

Significance of Fixed Costs on Break-even

The greater the fixed expense, the higher will be the break-even point, as demonstrated in Model 43. An increase of $14,000 in fixed expense resulted in the break-even point rising 38.9% ($163,636 to $227,272). In the short-run, fixed costs cannot be immediately reduced to meet declining customer sales product demand. Certain fixed costs remain fairly constant, such as taxes, insurance, rent or lease costs, depreciation, security and certain aspects of administration (accounting, supervision, marketing). Most of the fixed costs are essential in order to maintain the integrity and environment survival of the organization.

As sales revenue decreases and fixed costs remain fairly constant, the earnings will naturally decline accordingly because of the fixed cost

MODEL 43. Cost-Volume-Profit Relationships and Break-even Points.

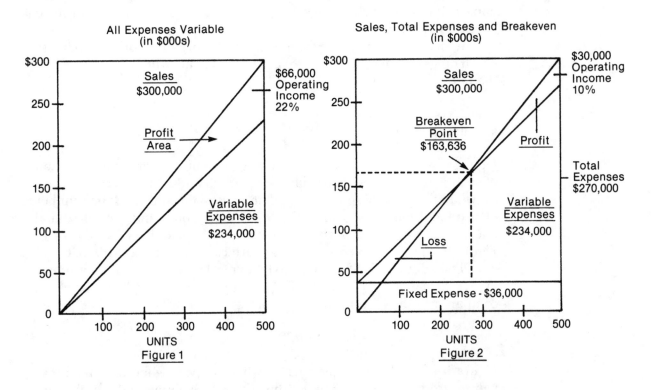

All Expenses Variable
(in $000s)

Sales $300,000

$66,000 Operating Income 22%

Profit Area

Variable Expenses $234,000

UNITS
Figure 1

Sales, Total Expenses and Breakeven
(in $000s)

Sales $300,000

$30,000 Operating Income 10%

Breakeven Point $163,636

Profit

Total Expenses $270,000

Variable Expenses $234,000

Loss

Fixed Expense - $36,000

UNITS
Figure 2

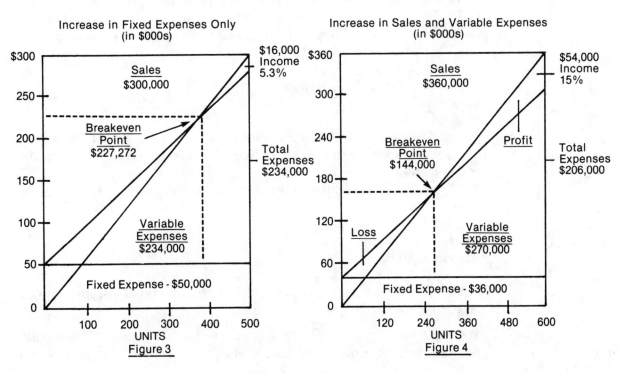

Increase in Fixed Expenses Only
(in $000s)

Sales $300,000

$16,000 Income 5.3%

Breakeven Point $227,272

Total Expenses $234,000

Variable Expenses $234,000

Fixed Expense - $50,000

UNITS
Figure 3

Increase in Sales and Variable Expenses
(in $000s)

Sales $360,000

$54,000 Income 15%

Breakeven Point $144,000

Profit

Total Expenses $206,000

Loss

Variable Expenses $270,000

Fixed Expense - $36,000

UNITS
Figure 4

227

impact. It is only logical to assume that an organization with greater fixed expenses must have larger sales revenue to break even.

If sales revenues increase, however, the organization can increase its earnings position because the increased income will more than offset the fixed cost needs.

Sales, Total Expenses, and Break-even

Figure 2 in Model 43 shows the break-even point to be at the intersection of sales and the total expense line. Horizontal and vertical dash lines are drawn to the point of intersection. The vertical line indicates the number of product units to be sold at the break-even point, and the horizontal line represents the sales volume in thousands of dollars. As shown in Figure 2, the break-even sales dollars are calculated to be $163,636.

The addition of $36,000 in fixed expenses (shown at the bottom of Figure 2) led to a reduction of operating income to 10% of sales, as compared to the 22% results in Figure 1.

Increase in Fixed Expenses Only

Figure 3 in Model 43 demonstrates what happens when only fixed expenses are increased by $14,000 but the sales volume and variable expenses remain the same. The break-even point increases from $163,636 to $227,272. The break-even point is thus raised to a higher level on the chart. Conversely, the opposite effect (a downtrend) is experienced if the fixed expenses decreased.

Increasing Sales and Variable Expenses

Figure 4 in the model shows the results of increasing sales by 20% ($60,000) and variable expenses by 15.4% ($36,000). Fixed expenses remain at the original $36,000 level.

The ratio of operating income to sales is calculated to be 15%. The break-even point is reduced to $144,000, as plotted on the graph.

Analyzing Data by Means of Alternate Methods

Model 44 demonstrates two alternate cost volume relationships that can be used for analyzing and assessing data.

Method 1. In Figure 1, the scattergraph technique is used. The plotted points represent two years of historical experience; costs were measured

MODEL 44. Cost-Volume-Profit Relationships: Alternate Plotting Techniques.

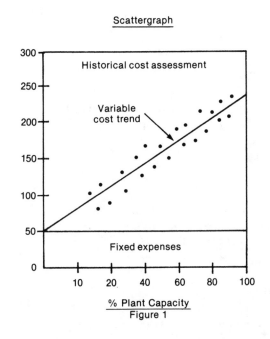

Scattergraph

% Plant Capacity
Figure 1

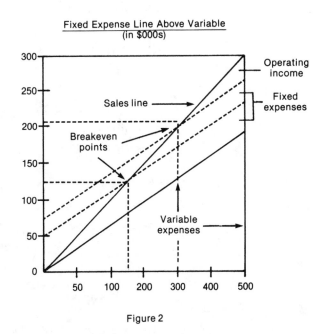

Fixed Expense Line Above Variable
(in $000s)

Figure 2

against sales based on percentage of plant capacity. Fixed expenses are presumed to be constant in this illustration, but variable expenses fluctuate with production volume.

Using the least squares correlation approach, you can calculate a representative line (a pattern of cost behavior) and fit it to the data, or you can just determine the line from visual observation. The regression line represents the average location of the plotted points. By extending the line slope, you can estimate costs based on past performance results.

APPLICATION   The break-even point formula can be used to determine the intersection between cost and volume, which indicates the sales break-even and the percentage of plant capacity.

Method 2. In Figure 2 in Model 44, the fixed expense line is drawn parallel and above the variable line slope. In other words, the fixed line represents the expenses added to variable costs.

Let's assume that costs are the only production expense. The vertical distance between the total variable expense line and sales then represents the *contribution margin,* whereas the distance between the total expense line and sales is indicative of the *operating income.* If the variable expenses maintain a constant pattern, then any change in the fixed expense results in *raising or lowering* the break-even point depending on whether fixed costs increase or decrease. You can draw fixed expense lines to reflect various situations and ascertain estimated break-even points for gaming and/or planning purposes.

Putting Break-even Analysis to Work

Break-even analysis enables you to highlight the factors relevant to expenses and sales. The practical applications will be illustrated through the use of equations.

Example:

S = Net sales	$400,000	100.0
VE = Variable expense	(238,000)	(59.5)
FE = Fixed expense	(42,000)	(10.5)
Operating income	$120,000	30.0

1. Current break-even point:

$$\text{Break-even sales} = \frac{FE}{1 - \dfrac{VE}{S}} = \frac{\$42,000}{1 - \dfrac{\$238,000}{400,000}} = \frac{\$42,000}{.405} = \begin{array}{c}\$103,704 \\ \text{(break-even)}\end{array}$$

2. Plant expansion will create higher fixed expenses of $30,000:

$$\text{Break-even sales} = \frac{\$72,000}{1 - \dfrac{\$238,000}{\$400,000}} = \frac{\$72,000}{.405} = \begin{array}{c}\$177,778 \\ \text{(break-even)}\end{array}$$

3. Sales will have to increase by $74,074 ($177,778 − $103,704): Hence the difference in break-even points to achieve the current operating income of $120,000:

Current sales of $400,000 + $74,074 = $474,074.

4. To verify the sales increase required to maintain current income:

$$\text{Sales} = \$72,000 + .595S + \$120,000$$
$$S - .595S = \$72,000 + \$120,000$$
$$.405S = \$192,000$$
$$S = \underline{\$474,074} \text{ (revised as shown above)}$$

5. Verifying current net income results through increased sales needs:

		%
Revised net sales	$474,074	100.0
Less: Revised FE	(72,000)	(15.2)
Revised VE	(282,074)	(59.5)
Current operating income	$120,000	25.3

6. Summation of calculations illustrated above:

   a. *Sales* have to increase by $74,074 to maintain current operating income.

   b. *Fixed expenses* have to increase by $30,000 to meet plant expansion needs. *Variable expenses* increased to $282,074 ($474,074 × 59.5%).

   c. *Current operating income* now represents 25.3% of sales versus 30% previously. The difference of 4.7% is reflected in the increased fixed expense as a percentage of sales (from original 10.5% to 15.2%).

   d. If sales do not increase as required to maintain current income, then the higher fixed expense of $30,000 will reduce current income results to $90,000. Plant expansion is assumed to result in greater sales volume achievement.

These computations are merely approximations based on the assumption that all expenses are either fixed or variable.

Calculating the Percentage of Plant Capacity at Which an Organization Will Break Even

Example: Let's make the following assumptions:

- Present level of production is 80% of plant capacity.
- Fixed expense is established at $72,000.
- Sales are $474,074; variable expenses are $282,074.
- The relationship between plant capacity and dollar sales is constant.
- x represents the percentage of plant capacity at break-even.

We use the following formula:

$$x = \frac{FE \times \% \text{ plant capacity}}{\text{Sales} - VE}$$

And here is the calculation:

$$x = \frac{\$72,000 \times 80\%}{\$474,074 - \$282,074} = \frac{\$57,600}{\$192,000} = 30\%$$

CAUTION   These hypothetical data are used only to illustrate the computation process. This application can, however, be used to *approximate* an estimated percentage of plant capacity at the break-even point based on the realistic data available. The objective is to ascertain plant capacity requirements.

Example: Let's make the following assumptions:

x = Sales volume required at present prices to produce an operating income of 120,000.

OI = Income required to compensate for plant expansion costs.

FE = $42,000.

VE = $238,000.

S = $400,000.

A = Additional FE of $30,000.

Here is the formula with the calculations:

$$x = \frac{OI + FE + A}{1 - \dfrac{VE}{S}}$$

$$= \frac{\$120,000 + \$42,000 + \$30,000}{1 - \dfrac{\$238,000}{\$400,000}}$$

$$= \frac{\$192,000}{1 - .595} = \frac{\$192,000}{.405}$$

$$= \$474,074$$

This is another version of Item 4 in the first example. If the organization's objective is to maintain the same operating income level in spite of increased expenses, it needs a sales volume of $474,074.

ASSUMPTIONS TO REMEMBER IN BREAK-EVEN ASSESSMENT

If variable costs remain constant, the increases or decreases in fixed expenses change the break-even position (either higher or lower on the chart). This factor should not affect volume changes.

If the general price level changes significantly, you should review the break-even point and make revisions accordingly.

For more realistic results in the analysis, identify fixed and variable costs based on historical experience and your own judgment. Segregating semivariable expenses into fixed and variable is highly desirable.

In the preceding discussion and analysis, only one product is assumed. If there is a varying number, however, the sales mix is presumed not to change, with its incorporated different sales mix gross margins.

Selling prices are generally assumed not to change with volume; hence, the sales line is straight. As price changes occur, supplemental sales lines can be drawn to reflect this situation.

Weighing the Pros and Cons of Break-even Analysis

Like most techniques, break-even analysis may have a degree of inaccuracy in its use and interpretation, and it has its advantages and disadvantages.

Advantages

1. Break-even analysis provides a forceful communication tool in demonstrating the relationship and interaction of cost, volume, and profit. If properly utilized and relevant, it aids in establishing realistic profit objectives and operating budgets.

2. It provides management with a distinctive insight into the economic characteristics of its business, not only in terms of the fixed and variable expenses at varying sales volumes, but also of the break-even relationship and its effect on the consequences of unearned income required to support the investors' return on both the preferred and common stock equities. Through break-even chart presentations you can readily determine the effect of changes in these relationships.

3. You can advantageously employ "what if" gaming to determine the anticipated results from contemplated managerial decisions. The break-even process may involve such planning questions as plant expansion, equipment modernization, change in product mix or sales prices, and the introduction of new product lines.

4. Management is often confronted with the decision to increase sales volume with an optimistic view toward enhancing profit. Profit enhancing is a possibility, providing costs are controlled within prescribed limits. The break-even technique can be an important tool

in establishing expenditure constraints and control by adequate surveillance.

5. An important influence on profit is the product sales mix with variable gross margins. The break-even chart can highlight problem situations requiring corrective management action, but you must first be aware of the problem.

Disadvantages

1. Break-even analysis is not panacea. It cannot be used unquestionably without a thorough understanding of its concept and limitations.

2. The break-even chart generally reflects a number of estimates and judgments, which may be misleading as to the resultant data developed and their implication. For example, measuring costs and sales volume at a particular output level may be an inaccurate method of assessment, particularly when the volume approaches the break-even point, which can change depending on operating circumstances.

3. Usually, the break-even is developed at a point that represents a static position. Changes in relationship factors should be correctly and logically reflected in a revised chart or a series of charts.

4. The improper understanding and usage of the charts can lead to inadequate decision making, inaccurate planning assumptions, and possibly inhibited control actions.

5. Fixed and variable expenses may be inaccurately segregated with the resultant effect on the break-even position. Plotting sales as a function of production volume may be misleading; the assumption that sales equals production activity may not necessarily be true because of the buildup or reduction of inventories at varying business cycles. Exercise extreme care in compiling homogeneous and compatible data for the break-even analysis.

USING THE PROFITGRAPH TECHNIQUE

APPLICATIONS   The profitgraph technique is used principally for profit measurement and control. It is concerned with management decisions involving product and plant profitability, improvement and/or expansion of plant facilities, performance measurement and operational control. In our discussion, the emphasis is on determining the probable pattern of gross margin, net income, and return on investment.

In constructing a profitgraph, you must understand the underlying principles of product price and costs and how, particularly, changing volume affects costs. Profitgraph construction and usage involve (1) break-even analysis and (2) the principles of variable budgeting.

Relating Break-even Assessment to the Profitgraph Technique

A break-even analysis reflects two separate measures of the relative profitability of varied product line: fixed and variable costs. In long-range planning, for example, fixed costs are generally flexible over longer time spans, and you can compare and assess product line profit potentials. In the immediate period(s), fixed costs are fairly stable; the contribution margin as a percentage of or ratio to sales provides a more realistic measure of individual product profitability and the effect resulting from the sales mix.

APPLICATIONS

Relative to operating efficiency, you can use the break-even charts to compare alternate planning courses of action and their effect on proposed projects. In facilities planning, the cost for additions can be compared to lower cost producton or increased capacity.

In reviewing cost-reduction projects as an analyst, you can compare the cost of new methods with the anticipated savings. Further, break-even analysis can be used as a budgetary control tool for measuring performance and the results from decision making.

Example: Let's see how break-even principles are reflected in the break-even charts.

Sales Volume	Variable Expenses 70%	Contribution Margin 30%	Fixed Expenses	Pretax Profit (Loss) Value	Pretax Profit (Loss) % of Sales
$20,000	$14,000	$6,000	$6,500	$(500)	(2.5)
$22,000	$15,400	$6,600	$6,600	*Break-even	0
$25,000	$17,500	$7,500	$6,600	900	3.6

*$6,600 ÷ 30% = $22,000 sales. Sales under $22,000 result in a loss, but above that value there are anticipated profits.

Understanding the Principles of Variable Budgeting

The variable budget is a management tool used primarily for monitoring and controlling production costs. Comparative analyses are made between allowed and actual costs, and variances are assessed relative to cost control performance.

In the production process, certain expenses are generally fixed and others are variable. When related to *unit costs,* fixed expenses actually become variable with volume changes, whereas variable expenses become fixed with volume changes. Generally, fixed costs remain constant regardless of sales volume changes (which is untrue for unit costs).

Examples of fixed costs include depreciation, property taxes, rentals, and so on. Variable costs fluctuate in direct proportion to product output or sales volume. Typical examples include direct labor, material, maintenance, utilities, supplies, and so on. Semivariable expenses may vary with production output but not in the same relative proportion; in other words, their increases are periodic or "step movement" with volume.

Volume, representing the rate of activity, is measured in terms of production or sales units or dollars, direct labor hours or dollars, machine hours, weight, and so on. Product unit measures are probably more significant than dollars because they do not reflect the effect of changes in price and wage levels. For purposes of management presentation, however, unit volumes should be converted to dollars, which are more readily interpreted and understood.

The basic considerations in constructing the variable budget include the following:

- Generally, use at least five volume levels, with the range from 40% to 100% of plant capacity.
- For each account and selected volume level, develop budgeted expenses by cost center and department—both production and service.
- Express the data in terms of the number of employee (as applicable) and of dollars by time period.
- The budget reflects the best judgment and experience of the individual supervisors and their management.
- Develop scattergraphs for each expense item that illustrates the principle of segregating fixed and variable expenses.

Model 45 illustrates a variable budget scattergraph chart for operating supplies. The horizontal line at the bottom of the chart represents units of production, and the vertical scale indicates the weekly expense allowance. The plotted points reflect the budgeted expense for the various volume levels. A trend line is drawn so that it either passes through the points or as close as possible to them, since it represents the median of the various points. At the intersection of the diagonal line on the left vertical axis, the point represents the fixed expense value, which is $875 in this case.

Establishing the Ratio of Variable Expenses to Production Volume

Calculate the variable expenses by means of the following equation:

**MODEL 45. Variable Budget Scattergraph Chart:
Production Department.**

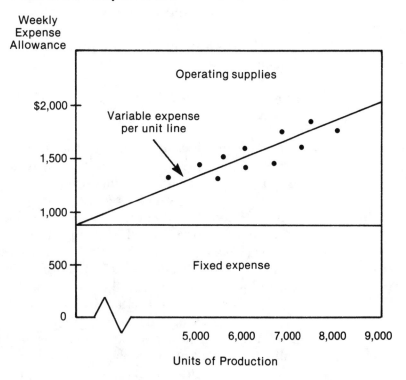

$$\text{Variable expense} = \frac{\text{Total expense allowance} - \text{Allowed fixed expense}}{\text{Production volume}}$$

Example:

$$\text{Variable expense} = \frac{\$2,000 - \$875}{9,000}$$

$$= \frac{\$1,125}{9,000}$$

$$= \$0.125$$

ASSESSING THE PROFITGRAPH TECHNIQUE

While the break-even displays the profit-volume relationship based on the segregation of fixed and variable expenses, the profitgraph presents a broader view of the business. To obtain more comprehensive information for management decisions, the technique makes use of both the break-even and investment analyses. These data relate primarily to profit measurements, such as gross margin, net income, and return on investment. The profitgraph provides not only the sales break-even and the profit at any level of capacity, but also the trend patterns of gross margin, net income, and return on investment *ratios* under a given set of conditions.

Model 46 summarizes the profitgraph principles. The terminology is commonly used in the accounting profession.

Analyzing Cost and Operating Income

Model 47 provides an overview of an income statement to the point of gross margin from operations and its ratio to sales revenue. The statement is segregated into four volume levels (or capacities)—40%, 60%, 80%, and 100%. Dollar values are shown for the various elements plus the estimated number of employees (as applicable) for direct labor activities and indirect support based on volume levels. In a more detailed analysis, the overhead expenses are typically arranged by individual accounts and their associated headcounts. This information serves as a comparative control tool in analyzing and planning performance results.

The expense information in Model 47 is similar to that in a break-even analysis except that it is segregated into fixed and variable costs. Under the variable caption are also reported the direct labor and material values representing percentages of *x* dollar values of sales revenue. The fixed and variable costs of sales are developed for the break-even analysis presentation.

The *ratios* of operating income to sales range from 6% at 40% volume to 20% at the 100% level. The principal cause for the increased operating income is a *250%* higher sales volume at the 100% capacity versus the 40% level, whereas cost of sales increased by only *222%*.

Assessing Investments

At this point in developing the profitgraph, you have to assess net investment. To do so, consolidate the gross current assets (including short-term marketable securities if existent but excluding prepaid expense) with the gross fixed assets to obtain a total as shown in Model 48. From this total, deduct the reserve for receivables (doubtful accounts), inventories, and fixed assets (depreciation). Some organizations may have other reserves in this presentation. Combine short-term liabilities, such as accounts payable, with the reserves; this total represents a reduction to gross investment. The result is net investment by the categorized sales volumes.

Example: Note, in Model 48, that *net* investment is estimated to increase by 35% in the 50 million sales volume level, as compared to the $20 million level. This is due to an anticipated 31% higher *gross* investment, which

MODEL 46. Fundamentals of Profitgraph Analysis.

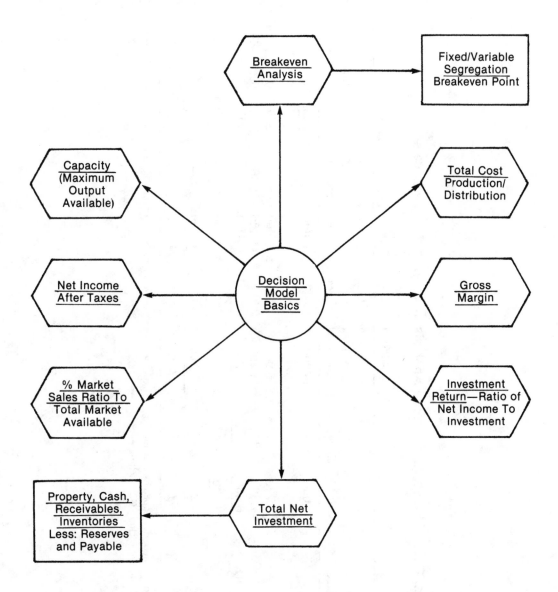

results from a greater current asset value with only a 17% increase in reserves.

Net investment may be computed in other ways depending on an organization's policies and procedures. Three of the more common methods are as follows:

1. Net *working capital* (excluding reserves) plus net fixed assets and owners' equity (including retained earnings).
2. Total net assets less current liabilities equals owners' equity and cred-

MODEL 47. Sales, Cost of Sales, and Income Analysis at Varying Volume Levels.

(in $000s)

| | Volume Levels—% Capacity | | | | | | | |
| | 40% | | 60% | | 80% | | 100% | |
Income Statement Data	Value	Employed	Value	Employed	Value	Employed	Value	Employed
Net sales	$20,000	—	$30,000	—	$40,000	—	$50,000	—
Cost of Sales								
Direct labor	$ 4,700	313	$ 6,900	445	$ 9,000	560	$11,200	710
Overhead*	7,500	234	11,200	290	14,400	360	17,600	440
Direct material/ODC	6,600	—	8,600	—	10,200	—	11,200	—
Totals	$18,800	547	$26,700	735	$33,600	920	$40,000	1150
Operating income	$ 1,200	—	$ 3,300	—	$ 6,400	—	$10,000	—
Ratio to sales	6.0%		11.0%		16.0%		20.0%	

*As required, expense data can be developed by individual major expense account (segregated, fixed and variable) using the scattergraph technique. These overhead dollars do not include G&A/selling expenses.

MODEL 48. Capital Investment Assessment (Profitgraph).

(in $000s)

	Sales Volume Levels			
Item Description	*$20,000*	*$30,000*	*$40,000*	*$50,000*
Current Assets				
Cash	$ 1,300	$ 1,600	$ 2,200	$ 2,800
Receivables	1,660	2,400	3,200	4,000
Inventories	1,070	1,300	1,500	1,600
Subtotal	$ 4,030	$ 5,300	$ 6,900	$ 8,400
Gross Fixed Assets	10,000	10,000	10,000	10,000
Total Gross Investment	$14,030	$15,300	$16,900	$18,400
Ratio to sales volume	.715	.510	.423	.368
Return on operating income*	.085	.216	.379	.543
Reserves				
Receivables	$ 60	$ 70	$ 110	$ 120
Inventories	100	110	120	120
Depreciation	2,500	2,500	2,500	2,500
Subtotal	$ 2,660	$ 2,680	$ 2,730	$ 2,740
Accounts payable	430	600	720	870
Total reductions	$ 3,090	$ 3,280	$ 3,450	$ 3,610
Net Investment	$10,940	$12,020	$13,450	$14,790
Ratio to sales volume	.547	.401	.336	.295
Return on operating income*	.110	.275	.476	.676

*Dollar values of operating income are shown in Model 47.

itor investment. In this case, long-term debt is recognized as a *creditor* investment.

3. Total net assets less current liabilities plus owners' equity.

Summarizing Profitgraph Data

Model 49 provides a summary of sales volume levels and net income plus the *ratio* of net income to net investment. The ratios range from .9% at the $20 million sales volume level to 25.4% at the $50 million level. The primary cause for the dramatic increase in the ratio is the rise in net income from $100,000 to $3.75 million at the $50 million sales volume level. On the other hand, net investment is only 35% greater at the $50 million volume.

   Although not shown in the model, summary data are highly desirable in a profitgraph chart. They should display the break-even analysis (cost

MODEL 49. Profitgraph Data Summary.
(in $000s)

Income Statement	Values	% Sales	Values	% Sales	Values	% Sales	Values	% Sales
Sales volumes	$20,000	100.0	$30,000	100.0	$40,000	100.0	$50,000	100.0
Cost of sales	18,800	94.0	26,700	89.0	33,600	84.0	40,000	80.0
Operating income	$ 1,200	6.0	$ 3,300	11.0	$ 6,400	16.0	$10,000	20.0
Less: G&A/selling	1,000	5.0	1,500	5.0	2,000	5.0	2,500	5.0
Pretax profit	$ 200	1.0	$ 1,800	6.0	$ 4,400	11.0	$ 7,500	15.0
Less: Reserve for taxes	100	.5	900	3.0	2,200	5.5	3,750	7.5
Net Income	$ 100	.5	$ 900	3.0	$ 2,200	5.5	$ 3,750	7.5
Net investment	$10,940	54.7	$12,020	40.1	$13,450	33.6	$14,790	29.6
Total costs (excluding taxes)	19,800	—	28,200	—	35,600	—	42,500	—
Ratio: *Net income to investment*	.9%		7.5%		16.4%		25.4%	
Total costs to investment	1.81%		2.35%		2.65%		2.87%	

242

and sales lines) and a percentage scale on the *right vertical axis*, which indicates the percentage of return on net investment as well as the gross margin return on sales. The summary graphic numeric display in Model 49 provides an immediate visual view of the profit situation in relation to sales volume levels, associated cost and income, as well as the return on investment.

How to Apply the Profitgraph

The profitgraph helps management to assess its planning actions/decisions relative to anticipated profits and performances at varying sales volume levels. This type of aid is extremely important in achieving profit objectives, in attracting equity investments, and in providing a reasonable return on the investors' capital. Further, a sound profit position aids the organization in obtaining financial institution loans at favorable rates and in generating good working relationships with current and anticipated creditors.

APPLICATIONS   The profitgraph technique can be used in a number of ways. Some of the common areas of usage include:

- product line/product mix assessments
- performance measurement
- establishment or verification of pricing policies
- facility expansion/modernization decisions

Product line mix contribution. Profits must be measured by product line to "weed out" the current or potential losers so that you can direct concentration on more promising or potential profit-makers. In reality, each product line is a separate entity. Supervision has direct responsibility for its profitability. Product line managers are generally notified in advance of the amounts to be charged against their products for the operation of each service section. The data are expressed in terms of fixed dollars per week and of variable dollars per output unit. This procedure may vary among organizations. Having knowledge of their activity units and requirements, supervisors can then approximate what their charges will be for service expenses (power, maintenance, production, and the like). Service expenses are often allocated on an accepted and equitable basis, such as direct labor hours, machine time, percentage of occupancy, number of personnel, units produced, and so on.

Scattergraph charts based on historical experience and break-even analysis play an important role in determining fixed and variable costs by direct element and expense account. Segregating the investment data by product line may require some arbitrary decisions and judgments, but there are some key considerations. Space occupancy and property possession dictate fixed asset allocation. Material procurement and usage can be the keys to inventory status. Sales volume is a major consideration in receivables, and estimated cost expenditures are a basis for projecting payables.

Profitgraphs have proven to be, in some organizations, most effective at the product line and productive cost center levels. Similar product line profitgraph exhibits for the total organization would be developed for the individual product line. A final plant summary from the detailed data would highlight specific overall problem areas and their causes.

Performance measurement. By segregating costs into finite detail such as labor (productive, setup, support), you gain an immediate insight as to variances in actual performance versus projected goals. Direct material basically follows units of production—planned versus reality. Variable expense deviations can indicate either inefficiencies or improvement on planned anticipations. Measuring performance and establishing controls in any operational area are essential in monitoring and evaluating an organization's progress. The profitgraph is a suitable procedure.

Decision making for pricing. Pricing policy decisions are never-ending, and the effect on the profit picture is inevitable. Management often faces the problem of deciding on appropriate product pricing. Their decisions can have either short- or long-range consequences. Long range, the question arises as to the alternatives for correcting the situation. Should the product line be eliminated, should they increase the sales price, reduce costs, seek new markets, accept less profit, or what? In introducing a new product, what is a customer acceptable sales price, while maintaining a reasonable profit margin? Suppose the product demand is greater than the productive capacity—or vice versa—what is the decision?

APPLICATIONS

The profitgraph technique may provide a suitable answer. At least, it might assist management in evaluating the problem and possibly in assessing alternative courses of action.

Facility expansion/modernization. Another major decision facing management is whether to expand the facilities and/or modernize the plant in terms of automation and acquisition of highly advanced machinery/equipment. This action can be highly expensive, affecting profitability, and may not lead to the results anticipated. Before the decision is made, you should conduct justification studies to ascertain the advantages and disadvantages, including the impact on financial position.

What the Profitgraph Can Do for You

Profitgraphs help you to assess and project varied profit patterns given alternate courses of management action. Variable profit factors result from changing sales volume and costs. The break-even point is influenced, as well as the return on investment. The anticipated savings in variable costs from facility expansion and/or modernization may, however, be more than offset by added fixed costs and investment. The profitgraph technique is a reasonable approach to determining potential results from a changing operational environment. It is an aid to management in making decisions before committing resources.

MAKING ASSESSMENTS BY MEANS OF THE CAPITALGRAPH TECHNIQUE

The capitalgraph technique assumes that fluctuations in sales volume influence current assets and liabilities, which, in turn, have an impact on working and operating capital. In this discussion, *operating capital* represents the combined working capital and net fixed assets. Basically, increases or decreases in sales volume result in higher or lower receivables, inventories, and cash balance requirements. Current liabilities are influenced because large cost commitments (labor, material, overhead, taxes payable, and the like) are involved in producing products or performing necessary services. Capital assets, in the form of expanded facilities or new machinery, may be necessary to support operations.

How to Construct the Capitalgraph Model

Like the development of most analytical and planning models, the capitalgraph technique assumes that the data derived from historical experience are relevant to the current and future operating environment. In some instances, determining relevance may be difficult because of the constantly changing economic and business climate and/or rapidly moving events in the organization itself (such as accelerated sales volume growth, plant expansion or acquisition, increased manpower and costs, or possibly a reduction in operational activity). A realistic assessment of current and anticipated events is the key requisite for adopting and using the results from historical data analysis and interpretation.

The capitalgraph procedure includes the following steps:

1. Determine the relationship between sales (the independent variable) and other dependent variables (such as major current asset and liability elements). For this purpose, the regression analysis technique is employed.

2. Use scattergraphs to plot asset and liability balances by sales volume levels. (This is a common statistical process.) One or two years of monthly data should be represented in the graph depending on their particular relevance at a given point in time. Some organizations may find that monthly annualized sales are appropriate, and others may use monthly sales results. Annualized sales generally provide a smoother curve line than monthly sales.

3. Upon completion of the plotting, draw a regression line to represent the median location of all the plotted points. In developing the formula, eliminate points located in extreme locations, due to unusual circumstances, to avoid their influences on the data relationships.

4. Model 50 illustrates the scattergraph plotting for current assets, current liabilities and net fixed assets. Ordinarily, each major asset and liability element is plotted against sales, but for illustration and brevity, only the totals were used in this model.

5. The following capitalgraph relationships were developed based on the least squares equations:

$$(1) \quad Y = Na + b\Sigma X \quad (Y \text{ represents current assets, current liabilities and net fixed assets in Model 50})$$

$$(2) \quad XY = a\Sigma X + b\Sigma X^2 \quad (X \text{ represents sales volume})$$

Figure 1. *Current Asset Relationship to Sales*

Developed formula: $Y = \$203 + .257\,X$
Regression line locations:

Point A: $\$203 + .257 \times \$36$	Point B: $\$203 + .257 \times \$45$
A = 203 + 9 or *212*	B = 203 + 12 or *215*

To locate the slope of the regression line, Points A and B were calculated as shown; $36 million sales were used for Point A and $45 million for Point B. The results are shown above.

Figure 2. *Current Liabilities Relationship to Sales*

Developed formula: $Y = \$129.8 + .09\,X$
Regression line locations:

Point A: $\$129.8 + .09 \times \$40$	Point B: $\$129.8 + .09 \times \$55$
A = 129.8 + 3.6 or *133.4*	B = 129.8 + 5.0 or *134.8*

MODEL 50. Developing the Capitalgraph.

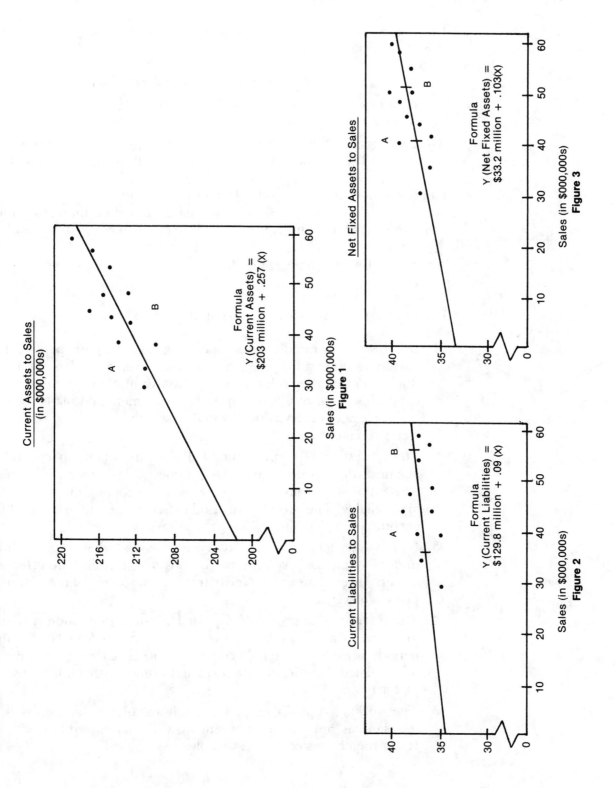

Current Assets to Sales
(in $000,000s)

Formula
Y (Current Assets) =
$203 million + .257 (X)

Sales (in $000,000s)
Figure 1

Current Liabilities to Sales

Formula
Y (Current Liabilities) =
$129.8 million + .09 (X)

Sales (in $000,000s)
Figure 2

Net Fixed Assets to Sales

Formula
Y (Net Fixed Assets) =
$33.2 million + .103(X)

Sales (in $000,000s)
Figure 3

The regression line was drawn as shown in Model 50 for sales volumes of $40 and $55 million.

Figure 3. *Net Fixed Asset Relationship to Sales*

Developed formula: $Y = \$33.2 + .103\ X$
Regression line locations:

Point A: $\$33.2 + .103 \times \$40$ Point B: $\$33.2 + .103 \times \$50$
    $A = 33.2 + 4$ or *37.2* $B = 33.2 + 5.1$ or *38.3*

The regression trend line is displayed in Model 50.

Develop points A and B as shown above. Based on the sales values, locations of Points A and B were established as shown in Model 50.

Putting the Capitalgraph Method to Work

The capitalgraph approach may be applied as follows:

1. It helps you to rapidly assess operating capital trends pertinent to current assets and liabilities, as well as net fixed assets based on past fluctuations in sales volume. The main assumption is that you may expect historical results to continue. If judgment and plans indicate major changes or deviations from the past, then you must revise the trend equations accordingly.

2. You can estimate the individual balances for current assets and liabilities based on projected sales volumes, at least on a preliminary basis, until more conventional and detailed planning method results are available. The process can also be used at the summary level for current assets, liabilities, and net fixed assets.

3. It gives you a gaming capability. You can assess "what if" possibilities under varying sales volume projections to determine the effect on balance sheet items and to verify the reasonableness of the planning process objectives.

4. The correlation approach under the least squares method is simple to apply on an automated basis, and, further, it can be updated periodically as new actuals become available. The data can be readily manipulated to reflect any anticipated events not characterized by past actuals.

5. The working capital can be selectively calculated and assessed in terms of past and future requirements without detailed calculations. It can then be tested for reasonableness.

**A PRACTICAL
APPLICATION**

Example: Based on the relationship equations developed above, the following illustration is provided relative to the projection process at varying sales volumes.

Capitalgraph Projection Process

Summary Balances	Developed Average Factors		*Monthly Sales Projections		
	*Fixed	Variable	$45.0	$55.0	$65.0
Current assets	$203.0	.257	**$214.6	$217.1	$219.7
Current liabilities	129.8	.090	133.9	134.8	135.8
Working capital	$ 73.2	.167	$ 80.7	$ 82.3	$ 83.9
Net fixed assets	33.2	.103	37.8	38.9	39.9
Operating capital	$106.4	.270	$118.5	$121.2	$123.8
Ratio current assets to current liabilities	1.56	—	1.60	1.61	1.62

*Millions of dollars.
**Equation calculations: $203 million + .257 ($45 million sales); $203 + 11.6 = *$214.6 million*

This example demonstrates the use of the capitalgraph to project summary balance sheet items at *three* varying sales volumes. This technique provides management with a tool to simulate anticipated balance sheet results using estimated sales volume levels and factors developed from historical experience.

UNDERSTANDING THE LEAST SQUARES CORRELATION

The least squares procedure establishes a most probable relationship between two sets of variables based on historical experience. The x (horizontal) axis represents the independent variable, and the y (vertical) axis signifies the dependent variable. The primary assumption is that, if past conditions caused a particular *relationship or ratio* between or among variables, then similar conditions will create the same relationships in the future. The premise is that the relationships have been tested and verified.

Using the Correlation Method

Mathematical measures of correlation are proof only of covariation among two or more variables not of functional or causal relationships. The scattergraph itself provides only a visual indication of the type and degree of association among variables. The basic concepts in correlation analyses are the regression line, the standard error of estimate, and the coefficient of correlation. You must exercise judgment in the use of the correlation technique as an absolute and valid means of making estimates or projections.

Historical experience has proven a definite relationship between:

- direct labor hour activity and overhead expenses
- production and materials usage
- sales volume and costs
- sales/costs and net income
- sales/production and current assets and liabilities, and so on

The least squares approach verifies the validity of the relationship among variable sets of data. Only adequate investigation can assure that the results of this procedure can be used for measuring performance and planning future objectives.

10

Employing Ratios to Assess Investments

CHAPTER HIGHLIGHTS

This chapter looks at investment analysis from the standpoint of both the investor and the organization. First, capital structure is defined and its importance highlighted.

The following types of ratios are explained and demonstrated:

- *Bond measurement ratios*—times interest charges earned, working capital to funded debt, fixed assets to funded debt.
- *Preferred stock measurements*—earnings per share and times preferred dividend earned.
- *Common stock measurements*—earnings per share, price-earnings ratio, market to book value ratio, and so on.

The various aspects of dividend yield are described and its significance defined.

The important subject of increasing equity capital is presented, particularly with respect to the use of leverage. Subsidiary or supplemental leverage ratios are described in terms of source of funds and borrowing constraints, with the focus on liquidity ratios.

DEFINING CAPITAL STRUCTURE

The term "capital structure" may have different connotations to various users. Organizational accountants and analysts generally use the term "capital" to identify the organization's proprietary/ownership equity. Investment analysts, concerned with a broader aspect of the capital structure, consider not only the owners' equity but also the long-term creditors' investment in the form of bond issues or notes to financial institutions. In some instances, even current liabilities may be included.

In the following discussion, the term *capital structure* encompasses the total book value of all stocks and bonds and/or long-term notes, retained earnings, and other additions to the outstanding capital. Thus, the data and its relative assessment include the total equity investment of both the stockholders and long-term creditors.

Gauging the Effect of the Relative Investment

The relative equity position of the stockholders (common and preferred) and bondholders is of major concern to the investment analyst. As the investment in bonds becomes larger in proportion to that in stocks, the stockholders' position becomes weaker due to the greater prior claims of the bondholders. Further, the position of the bondholders becomes less attractive because of the smaller margin of safety provided by the stockholders' investment. Generally, the capital structure of a business enterprise becomes unsatisfactory—or possibly even detrimental—when the bonds exceed 25% of the total investment.

Example: Three types of securities are proportioned as follows:

Capital Structure

Preferred stock	$ 600,000	23.1%
Common stock and retained earnings	1,600,000	61.5
Bonds/long-term loans	400,000	15.4
Totals	$2,600,000	100.0%

These proportions indicate that 84.6% of the capital structure is contributed by the stockholders (common and preferred), whereas only 15.4% is provided by the bondholders. In assessing the dollar value contributions, note that the stockholders' equity provides $5.50 ($2,200,000 ÷ $400,000) for each dollar by the bondholders.

Another variation of the contribution measure is to *price the stocks at market value*. This reveals the extent to which the bond commitments are covered by the stockholders' equity on the basis of the investing public's opinion of the prevailing stock values.

Example: Based on stock pricing at the annual average market quotation, the capital structure is as follows:

Revised Capital Structure

Preferred stock *at market*	$ 540,000	27.3%
Common stock and retained earnings	1,040,000	52.5
Bonds/long-term loans	400,000	20.2
Totals	$1,980,000	100.0%

On this basis, the stockholders contributed $3.95 ($1,580,000 ÷ $400,000) for each dollar provided by the bondholders, which is 28.2% (5.50 − 3.95 = 1.55 ÷ 5.50) less than the $5.50 calculated in the prior example. This difference can be of significance in the investment assessment.

CONSIDERATIONS IN EARNINGS PER SHARE ASSESSMENT

Earnings or loss per share of stock are commonly shown on the income statement by a number of organizations. They are calculated on the basis of income *before* extraordinary items and net income *after* reflecting extraordinary items such as: goodwill write-off, realized operating loss carryover from prior periods, sale or abandonment of a plant or segment thereof, and foreign currency devaluation. Some organizations may report earnings per share, if important or applicable to their presentation, on extraordinary items less the appropriate income tax.

In the simplified capital structure, earnings per share are reported on outstanding common shares or equivalent type of securities. There are situations that involve the fully diluted earnings potential such as convertible securities, retiring preferred stock or debts, warrants, stock options, or possible other preemptive rights that would reduce the earnings' position per share had they occurred at the beginning of the year. In calculating fully diluted earnings, the number of treasury shares is determined by using the market value at period end.

If any organization has preferred stock, the rate of return on the *common equity* would be accomplished by using the following calculating procedure in order to reflect the removal of preferred stock from the common equity ratio:

$$\text{Rate of return} = \frac{\text{Net income less preferred dividends}}{\text{Total net worth less preferred stock}}$$

The rate of return on owners' capital can be obtained based on year-end data or using weighted averages during the year. In the latter process, data distortions are minimized in ratio results and assessment. It further provides the means to isolate specific changes and causes.

Some organizations may use pretax income from operations plus interest expense while others elect to use net income after taxes plus interest expense. The method used is based on an organization's established practices, past experience, and results.

PUTTING BOND MEASUREMENT RATIOS TO WORK

In analyzing the safety of a bond investment, you must determine the asset protection of the principal, as well as the stability and adequacy of the organization's earnings to meet the bond interest payment schedule.

Four types of ratio analyses are common in the measurement process:

1. times interest charges earned
2. ratio of working capital to funded debt
3. ratio of fixed assets to funded debt
4. disposition of bondholders' investment

Calculating Times Interest Charges Earned

How adequately do earnings compare with the payment of bond interest? To answer this, determine the number of times the interest charges have been earned.

Example:

Pretax income before bond interest	$200,000
Less: Bond interest	18,000
Pretax income after interest	$182,000
Less: Provision for taxes (50%)	91,000
Net income	$ 91,000

By dividing the pretax income before interest ($200,000) by the bond interest ($18,000), you determine that the bond interest was earned 11.1 times. This factor is generally considered to be more than adequate to meet bond interest payments.

Some organizations take a more conservative approach. They may elect to reduce the pretax income by the estimated federal income taxes before dividing the value by the bond interest.

Calculating the Ratio of Working Capital to Funded Debt

In this approach, you determine whether sufficient liquid capital is being maintained to meet bondholder (long-term debt) obligations. The ratio of working capital to funded debt indicates the information required.

Example:

Funded debt	$180,000
Working capital	$270,000

If you divide the working capital by the funded debt, you get the computed ratio of 150%. This ratio indicates that there is *$1.50* of liquid capital for each dollar of funded debt, which is generally considered to be adequate.

Calculating the Ratio of Fixed Assets to Funded Debt

Comparison of the funded debt with the fixed assets indicates the general degree of protection for the bondholders' investment, providing the bondholder has priority claims on the assets. To assess the results of this comparison, compute the ratio of fixed assets to funded debt.

Example:

Funded debt	$180,000
Fixed assets	$900,000

The resultant ratio is 500% ($900,000 ÷ $180,000). The ratio indicates that, for every dollar of funded debt, there is $5.00 in book value of fixed assets (real property, plant, and equipment). Historical experience and comparative industry averages would reveal the adequacy of this ratio.

Measuring the Disposition of the Bondholder's Investment

An alternative approach in the analysis of the bond position is the measurement of the disposition of the bondholder's investment in the organization.

Example:

Distribution of the Investment

Current assets	$ 150,000	Current liabilities	$ 80,000
Noncurrent assets	900,000	Funded debt	180,000
		Equity capital	790,000
Totals	$1,050,000		$1,050,000

Another method for measuring the disposition relationship is to compare current assets with total liabilities. In this case, compare current assets of $150,000 to total liabilities of $260,000, with the difference of $110,000 being invested in noncurrent assets.

Other Considerations

In addition to these data comparisons, the analyst or investor must consider other pertinent facts, such as the very important maturity date of the funded debt. If the redemption date is near, then a greater degree of liquidity is required.

WORKING WITH PREFERRED STOCK MEASUREMENTS

Computing Earnings per Share

The earnings on preferred stock are commonly expressed in terms of earnings per share. To obtain the data, divide the net income by the number of shares outstanding.

Example: Investors hold 5,000 shares of preferred stock.

Earnings per Share

Income before bond interest	$400,000
Less: Bond interest	50,000
Pretax income	$350,000
Less: Provision for income taxes (50%)	175,000
Net income	$175,000

The net earnings after taxes is calculated to be $35/share ($175,000 ÷ 5,000 shares).

Calculating Times Preferred
Dividend Earned

Earnings per share does not consider the margin between earnings per share and the dividend requirement. The dollar amount of the dividend has a decided influence on the *times earned factor:* the larger the margin, the greater the common stock equity. The situation results in a strong preferred stock position. A more meaningful measure of preferred stock earnings would be the number of times the preferred stock dividend has been earned.

Example: The preferred stock dividend is $5.00 per share, and there are 5,000 shares outstanding. The dividend requirement is therefore $25,000 (5,000 shares × $5.00). Dividing the net income of $175,000 in the prior example by $25,000 shows that the preferred stock has been earned 7 times.

Comparing Times Bond Interest and
Preferred Dividend Earned

The times preferred dividend earned is adequate if no bonds (long-term creditor debt) are outstanding. If bonds are outstanding, as in the prior example, the bond interest represents a fixed lien on the income prior to that of the preferred stock dividend. Investment analysts therefore compute the number of times the preferred dividend has been earned on an aggregate basis.

To make the calculation, combine the bond interest and the preferred dividend. Then compute the number of times the *total of the two* has been earned.

Example: Using the data from the prior example, divide the net income of $175,000 by $75,000 ($50,000 plus $25,000). The result is 2.3 times.

EMPLOYING COMMON STOCK MEASUREMENTS

To obtain the book value of a share of common stock with no preferred stock outstanding, divide the total equity capital by the number of shares outstanding. The equity per share includes retained earnings and any other additions to capital. If preferred stock is outstanding, deduct its dollar amount value from the total owners' equity before dividing by the number of common stock shares outstanding.

Computing Earnings per Share

Common stock earnings per share is generally the most important single ratio for the investor. Earnings per share is used by the investor to appraise the market price of the stock. To derive it, divide the net income available for the common stock by the number of shares outstanding.

Example: If the available net income is $300,000 and 40,000 shares are outstanding, the earnings are $7.50 per share.

Computing Price-Earnings (P-E) Ratio

To calculate the price-earnings ratio, divide the average market or selling price of the stock by its earnings.

Example: The market price of the stock is $50.00 per share, and the earnings per share are $5.00. The price-earnings ratio is therefore 10 times, or 10 to 1. If the ratio is reversed, it then represents the *capitalization rate*, the rate at which the stock market is capitalizing the value of the earnings. Here are the two calculations:

$$\frac{\text{Market price}}{\text{Earnings}} = \frac{50.00}{5.00} = 10 \text{ P-E}$$

$$\frac{\text{Earnings per share}}{\text{Market price per share}} = \frac{5.00}{50.00} = 10\% \text{ capitalization}$$

INFLUENCES ON THE P-E RATIO

The price-earnings ratio is strongly influenced by how rapidly the organization is growing, the inherent operating risks, its financial stability, and its policy with respect to retained earnings. Increases in financial risks generally cause a downward trend on the price-earnings ratio; anticipated earnings have the opposite effect. To gauge the integrity and reasonableness of the price-earnings ratio, compare it to those of similar organizations and industry averages.

APPLICATIONS

The ratio is also used to come up with a realistic value of an organization's common stock. To do so, estimate the earnings per share for a given time period and the ratio that the investors will pay for the organization's earnings. Then multiply the price-earnings ratio by the earnings per share. The result represents a projected estimate of the common stock value. Based on this information an investor can judge whether to buy or sell off certain stocks.

Computing the Ratio of Market to Book Value

Another ratio sometimes employed to assess the risk in investing in an organization's common stock is *market versus book value*. To calculate this ratio, divide the market price per share by the book value per share.

To obtain the book value, as already indicated, divide the owners' equity (excluding preferred stock) by the number of common stock shares outstanding.

Example:

$$\text{Market price} \quad \$25.00/\text{share}$$
$$\text{Book value} \quad \$20.00/\text{share}$$

$$\frac{\$25.00}{\$20.00} = 1.25 \; ratio$$

The 1.25 ratio indicates that the market price is greater than the organization's book value. This ratio represents an investment risk factor, particularly if the ratio becomes much greater than 1. Conversely, if the book value is substantially greater than the market price, then the stock is considered to be underpriced. The organization could come under scrutiny as a possible acquisition by other interested investing organizations.

Figuring the Dividend Return Ratio

The *yield* of a common stock investment is the ratio of the dividend declared to the stock's market price.

Example: If the market price is quoted at $25.00 per share and the dividend rate is $2.00, the yield ratio is 8%.

Note that the *dividend yield* represents the actual gross current rate of return being earned by the stockholder on the investment.

The dividend yield differs from the rate of dividend declared in that the latter ratio represents the total gross dividend as a percentage of the value of the common stock. However, when the market price per share equals the book value, then the dividend yield and dividend rate are equal; otherwise, the dividend rate is of minor importance.

THINGS TO REMEMBER ABOUT THE DIVIDEND YIELD

Here are some points about the dividend yield to keep in mind:

- The dividend yield result depends on the earnings yield (net income divided by the market value of the common stock). The advantage of using price-earnings ratios is that they represent an accepted measure of common stock results. Further, P-E ratios are commonly quoted in trade/financial publications (such as Standard & Poors, Moody's Book of Industrials, *The Wall Street Journal,* and the like).

- The equity earnings per share ratio is influenced by the net income on owners' capital ratio. It is also affected by the net asset value per share ratio, which is derived by dividing the book value of the net assets by the number of shares outstanding.

- To a degree, the magnitude of the asset value per share provides a lower limit for the market price. If the asset value drops significantly below the market price, then the stock's marketability may be jeopardized. If the asset value measurably exceeds the market price, then its marketability is enhanced considerably and the organization may be subject to takeover attempts. If the assets are oriented to a specific use, the asset value provides very limited protection to the market price.

- The magnitude of an organization's net income to owners' equity ratio poses such questions as:

  —If the net income on capital is extremely high, can it be maintained?

  —Is the size of the net income due to successful management, sole source product, or lack of competition?

  —If the net income on owners' equity decreases significantly, what are the consequences on market price and on the organization's financial stability? Will conditions improve on mediocre profitability or further deteriorate, with its ultimate effect on an organization's survival?

WHAT TO CONSIDER WHEN INCREASING EQUITY CAPITAL

Other than stockholders' investment, a primary source of capital acquisition is to increase the rate of return on the capital available.

Example: An organization borrows funds that cost $x\%$ in interest and invests these funds in assets that yield $y\%$. If the $y\%$ yield is greater than the $x\%$ cost, then the difference represents pure gain to the equity stockholder. This process is known as *leverage*.

ADVANTAGE   There is another advantage to the use of leverage. Although profits and asset values tend to increase in a period of inflation, the repayment liability on borrowed capital is fixed in dollar terms. So, in actual or real terms the borrowed capital represents a decreasing liability.

RISKS   This type of activity entails inherent risks, particularly if the rate of interest paid increases and/or the rate of profit decreases. For example, if the interest rate paid is greater than the income earned, the difference represents a loss to the equity holder.

DISADVANTAGE   Another possible disadvantage of *leverage* is that it magnifies any change in the asset profitability to the extent that the return on equity capital fluctuates more widely than the return on the assets.

Example:

Leverage Ratios

	19X3	19X4
Income/Loss Accounts		
Asset profitability	$ 300	$ 200
Interest on borrowed capital	72	72
Net income	$ 228	$ 128
Balance Sheet Account		
Equity capital	$1,000	$1,000
Loan capital	1,000	1,000
Total capital and assets	$2,000	$2,000
Ratios		
Income to total assets	.15	.10
Interest to loan capital	.072	.072
Income to equity capital	.228	.128
Borrowed capital to equity capital	1	1

The ratio of income to asset decreased to 33.3%: 15% − 10% = 5% ÷ 15% = 33.3%. This decrease resulted in a decreased return on equity of 43.9%: 22.8% − 12.8% = 10% ÷ 22.8% = 43.9%. Note that the return to the equity stockholder for the two years is greater than it would have been if the organization had not financed part of its assets with borrowed capital. Debt, therefore, is used as a leverage to increase the owners' rate of return.

CALCULATING COMMON STOCK LEVERAGE   Let's see how the *leverage of common stock* is computed when the capital structure includes bonds and preferred stock.

Example:

1. $3,000,000 in 8% bonds.
2. $2,000,000 in $100 par value 6% preferred stock.
3. 400,000 shares of *no-par value common stock* with an equity of $2,800,000.

Capital Structure		*Common Stock Leverage*
Bonds	$3,000,000	$\dfrac{\$7,800,000 \text{ total equity}}{\$2,800,000 \text{ common stock}} = 2.79$ leverage
Preferred stock	2,000,000	
Common stock	2,800,000	
Total	$7,800,000	

The resultant leverage factor indicates that, for each dollar invested by the common stockholder, the bond creditors and preferred stockholders have invested $2.79. This common stock is in a relatively inadequate position: There is a heavy drain on the income for bond interest, and the claims of the preferred stock take precedence over dividends available for the common stock.

Generally, if the leverage factor is above 2, the indications are that the bonds and preferred stock investments represent twice the common stock equity. A low-leverage stock offers return advantages because interest and preferred dividend claims are so small—or nonexistent—that most of the earnings are available for common stock dividends.

Computing Earnings per Share

Refer to the prior example and further assume $1 million earnings before deducting the bond interest. The available amount for the common stockholders is calculated as follows:

Example:

Earnings per Share

Income before bond interest	$1,000,000
Less: Bond interest ($3 million × 8%)	240,000
Pretax income	$ 760,000
Less: Reserve for federal income taxes	380,000
Net income	$ 380,000
Less: Preferred dividend needs ($2 million × 6%)	120,000
Available net income for common stock	$ 260,000
Earnings per share (400,000 shares)	$ .65

When the leverage is high, an increase or decrease in the income before bond interest results in the available earnings being greater than the rate of that increase or decrease.

Note that, to achieve a more conservative position in determining the available net income for common stock, investment analysts may include current liabilities in the leverage calculations. In this situation, you must recognize the current creditors' claims against the assets.

DETERMINING THE ACTUAL COST OF INTEREST PAYMENTS

The true cost of interest to an organization reflects the influence of the following factors:

1. a decrease in federal income taxes if interest is an allowable deduction
2. less the inflation trend factors
3. issue expenses

Example: The assumptions are as follows:

1. 8% debenture, par value $100
2. Provision for federal income taxes, 50%
3. Inflation, 10%
4. Issue expenses, 2%

Calculations:

1. To pay the 8% on the issued debentures, earnings must be:

$$8\% \times 100 = \frac{8}{98\% \ (100\% - 2\%)} = 8.16\%$$
$$\text{for issue expenses}$$

2. Allowable deduction for taxes:

$$8.16\% \times (100 - 50\%) = 4.08\% \text{ in dollars}$$

3. The cost of inflation to the organization is 10%:

$$\frac{104.08\% \ (100\% + 4.08\%)}{110\%} = 94.6 - 100\% \text{ or } -5.4\% \text{ in real terms}$$

Compare the interest rate with the return on the project only after making allowances for the effect on costs of both federal income taxes and inflation *plus* debenture issue expenses. Since income tax, inflation, and issue expenses affect different sources of financing in varying degrees, use the real cost of raising funds in relevant management decisions and in planning activities.

ASSESSING THE BASIC LEVERAGE RATIOS

Four basic ratios are generally associated with the leverage assessment:

$$A: \textit{Pretax profit to owners' equity} = \frac{\text{Pretax profit}}{\text{Equity capital}}$$

$$B: \textit{Asset profitability to total capital} = \frac{\text{Asset profitability}}{\text{Total capital}}$$

$$C: \textit{Interest paid to borrowed capital} = \frac{\text{Interest paid}}{\text{Borrowed capital}}$$

$$D: \textit{Leverage of borrowed capital to equity} = \frac{\text{Borrowed capital}}{\text{Equity capital}}$$

Calculate the pretax profit to owners' (equity) capital ratio as follows, using the above alphabetic designations:

$$A = B + (B - C) \times D$$

Example: Assume the following calculated ratio data:

	19X3	19X4
B. Income to equity (total assets)	15.0%	10.0%
C. Interest to borrowed capital	7.2%	7.2%
A. Pretax income to equity capital	22.8%	12.8%

Using the formula:

19X3	19X4
A = 15% + (15% − 7.2% or 7.8%) × 1	A = 10% + (10% − 7.2% = 2.8%) × 1
A = 22.8% × 1 = 22.8%	A = 12.8% × 1 = *12.8%*

The analysis indicates the results of reduced profits in 19x4 with the total equity capital remaining constant. When involved in leverage, you must consider the long-term movements of interest rates and their anticipated effect on an organization's financial stability and ability to meet its debt obligations.

Using Subsidiary Leverage Ratios

In addition to leverage analysis, give some consideration to important subsidiary ratios. The two major category ratios to be considered are:

1. primary source of funds
2. borrowing constraints

Primary source of funds. Excluding stockholders' investment and retained earnings, the primary source of funds consists of credit bond debentures and bank loans. Other sources are less significant. In addition to the sources of borrowed capital, examine the rate of interest paid to each type of lender, to determine which capital source has the greatest or lowest rate of interest. Since objective of management should be to borrow capital at minimal cost, it definitely has an interest in this comparison.

The formulas are as follows:

$$\text{Percentage ratio} = \text{a.} \quad \frac{\text{Debenture bond interest}}{\text{Value of the debentures}}$$

$$\text{b.} \quad \frac{\text{Interest on the bank loans}}{\text{Averaged value of the loans}}$$

Borrowed capital constraint ratios. These ratios enable you to measure the factors governing the amount of capital that can be borrowed. Potential investors and lenders use these ratios to assess an organization's financial strength. The ratios are

1. asset coverage
2. interest coverage
3. liquidity factors

1. To derive the *asset coverage ratio,* divide the total assets by the amount of borrowed capital. This ratio indicates the safety of the lender's capital—both the investor's and the creditor's.

2. Obtain the *interest coverage* ratio by dividing the total profit by the amount of interest paid. The objective of this ratio is to indicate the *vulnerability* of the lender's interest when the borrower's profits decline. In such a case, the interest payments reflect a greater portion of the profits. Note that interest coverage is considered to be more important in the constraint assessment than the asset coverage due to the more immediate need for payment.

3. An *adequate liquidity position* is a prime and positive constraint on the organization's borrowing action. Two major considerations, relative to liquidity, need mentioning and monitoring:

The *marketing (sales)* organization must select reliable customers to assure their liquidity status and their ability to meet their debt obligations. The *procurement* organization must ensure the vendor's liquidity position to *preclude the possibility* of an interruption in the flow of material and supplies to support an organization's manufacturing process.

The primary ratios and their role in the data analysis assessment are as follows:

$$\text{Current ratio} = \frac{\text{Current assets}}{\text{Current liabilities}}$$

This ratio provides an insight as to whether sufficient current assets are available to meet current debts outstanding.

$$\text{Quick ratio} = \frac{\text{Quick assets}}{\text{Current liabilities}}$$

This determines the status and value of their most liquid assets: cash, receivables, and short-term marketable securities. A generally accepted standard for this ratio is 2 to 1, but there may be other influencing factors, such as inventory turnover, velocity of collections, prospect of auxiliary capital acquisition, borrowing capacity and extension, and so on.

$$\text{Funded capital ratio} = \frac{\text{Long-term debt} + \text{Owners' equity}}{\text{Fixed assets}}$$

The ratio's objective is to determine the extent to which required fixed assets are financed by long-term commitments, both creditors' and investors'.

Index